the experience of dynamic media

works
from the Dynamic Media Institute
at Massachusetts College of Art and Design

2006 – 2010

the

experience *n.*
—an event or occurrence that leaves an impression on someone
—a collection of events or activities from which an individual or group may gather knowledge, opinions, and skills
—the knowledge and skills accumulated as a result of learning

of

dynamic *adj.*
—relating to or caused by motion
—characterized by continuous change or progress
—an interactive system or process

media *n.*
—from "media of communication" referring to means of dissemination of information
—form through which something else is represented or transmitted
—materials used in a specific artistic technique

the experience of dynamic media

works
from the Dynamic Media Institute
at Massachusetts College of Art and Design

2006 – 2010

edited by Jan Kubasiewicz

with contributions by Joe Quackenbush
Brian Lucid
Gunta Kaza
Evan Karatzas
Toby Bottorf
Ronald Bruce Smith
Colin Owens
Heather Shaw
Dennis Ludvino
Lou Susi

On the occasion of our tenth anniversary, I am very pleased to present *The Experience of Dynamic Media* — the second book publication of the Dynamic Media Institute, the graduate program in communication design at Massachusetts College of Art and Design in Boston. Combined with the previous, entitled *The Language of Dynamic Media* published in 2005, the books cover work from the Dynamic Media Institute between 2000 and 2010.

This edition is organized in several sections. "Faculty Perspectives" includes short essays by DMI professors and visiting faculty, each sharing their individual philosophy and various approaches to dynamic media design education. "Featured Projects" presents student work through articles excerpted from the larger thesis documents — the required component for the MFA degree. "Collaborations" presents examples of extracurricular projects which were developed between DMI and outside partners, as well as a series of DMI student-curated exhibitions. "Student essays" includes a selection written by current DMI student in their seminar classes. "Alumni Stories" presents short accounts of six DMI alumni sharing their thoughts on the DMI experience. "Thesis Abstracts" presents all MFA degree thesis abstracts from 2006 to 2010, organized by year and alphabetically within each year. The last section, "About DMI," describes who we are and what we do — from course descriptions to a list of faculty, visiting lecturers, and all DMI alumni since 2000.

The Experience of Dynamic Media represents an effort of many individuals and institutions, whom I would like to thank for their support and help:
— Each and every DMI student for contributing to the great success of our first decade.
— The DMI former and current faculty for contributing original essays, as well as former and current students for the opportunity of presenting their work in this publication.
— My faculty colleagues in the undergraduate graphic design department for supporting the DMI post-baccalaureate program.
— Joe Quackenbush for his invaluable help in this project. He helped select student-featured projects and essays and then with his excellent editing skills helped make all texts in this publication comprehensible.
— Dennis Ludvino for his idea of interviewing and then writing alumni stories, as well as for his and Andrew Ellis' help in editing.
— Joseph Liberty, Katelyn Rezza, and Rumiana Williams for their meticulous work on this book design and production.

I would like to express my gratitude to Massachusetts College of Art and Design administration and especially President Kay Sloan and Dean of Graduate Programs George Creamer for their continuous support of the Dynamic Media Institute.

Jan Kubasiewicz, Coordinator of the MFA Program in Design, the Dynamic Media Institute

contents

faculty perspectives

Mapping the Experience of Dynamic Media

JAN KUBASIEWICZ

MAPS AND MAPPING AS METAPHORS

Maps are made for different territories and different themes — real or imagined — not necessarily related to geography. As symbolic depictions of those territories, traditional maps were limited to a static, two-dimensional representation, whereas today's maps may be multidimensional, dynamic and interactive. Regardless of the medium, maps are tools of reasoning revealing relationships between elements, properties, and concepts. Mapping creates associations between equivalent groups of qualities that are organized according to rules of correspondence based on a particular system. The word "map," both as verb and noun, seems very appropriate to describe the essence of dynamic media.

This text, metaphorically speaking, is a concept map describing the territory of dynamic media and its pedagogy as practiced at the Dynamic Media Institute. It represents the humanistic approach to the study and practice of dynamic media with its central focus (as the humanities) on the creation and documentation of cultural artifacts. Those artifacts are human experiences mediated, or perhaps the better term would be "curated," within the computational complexity of social communication.

Communicating in the language of dynamic media requires fluency in multiple "languages," "dialects," and "codes" that have traditionally been segregated into distinct disciplines. It demands a synthesis of multiple points of view on communication. At the Dynamic Media Institute we take advantage of the fact that each participant in the program brings a unique background and vision to the discourse.

Graphic designers and information architects, filmmakers and writers, musicians and programmers all offer diverse points of view and use the different "native" languages of their respective professional fields in describing the human experience of communication. To adequately address the multiple aspects of dynamic media requires a combination of these expert points of view, accomplished through a difficult dialog along the borderlines of multiple disciplines.

As the DMI program focuses on communication design, our notion of dynamic media is closely related to information and its broad range of meanings from information architecture to data visualization.

Furthermore, the notion of dynamic media is also closely related to motion — and therefore time. Motion, as integral to design, is considered a language of communication in our curriculum, and consequently "motion literacy" — the act of understanding how motion can be used to communicate more effectively — becomes an essential component of our pedagogy.

Lastly, dynamic media is related to interaction. The terms "interaction" or "interactivity" describe an interdisciplinary field encompassing those aspects of art, design, science, and engineering involved in bringing meaningful experiences to people. Interactive systems — human-to-computer, human-to-artifact, and human-to-human — mediate the process of communication and therefore augment the participant's experience as well as the environment where communication occurs.

Accordingly, in this text the mapping and discussing of dynamic media is arranged within the following groups of concepts: Design for Information; Design for Time and Motion; Design for Interaction.

DESIGN FOR INFORMATION

The beginning of the Information Age was marked by the concept of "information" as defined by mathematicians and computer scientists to solve the problems of sending and receiving messages. As a concept, information was abstracted and extracted from the news, or image, or sound. Cybernetics — an interdisciplinary approach to the study of systems and structures of information born in the 1950s — considered information an abstract sequence of signs. Such definitions of information allowed then, and now, for comparisons and analogies between scientific disciplines as well as for finding parallels between science and art.

Dynamic media designers see the world as an information structure that communicates continuously. For dynamic media designers information relates very closely to the essential notions of communication design: knowledge, learning, language, perception, and many others. Consequently, the subject of information requires a unique and highly analytical approach from designers and design educators.

In everyday conversations we often use the words "data," "information," and "knowledge" interchangeably. However, they are not synonymous and, in fact, refer to different levels of information structure. In his multiple publications related to information design, Nathan Shedroff uses the following progressive sequence of terms to explain the hierarchy of information organization: "Data–Information–Knowledge–Wisdom." [1] "Data is not information …" and "… information is also not the end of the continuum of understanding," [2] This is a critical realization for communication designers.

Data represents only a potential to become information. It is context that gives data a structure that the human brain is able to process. Similarly, information is not knowledge. Only in the context of knowledge — a larger volume of highly organized information accumulated as a result of experience — can new information become "visible" or "recognizable." It can then be processed, verified, and eventually become part of knowledge.

We have just described the process of learning — a change in information processing pattern that occurs as a result of experience. Learning, and subsequently knowledge, is a result of a communication process that can only be completed by an individual's brain. The designer can help, but cannot complete this process for the learner.

Human communication is a process that "relies on artistic techniques, on inventions, on tools and instruments, that is, on symbols ordered into codes." (Vilém Flusser) [3] Homo sapiens are born with some of these "tools and instruments" — or rather we adapt our body to become "tools" able to articulate symbolic languages. We invent these languages as well. And our ability to create stories is a powerful, primordial communication model.

In his overview of narrative, Roman Jakobson uses the terms "context" and "contact" to describe "… a physical channel and psychological connection between the addresser and the addressee enabling both of them to enter and stay in communication." [4] We've already concluded that it is the context which gives data a structure that the human brain is able to process. The term "context" also refers to the complexity of technology and the various degrees of participation by multiple users.

The notion of "contact" is very relevant today. In contemporary practice of dynamic media design the term "contact" — or its contemporary equivalent "flow" (Mihály Csíkszentmihályi) — relates to the situation of full focus and involvement, usually within multi-sensory environments, where and when a person is entirely immersed in the process of communication and interaction. Today such experiences — mediated by interactive systems often in the background or peripherally — are capable of simulating the complexity of a true multi-sensory human experience.

Multi-sensory experience — as a model for dynamic media communication — makes a clear argument for multiple modalities of information. In his book *Multiple Intelligences,* Howard Gardner reveals several distinguishable preferences of individual competence and creativity. [5] This brilliant concept, so influential among educators, simply acknowledges the fact that people think differently. These types of personal preferences in learning — "intelligences" according to Gardner — also describe participants in any process of communication, including designers and audiences of dynamic media.

"An intelligence is a computational capacity — a capacity to process a certain kind of information — that originates in human biology and human psychology." [6] Gardner identifies seven preferable learning styles: Linguistic intelligence (involving words); logical-mathematical intelligence (numbers and logic); spatial intelligence (visual and spatial thinking); musical intelligence (music and sound); bodily-kinesthetic intelligence (natural sense of body movement); interpersonal intelligence (involvement with others, understanding them); intrapersonal intelligence (self-reflection and self-understanding).

Mapping may be considered another form of natural intelligence. Among many strategies for communicating in the language of dynamic media, mapping seems to be a dynamic media designer's natural way of thinking. It is a unique cognitive skill of finding connections among things, and making them visible to others who cannot see on their own. It requires both types of skills: the intellectual skill needed in research and theory, and the manual dexterity needed to translate concepts into visualizations. For users, mapping is a process whereby knowledge may be created, rather than revealed. It is a tool of the thought process.

Images are one means of representing information — different obviously from numerical and verbal description. Yet logic, not imagery, communicates the true intention. Application of logic tied strategically to visual form — in other words visual logic — creates a unique way of interacting with information for both designers and users. By viewing, reading, and scanning visual patterns — static or dynamic — and by selecting subjective paths through the content of maps and diagrams, users learn in their own unique way.

Visualization of information supports our intuition toward abstract thinking and therefore understanding. Understanding combines the rational and the emotional: the knowledge frozen in words and numbers, and the knowledge vested in sensory experiences. The best examples of visualization are always charged with imagination — and often with poetry. Visualization extends to discovery. These images can teach us something, as their forms seem inseparable from the information they convey and knowledge they create or reveal.

Researchers of all disciplines apply computational tools — including dynamic visualization and simulation tools — to "observe" and analyze the data in search of patterns and connections, often prior to defining scientific hypothesis. This is what some call "the fourth paradigm of science" (the term coined by James Nicholas Grey).

In processing and analyzing unprecedented amounts of data collected via sophisticated tools of observation, researchers are helped by designers — contemporary cartographers — who aid in developing systems of visualization and mapping to navigate large scale patterns of information, that not so long ago were totally invisible to us.

DESIGN FOR TIME AND MOTION

Motion is integral to design. It is considered a language of communication in the curriculum of the Dynamic Media Institute. Consequently, "motion literacy" — understanding how motion can be used to communicate more effectively — becomes an essential component of our pedagogy. The notion of time, intertwined with motion, is considered the organizing principle to which all other design elements must relate. It gives emphasis to the process of forming rather than form. The meaning of motion has already been explored within multiple disciplines of art and science. Various expert languages, codes, and dialects of motion have been developed in cinema, music, choreography, etc. Communication designers must learn these languages.

"Communicating in the language of motion involves issues of what is moving and how that something is moving. The how question refers to the kinetic form and its grammar defined by space and time dimensions." [7] Kinetic "behavior" of typography, cartoon or diagram, contributes an additional layer of meaning to the objects that already convey messages expressed in their own native languages of pictures, words, or numbers.

One of the most spectacular historical examples of the dynamic media design process is a post-production diagrammatic storyboard for "Alexander Nevsky," a 1938 film by Sergei Eisenstein, a Russian film director and one of the first theorists of the medium. [8] That storyboard is a timeline in which visual representation of the film components are precisely synchronized into a sequence of "audio-visual correspondences" including film shots, music score, a "diagram of pictorial composition," and a "diagram of movement." The "diagram of movement" represents specifically the camera work resulting in on-screen motion. Choreographed very precisely, in fact to a fraction of musical measure, this "diagram of movement" attests to how essential, for the cinematographer, was on-screen motion and its meaningful integration with all other elements of his vocabulary. The same challenge of integrating motion as a meaningful component of communication design remains the focus of research and practice in our curriculum.

Studying cinematic narrative is always a source of inspiration for designers. In its hundred-year history, the cinematic vocabulary has evolved into a complex, universally understood system of communication, a system capable of translating a multi-sensory human experience into a kinetic sequence of audio-visual events, where motion serves to integrate all other channels of communication.

"As the mind perceives visual, sonic, and kinetic information over a period of time, it continuously organizes discrete units or messages into a story, however abstract that story might be." [9] A story is a sequence. It must have a beginning, middle, and end (after Aristotle), though (after Godard) they need not necessarily be told in that order. A designer's awareness of two distinct timelines — one for the story, another for the storytelling — is therefore essential. Equally essential is the designer's awareness of the "plasticity" of time, and consequently, the designer's skill in manipulating time — real time, its representation and perception — through motion and sequencing.

Since Charles and Ray Eames' "Powers of Ten" (1977) integration of motion and sequencing with information design has demonstrated a tremendous potential for contributing, through sequential visualizations, to various disciplines of science, economy, and education. [10] Similarly, there is no need to argue any more that dynamic visualizations seem to be the only practical solutions for managing complexity of large-scale information structures.

The history of dynamic visualization seems to accelerate. It is difficult to realize that widely accepted concepts and metaphors of dynamic visualization and interaction with data — such as transparent intersecting planes, infinite zoom, dynamic points of view, manipulablility, zero-gravity 3-D space — did not exist before Muriel Cooper presented the MIT Media Lab Visible Language Workshop projects to the TED conference audience in 1992. [11]

Of course motion has been an essential structural element in various forms of expression. The art of music provides extraordinary case studies of using the expert language of motion for the purpose of communication. In "The Seventh Door," a documentary film on Peter Eötvös, there is a scene where three music conductors Pierre Boulez, Peter Eötvös, and David Robertson rehearse Karlheinz Stockhausen's "Gruppen" — the composition for three orchestras placed to the left, centre, and right of the audience. [12] In this piece Stockhausen explores the spatial location of sound by separating music themes from orchestra to orchestra, and creating an effect of sound moving in space. In the documentary only the three conductors are rehearsing the composition. They communicate among themselves in a very precise language of gesture while reading the score and translating musical text into their own interpretation of the piece. Without other musicians, Boulez, Eötvös, and Robertson seem to have an intense conversation, yet they conduct without producing any sound.

Gesture, understood as motion that has meaning, has already become part of the vocabulary of communication design. Computer users widely accept the kinetic behavior of icons that move or jump a certain way, in order to tell us something. Through their "gestures" icons notify us, warn us, and prompt us to action. These behaviors are not formally codified, but perhaps they should become a convention, in order to be even more precise in "what" and "how" they communicate.

The success of multiple-touch displays has elevated gesture to a new role in interface design. "We're just scratching the surface of multitouch" optimistically proclaims Jeff Han, one of the pioneers in designing and engineering multitouch technology. [13] It seems that gestural interface introduced in the well-known science fiction movie, "Minority Report," became reality, and according to Jeff Han, perhaps in its better version. Better, "because purely gestural interfaces actually work very poorly. It's been proven. The human body really needs that kind of tactile feedback." [14] Multitouch technology delivers that tactile experience, and is now migrating away from stationary to mobile multitouch displays to be combined with other devices. Current popularity of the "Wii" gaming platform, iPhone, and iPad are precursors of things to come, where integrating the function of gesture and touch "may actually be more successful that each one on its own." [15]

DESIGN FOR INTERACTION

Bill Verplank asks three fundamental questions of interaction design while drawing his brilliant diagram in "Designing Interactions." [16] The first is: "How Do You Do?" a question that relates to a possibility of an action the interface offers the user — "… you can grab a handle … or push the button." The second is: "How Do You Feel?" a question that relates to feedback the interface gives to the user — "… feelings come from … the sensory qualities of media." And the third is: "How Do You Know?" a question that relates to learning and understanding the interface — "… [the] map shows the user an overview … the path shows them what to do." [17] Verplank's questions focus on three essential areas of concern to dynamic media designers creating user experiences — regardless of the environment in which the interaction occurs. "Doing" means acting. "Feeling" means reacting to feedback. "Knowing" means learning and understanding the system.

The user interface is the front-end of an interaction. The back-end of any dynamic system of information — invisible to the user — is a database. Information architecture addresses the issues of structure and organization of information from the user's point of view. By running hypothetical user scenarios, the goal of the information architect is to design appropriate information flows within the system — often very complex systems with multiple "touch-points" and multiple modes of interaction.

Consequently, information architecture is part of the design process in almost all work developed at DMI. However, it should not be considered a discipline of design. Information architecture represents an approach to design that allows the designers to see the information flow in any design product. It can be applied to traditional communication design as well as to other design disciplines, since information flow defines not only digital interfaces, but also analog interfaces of objects, as well as services and environments.

Dynamic media designers see the world as an information structure that communicates continuously and persistently. Any human experience involves dynamic information flow, therefore communication process, therefore learning. Communication and learning are as inseparable from human experience as from time and motion. Even if we do not want to communicate — by not doing so — we communicate. "You cannot not communicate." (Paul Watzlawick) But as communication designers you can always learn how to communicate more effectively in the language of dynamic media.

As DMI educators in this age of "tsunami of data" (Richard Saul Wurman) we choose to focus our curriculum on the role of dynamic media. In doing so we are helping ourselves and others to participate in the complexity of information in the world today — in learning and understanding, making informed decisions, articulating meaningful thoughts, creating, entertaining, telling stories and enjoying the experience of all of the above.

Jan Kubasiewicz is Professor at Massachusetts College of Art and Design

REFERENCES

1. Nathan Shedroff, "Information Interaction Design: A Unified Field Theory of Design," http://www.nathan.com/thoughts/unified/ (1994): 3.

2. Ibid.

3. Vilém Flusser, *Writings,* Andreas Ströhl, ed. (Minneapolis: University of Minnesota Press, 2002), 3.

4. Roman Jakobson, "Closing Statement: Linguistics and Poetics," in *Style and Language,* Thomas Sebeok, ed. (Cambridge, Mass. 1960), 353.

5. Howard Gardner, *Multiple Intelligences.* New Horizons (New York: Basic Books, 2006).

6. Ibid., 6.

7. Jan Kubasiewicz, "Motion Literacy," in: *The Education of a Graphic Designer,* 2nd ed., Steven Heller, ed. (New York: Allworth Press, 2005), 181.

8. Sergei Eisenstein, *The Film Sense,* Jay Leyda, ed. (San Diego: HBJ, 1975), 175.

9. Jan Kubasiewicz, "Motion Literacy and the Language of Dynamic Media," in: *The Language of Dynamic Media,* (Boston: MCAD, 2005), 15.

10. *Powers of Ten,* dir. Charles and Ray Eames, 9 min. 1977.

11. *Information Landscape,* MIT Center for Advanced Educational Services VHS tape. 1994.

12. Peter Eötvös: *The Seventh Door,* Juxtapositions DVD, 2005.

13. Bryan Gardiner, "Jeff Han: We're Just Scratching the Surface of Multitouch," *Wired* Magazine, 26 August 2008.

14. Ibid.

15. Ibid.

16. Bill Moggridge, *Designing Interactions,* (Cambridge, Mass.: MIT Press, 2007).

17. Ibid., 127.

History and the Virtues of Perspective

JOSEPH A. QUACKENBUSH

1.

Fifteen years ago I shared a graduate studio with Karen, a lovely woman who spent most days painting color swatches with gouache, exploring the over-my-head world of color, design, and meaning. The process required a good deal of patience as the true color of the swatch was revealed only after the gouache dried completely. Karen's process, her algorithm, if you will, allowed time for contemplation. She sometimes wondered aloud how that time would translate into the digital world, where a new color swatch was only a keystroke away. As her thesis title suggests, *Waiting for the Gouache to Dry*, her investigation ultimately became less about color, and more about the virtues of observation, reflection, and perspective in the creative process.

Perspective is a vexing problem for the dynamic media designer. Our tools work against us. Colors are changed with a keystroke, as are photos, videos, sounds, posts, tweets, profiles, blogs, pages, and applications. No drying necessary. Our tools favor action. Not reflection.

Our industry also works against us. A dizzying rate of innovation insures a permanently shifting landscape of themes, products, subjects, and characters. Consider, for example, the following subjective list of debuts since the inception of the Dynamic Media Institute: Wikipedia (2001), Apple iPod (2001), MySpace (2003), Apple iTunes (2003), Skype (2003), Facebook (2004), Blizzard World of Warcraft (2004), Flickr (2004), YouTube (2005), Twitter (2006), Nintendo Wii (2006), WikiLeaks (2006), Apple iPhone (2007), Google Android (2007), Amazon Kindle (2007), Harmonix Rock Band (2007), Apple iPhone App Store (2008), and Apple iPad (2010).

The furious pace of change leaves little room for contemplation. How do we distance ourselves from the foment enough to understand it? Can we be both a product of the rapid change and apart from it? Well, yes. In fact, it seems an apt job description.

2.

As in most disciplines, history can be an important lens for providing perspective. Without a better understanding of the forces at work in the field — their properties and origins — our own work can seem limited, disengaged from the issues the times bring.

Getting at the historical issues of dynamic media is a tricky business. There is no canon. Do we focus on the history of computing? Technology? Design? Communication? Yes. What about individual media forms like film, sound, and photography? Yes, those too. And what about when it all comes together? How do you parse a field that encompasses virtually all forms of human communication?

3.

Every Fall, incoming students enroll in Design Seminar I (DSGN611) a wide-ranging class that investigates key moments in communication, media, technology, computation, and inter-action design. Our objective is to give students a solid intellectual and historical framework for thinking about the work they create.

Readings include: essential essays such as Vannevar Bush's "As We May Think" first published in *The Atlantic* magazine (1945); J. C. R. Licklider's "Man-Computer Symbiosis" (1960); Douglas Englebart's "Augmenting Human Intellect: A Conceptual Framework" (1962); selections from Ted Nelson's self-published masterwork *Computer Lib/Dream Machines* (1974) that imagines a utopian media platform; Marshal McLuhan and designer Quentin Fiore's visual extravaganza, *The Medium is the Massage: An Inventory of Effects* (1967); John Dewey's chapter "Having an Experience" from his seminal book *Art as Experience* (1932), perhaps the most cogent analysis of the relationship between an artist and his audience; short stories by Jorge Luis Borges including "The Garden of Forking Paths" and "Funes the Memorious" that explore the nature of experience; selections from Walter Ong's *Orality and Literacy* which beautifully charts the demise of oral culture and the rise of visual cul-ture; several chapters from Janet Murray's superb *Hamlet on the Holodeck*: *The Future of Narrative in Cyberspace* (1998); selections from Neil Postman's *Technopoly: The Surrender of Culture to Technology* (1993); and William Gibson's cyber punk classic *Neuromancer* (1984). Lev Manovich's excellent *The Language of New Media* (2002) anchors the course with a vari-ety of essays on form, aesthetics, and history.

There's always a variable — a new device, product, application, service — something that touches a collective nerve. Dynamic media history, after all, is unfolding before us. In 2005, we were discussing the havoc Apple's iPod and iTunes was wreaking on the record-ing industry, and by extension, the consequences for any industry that could be digitized. In 2006, we examined the furious growth of blogs, which, naturally, led to lengthy discussions of authorship, audience, and editorial veracity. In 2009, we often spoke about how Google's Earth, Maps, and Street View applications were changing our sense of and relationship to space. Early odds for 2010 seem to favor social networking: Twitter and Facebook, certainly, but also Blippy, "a community of people helping each other discover interesting things by reviewing and discussing almost everything we buy"; StumbleUpon, "you'll only see content already filtered by like-minded users who share your passions and interests"; and the icky, but compelling Chatroulette, "one rule: obscene content is prohibited." What next?

Students also complete a major research project, Digital Analogs, in which they are asked to map the transition of an object, activity, or industry from its analog form to its digital form. The transition from analog to digital can be jarring. As Lev Manovich suggests, digital algo-rithms bring unexpected consequences:

> *Substantially speeding up the execution of an algorithm by implement-ing this algorithm in software does not just leave things as they are. The basic point of dialectics is that a substantial change in quantity (i.e. in speed of execution in this case) leads to the emergence of quali-tatively new phenomena.*
>
> **— Lev Manovich,** "New Media from Borges to HTML," *New Media Reader*

Of course, Manovich is also describing the algorithm by which the history and future of dy-namic media is made.

The student responses to the assignment always surprise. Projects range from Kent Millard's (MFA 2010) study of role-playing games (Dungeons and Dragons vs. The World of Warcraft) to Eun Kyoung Lee's study (MFA 2010) of the garage sale (humble garage vs. Craigslist) to Audrey Fu's study (MFA 2010) of the bulletin board (public walls vs. digital bulletin board in all their variations). Brian Moore (MFA 2009) explored the mores of analog dating and its modern corollary in online dating sites, revealing, among other things, a more than curious paradox: to get high rankings on many systems, rank being the equivalent of a digital pheromone, one needed to tend their profile carefully with frequent updates which deprived one of actual dating time — a Catch-22 for the new age.

The point of Digital Analogs? Not just to map the change from analog form to digital form, but to think deeply about what is lost in the transition. Loss and displacement are natural consequences of the digital age. The situation provokes a challenge for the dynamic media designer: how can we reclaim what is lost or reconsider it in our work.

It's no accident that many DMI students are investigating physical objects as interface — a reaction to the demise of the tangible. True, a new generation of smart phones and tablets invite touch, but the devices themselves are clinically born: their texture, weight, and feel serve no specific experience, but rather the dreams of 80,000+ applications. Erich Doubek (MFA 2008) uses a simple cube in *The Field* to help direct and reshape our sense of space (see page 101). Dan Johnston (MFA 2009) explored the communal object in *Sound Machine*, a multi-user musical instrument for exploring non-verbal communication between users (see page 108). Kate Nazemi (MFA 2006) investigates objects, sound, and space in her exhibit *InsideOut* (see page 73).

Nor is it an accident that so many students are exploring environments as interface — a reaction to the claustrophobic limitations of the screen. Evan Karatzas (MFA 2005) designed and built *Proximity Lab*, a large-scale physical platform on which users' interactions with one another are mediated by visual and aural data (see profile on page 66). Audrey Fu (MFA 2010), an architect, built three-dimensional sculptures for *Perceiving Interaction: Heartbeat*, then used projected light to radically change the way we experience space (see page 158). And Julia Griffey, (MFA 2005), continues her original thesis work through her company Animocation, where she builds interactive learning exhibits for zoos across the country (see profile on page 65).

4.

No project in dynamic media exists in a vacuum. Students are expected to have a deep understanding of the history of their particular subject, which more often than not, intersects with a host of other subjects.

In his thesis *Synaesthesia as a Model for Dynamic Media*, Colin Owens (MFA 2009) devotes an entire chapter to the history of synaesthetic media including visual music, video, music and color, motion and space, film music and sound, and computer sound. That history is richly expressed in his final thesis project, *ShapeMix*, a tablet-based audiovisual mixing board (see page 112).

Carolin Horn (MFA 2007) traces the history of computer-aided data visualization in her thesis *Natural Metaphors for Information Visualization*, which features the acclaimed *Anymails* project, a dynamic interface to her e-mails using microbes as a metaphor (see page 81).

Lauren Bessen (MFA 2006) meticulously analyzed over 100 major works of Paul Rand for her thesis project, *RandStudio*, an interactive laboratory for design students to explore principles of visual literacy (see page 46).

An historical perspective allows students to place their work in a larger intellectual context, revealing new connections and new opportunities. They build upon what's already been done, while becoming part of a continuum of thought.

5.

History, of course, also works on a personal level. DMI attracts a wide variety of students: industrial designers, engineers, architects, journalists, writers, graphic designers, photographers, teachers, and fine artists.

That students from so many walks of life see their future in dynamic media reveals something about its inherent potential. It also explains the kaleidoscopic variety of projects represented in this catalog. Our students work in virtually every area of the field: learning systems, physical interfaces, data visualizations, enhanced objects, social networks, smart environments, interactive narrative, and sound and motion design.

Each student brings their own experiences, their own personal history with technology, communication, and design. They are, at all turns, encouraged to align their history, their passions, to their work — to make it personal. Students quickly find that they have been working on their thesis all their lives.

The seeds of Agata Stadnik's (MFA 2009) kinetic *Motionary* project (see page 122) were born, literally, with her younger sister:

An important moment in my development as an interaction designer happened when I was five years old. My long awaited sister was born. I adored her and created new activities and challenges for her. She responded happily to puppet shows and games I designed. Of course, I challenged her to participate actively, to move and even stretch her body. When she was only two years old, I "trained her" to do a split and other gymnastic feats. My passion for finding ways for people to move and stretch themselves while at the same time communicating began when I was young and it continues to this day.

Brian Moore's (MFA 2009) touching *Camp Ta-kum-ta* project (see page 117) stems from his relationship as a volunteer at the cancer retreat: "My experience with this camp has had a profound effect on my own life's perspective. The individual stories of triumph, loss, joy, and pain are inspiring, heartbreaking, and all very real. In my short time volunteering with camp, I have watched campers grow up, some get better, some get worse, and some return as different kids the following summer and some don't return at all."

Our students' histories are best told in their own words. This catalog includes four biographical essays. Three, by Jason Bailey (MFA 2010), Dennis Ludvino (MFA 2010), and Scott Murray (MFA 2010), are responses to a writing assignment entitled "Why Dynamic Media." The fourth, by Alison Kotin (MFA 2011), was a response to an assignment from Design Seminar I class which asked students to critique an experience with digital media using John Dewey's "Having an Experience" from *Art as Experience* as a reference point. Alison's essay is a beautiful meditation on identity, experience, and personal history.

6.

Writing is a significant part of the DMI experience — it forces perspective. This catalog reflects the perspective of DMI at an important moment in its history. But it is only one of many contributions DMI makes to the future history of dynamic media. Our faculty lectures widely, develops new curricula, and organizes industry events such as the Massaging Media series of conferences. Our alumni work in design agencies, studios, and companies around the world. They teach in leading universities and colleges. And our students continue to pursue original work with passion and rigor.

Joe Quackenbush is an Associate Professor, Massachusetts College of Art and Design

System as Craft

BRIAN LUCID

How should we define craftsmanship in the age of dynamic media? In common usage, the term is often applied to the physicality of the man-made object — describing a material handled sensitively or worked skillfully. Students at the Dynamic Media Institute manipulate bits and photons in much the same fashion that other artisans work with wood or metal, yet they rarely produce work that would fit comfortably into the traditional definition of craftsmanship. How, then, do we connect our impermanent practice to the concept of craft?

Craftsmanship is more than "making." Craftsmanship is an inherently human element that transforms competent workmanship into something that is masterful or adroit. It is measured in quality of experience. Achieving it requires not only skill, but also sensitivity — sensitivity to material and medium, sensitivity to content and message; and sensitivity to the social, cultural, and myriad other highly complex systems within which the object must function.

One develops such sensitivities through doing a practice repeatedly, iterating though design decisions until the experience negotiates each in a balanced and holistic way. Getting these details right, therefore, implies that the practitioner has become adept at understanding how the elements that make up a work influence one another within the whole — an awareness to the systems that exist within our process, within the work, and the larger systems that exert force upon the work. The core of this essay will address these three systems in turn, from internal to external.

SYSTEMS OF PROCESS

There is no direct path between the designer's intention and the outcome. As you work a problem, you are continually in the process of developing a path into it, forming new appreciations and understandings as you make new moves.

– **Donald Schön and John Bennett [1]**

Craftsmanship requires a practiced and insightful approach to the process of making. It is important to recognize that the process of making a design is system in itself: a feedback loop of research, thinking, making, observing, testing, and reflection. Designers work their way around this loop repeatedly, comparing what they have made to a mental model of a desired outcome. Each fresh revision affects their response to the object as a whole. The process runs. The work "evolves." The prototype changes. Sometimes the desired outcome changes. In this way, the project becomes more rigorous.

Skilled designers have control over this process. They understand it as a conceptual framework for understanding and improving the things they design. They allow themselves to be open to the myriad possibilities that a good search allows. The curriculum at DMI has been designed to facilitate this type of deep and participatory design process. At the core of the DMI graduate program is a strong culture of design prototyping and the shared philosophy that making is a powerful form of design research.

While it is often compelling to dwell on the "what ifs" of ideas and possibilities within a concept, projects at DMI do not stay on the drawing board for long. Students quickly realize that a substantive discussion of their work cannot begin until they can present their ideas in some tangible, prototypical form. It is this requirement to make and present work that fuels the iterative design process. Once the work exists in some experiential form, the feedback loop becomes greatly expanded. The students write about what they have made. They observe and test what they have made. They respond to outside critique. All of this is transformed into better, more informed decision-making about the project.

Prototyping at DMI takes on many forms, each serving a different function within the process of making. Most prototypes start as simple proofs of concept, testing some aspect of an idea without attempting to simulate the fully-planned experience. Such early prototypes are often used to test certain assumptions about a design, define technology needs, and identify where further development and testing is necessary. Later form-study prototypes explore the experience of a project without simulating the actual function. This step is vital in assessing usability and other factors while providing insight into visual aspects of the product's final form.

The projects at DMI reach completion at the functional prototype level — attempting to simulate the complete design thought, aesthetics, materials, and functionality of the intended design to the greatest extent practical. The functional prototype is often reduced in size or scope to remain feasible. The construction of this working prototype is the ultimate test of concept, and is designed to force iteration and reflection at all levels of the project.

Kent Millard's (MFA 2010) *Sparks* project (see page 140), a project underway at the time of this writing, serves as an example of a conscientious design process. *Sparks* explores the concept of identifying and marking influences within filmmaking. Proposed as an online community, users can identify relationships and tag them within a film's timeline. The project has grown through a variety of conceptual design prototypes, supported by rounds of user-experience testing with paper prototypes. Each revision has subtly changed the scope of the project. Additional features have been added while the concept of the project has become more focused. Multiple forms of the visual relationship between film content and user-generated content have been explored. Encouraged by what he has learned so far in the process, Kent is now well prepared to move the project into the functional prototype phase.

SYSTEMS OF DESIGN

Once the designer's art was composition. Now it is choreography. In a fluid four-dimensional world, the problem is not so much to get the fixed thing right as to find an elegant sequence of evolving relationships.

– **Chris Pullman** [2]

Craftsmanship in the digital age is about developing work that is robust and responsive in the face of the unknowns of users and real-time content.

Communication design once focused upon the static representation of fixed ideas and concepts. The practice is now shifting to focus upon the movement of information [3.] In a day where so much of our valued content is fluid, real-time and reactive, our design products must be equally responsive. In his essay "Some Things Change…" Chris Pullman touches upon the re-definition of the designer's practice. "Once the designer's art was composition. Now it is choreography." Where the designer once spent a great deal of effort on getting elements in just the right relationship, Chris explains that the designer's product today should be flexible, fluid, and variable. "The new problem," he declares "is to design the rules for the relationship of things, not a single predictable outcome." [4]

As designers, we understand that the process of visualizing design has always involved the careful manipulation of a multitude of interconnected systems — composition, color, and hierarchy to name a few. But following Pullman, designers need to get better at planning and implementing design systems that describe how such elements interact in ways that are variable, responsive, and real-time.

The gap between "designer as compositor" and "designer as rule-maker" is a large one, and many experienced and sensitive designers struggle with the transition. The strategies for creating successful static design work do not necessarily scale to the development of highly systemic interactive design. Constructing a robust system requires the designer to design beyond specific instances. It requires having the ability to pre-visualize a wide range of possible outcomes — outcomes driven by differing situations and ever-changing user needs, content, and display devices. Planning for these outcomes requires empathic research into, and understanding of, the needs, goals, and abilities of the prospective users.

The role of rule-maker also requires the ability to relinquish control of an object or experience to the system designed to generate it. Dynamic design experiences are inherently unpredictable — as unpredictable as the users and network that drive them — so the designer must understand that while they may take ownership of the system, the resulting experience is owned solely by the user.

Faced with such infinite variation, one measure of quality for these types of design systems is robustness of the designed experience and its ability to respond to the unexpected. How does the practice of rule-making integrate into our previously defined feedback loop of design process? We must test, observe, and evaluate to fine-tune the rules of the system. However, because the interrelated systems required in such work quickly become too complex to map out as specific instances, the traditional sketching process must be mated with algorithm.

At DMI, programming is often viewed in relation to pre-industrial handcraft. Students write their software one line at a time, "sketching" their systems into life. Their work is rarely scalable, rarely formulaic. They code. They test. They evaluate the results and continue building the system from the bottom up. The nature of algorithmic design makes this technical process deeply compatible with the creative, and the prototyping, processes.

Often, it is not until a system is implemented that the full outcome of the designer's rules can be understood. By defining a set of rules, one cannot visualize the full impact of the result. Interrelated systems create unforeseeable results. It is only through observing the running program that we can fully understand the results of our systems in play. One by-product of this feedback loop is that it allows the work of the open-minded designer to become more improvisational — even within the rigid and logical world of code.

In the spring of 2007, DMI graduate student Carolin Horn (MFA 2007) presented her project *Anymails* as part of the defense of her thesis *Natural Metaphors for Information Visualization*. A collaborative project with programmer Florian Jennett, this dynamic, real-time data visualization serves as a useful case study regarding both the process and implementation of algorithmic or rule-based design. *Anymails* is an animated, real-time visualization of Carolin's email inbox. A "living" microbe represents each of her messages. How the creatures look, move through space, and order themselves in relation to others is defined by the properties of each message and visualized in real-time via a rigorous and complex system of rules.

The development of *Anymails* was aided by the development of a collection of small separate programs or "laboratories" that allowed Carolin to change specific parameters to observe how such rule modifications might affect the overall experience. These small interactive studies allowed Carolin to focus attention upon specific visualization properties — the movement or grouping of microbes for example — and fine tune the algorithms that define those specific interactions. Once properly sketched, the results of that experiment could be integrated into the larger application and observed in the context of the larger system. In this way, systems were layered upon systems via a process of algorithmic sketching.

COMMUNITIES OF SYSTEMS

When you are asked to solve a problem, look beyond it. Ask why that particular problem arose in the first place. Search beyond the technical: Question the business model, the organizational structure, and the culture. The path to a solution seldom lies in the question as posed: the path appears only when we are able to pose the right question.

– Donald Norman [5]

Craftsmanship demands a broad understanding of the contexts in which a design object or experience must exist and function.

Design methodologist Christopher Jones wrote in the 1970s about a hierarchy of design problems ranging from components, through products and systems, to something he called communities, or interacting systems. Jones' message was that the problems of contemporary post-industrial society reside at the levels of systems and communities, not at the level of components and products.[6]

The systems in play that Pullman describes in his essay are systems functioning at the micro- or component level. Jones challenges us to become aware of wider systems of influence. This means, increasingly, shifting the products of our design thinking from objects or simple interactions to the development of systems or services in themselves. As design planner and educator Hugh Dubberly perhaps more clearly explains: "Over the last century, the arc of development of design practice has been from objects, to systems, to communities of systems. Design practice has moved from a focus on hand-craft and form, through an increased focus on meaning and structure, to an increasing focus on interaction and services." [7]

Consider as examples the current Apple iPhone/iPod/iTunes and App store ecosystem, or the multiple components that make shopping on Amazon.com so streamlined. We often cite such systems as examples of "well-crafted" digital experiences without understanding the myriad components that are put in place to make them work. Designing such systems extends far beyond the intelligently designed interfaces and interactions — necessary components include issues of licensing, infrastructure, and distribution.

For the most part, communication designers are unprepared to function within the landscape that Dubberly calls service-craft. Designers often anchor themselves to the level of object or component systems, and have difficulty understanding the deeper influences and contexts of the things they make. This is understandable. "Trying to understand the community of systems that make up an online service such as Amazon is difficult, because we have nowhere to stand which affords a complete view." Dubberly explains, "Looking at Amazon through a web-browser is like looking at Versailles through a keyhole in a gate in the wall around the garden; you have a sense of a few parts but cannot easily grasp the complete structure." [8]

Like a designer learning through observing their computer algorithms iterating for the first time, we must train ourselves to look at our work as single elements in a wider construction. Meta-systems are difficult to prototype and test but it is imperative that, as designers, we widen the language of our practice to include them. Otherwise, the work we do becomes increasingly irrelevant, and our design solutions will have little lasting effect.

REFERENCES

[1] Schön, Donald and John Bennett. "Reflective conversation with materials" in *Bringing Design to Software,* (New York, NY: Association for Computing Machinery. 1996), 171 - 189.

[2] Pullman, Chris. "Some Things Change…" in *The Education of a Graphic Designer,* edited by Steven Heller, (New York, NY: Allworth Press. 2005), 168.

[3] Dubberly, Hugh. "Design in the Age of Biology." *Interactions,* XV.5 (2008). Journal on-line. Available from http://interactions. acm.org/content. Accessed 15 June 2010.

[4] Pullman, Chris. "Some Things Change…" in *The Education of a Graphic Designer,* edited by Steven Heller, (New York, NY: Allworth Press. 2005), 168 - 169.

[5] Norman, Donald. "Design as Practiced." Article on-line. Available from http://www. jnd.org/dn.mss/design_as_pract.html. Accessed 15 June 2010.

[6] Davis, Meredith. "Toto, I've got a feeling we're not in Kansas anymore…" *Massaging Media 2* Conference Keynote. Massachusetts College of Art and Design. Boston, 4 April 2008.

[7] Dubberly, Hugh and Paul Pangaro, (2007) "Cybernetics and service-craft: language for behavior-focused design," *Kybernetes,* Vol. 36 Iss: 9/10, pp.1301 - 1317

[8] Ibid.

Not all service-design work requires an extreme scale. Sometimes it only takes a few small components to transform a concept. Dan Johnston's (MFA 2009) project *Garden City* began with the simple desire to create an online community that would connect gardeners within an urban landscape — people growing local vegetables on rooftops, window boxes, and fire escapes — enabling them to define best practices and ask questions of each other. However, developing a channel of communication designed to be used by gardeners of all skill levels in many locations quickly presented problems of scale. By asking "How do we compare or relate one unique garden to another?" Dan realized that the subject required an agreed-upon set of benchmarks that would allow the site's users to collaborate in a productive way. Therefore, along with developing and designing a dynamic community-based website, he also initiated a common language to aid his users in communicating. One of the results of this study was the creation of an open-standard unit of measurement, the SGU (Standard Gardening Unit). This measurement is used to calculate the amount of soil within each user's garden. Once a common method of comparison was established, the community could better address issues such as water usage and crop density. The realization that the community could not flourish without a wider foundation of contextual development was an important one, and the measurements that were created may stand to be more important in the long run than the site for which they were originally created.

CONCLUSION

Many consider craftsmanship a throwback to the pre-industrial age. The work developed at DMI is very much post-industrial. Yet the DMI program, at its core, is rooted within the tradition of craft. By colliding theory and making, the program not only seeks to impart the necessary knowledge and skills to perform work in dynamic media, but challenges students to apply sensitivity and attention to detail to the systems that exist within their process, within their work, and the larger systems that exert force upon their work.

Of course, the three elements mentioned are not the only elements that define craftsmanship, but they serve as important touch-points in the making of dynamic media. By integrating these types of sensitivity, we hope the work we produce at DMI will go beyond simple "making" to become transformed into something profound, moving, and influential to the work that will come after it. In this way we, as a community, can continue to shape the growing body of work we call dynamic media.

Brian Lucid is Assosiate Professor at Massachusetts College of Art and Design

AaaaarrRRGGGgggHHHhhh!

or How to Maintain Equilibrium Between Frustration and Gratification

GUNTA KAZA

Designers are called to create and build visual relationships among other things. This process requires that we tolerate pleasure and frustration — the pleasure (and often suffering) that comes from original and unique thinking — with the frustration that our solution may be rejected, or labeled as ineffective. To achieve an internal balance between frustration and gratification is what is known as homeostasis, or being in a state of equilibrium or stability. How do we do this, and why is it important that we learn these techniques?

To be asked to create something (at times, out of nothing) requires a certain amount of aggression (to move toward something; to bring out something). "Civilization is a process in the service of Eros, whose purpose is to combine single human individuals, and after that families, then races, peoples and nations, into one great unity, the unity of mankind.... These collections of men are to be libidinally bound to one another.... The sense of guilt is an expression of the conflict due to ambivalence, of the eternal struggle between Eros and the instinct of destruction or death. This conflict is set going as soon as men are faced with the task of living together." (Freud, *Civilization and Its Discontents*, pgs. 122 & 132) The stimulus and response methods I use in teaching the Design as Experience class activate our most primal sense of survival. A striving for homeostasis must be achieved in a civilized way.

The technique by which I teach the class utilizes modern psychoanalytic techniques as a methodology where creative impulses are initiated, observed, and responded to. Understanding emotional communication becomes increasingly necessary to dynamic media interactions. "Emotions are measurable physical responses to salient stimuli: the increased heartbeat and perspiration that accompany fear, the freezing response of a rat in the presence of a cat, or the extra muscle tension that accompanies anger. Feelings, on the other hand, are the subjective experiences that sometimes accompany these processes: the sensations of happiness, envy, sadness, and so on. Emotions seem to employ largely unconscious machinery....[They] are brain states that quickly assign value to outcomes and provide a simple plan of action. Thus, emotion can be viewed as a type of computation, a rapid, automatic summary that initiates appropriate actions." (Eagleman, D., "Unsolved Mysteries of the Brain," *Discover Magazine*, August, 2007)

By paying attention to their feelings or sensations, students learn to pay attention to the moment, to what unfolds in front of them or beneath them or from within. These moments invite conversations as part of a developing relationship. "One cannot not communicate. Activity or inactivity, words or silence all have message value: they influence others and these others, in turn, cannot not respond to these communications and are thus themselves communicating." (Watzlawick, P., *Some Tentative Axioms of Communication*, pg. 49)

The introduction of objects, a word, a gesture, an experience or the like, induces uncertainty and we are faced with the unknown. The unknown sparks ideas that surface while individuals are directed elsewhere. It is as if the solution creeps into consciousness while the student is being directed elsewhere. While attempting to make some sense from the problem at hand, a revelation becomes apparent. "This new knowledge confronts us with dangers that we seemed to have mastered long ago, raises thoughts that we had not dared to think, stirs feelings from which we had anxiously guarded ourselves.... These psychological experiences are of such a nature that they must be suffered.... Suffering consciously experienced and mastered, teaches us wisdom." (Reik, T., *The Courage to Not Understand*, pg. 504) Theodore Reik states that it takes courage to not be influenced by the obvious explanations. At times, the path we choose to follow will be tested and perhaps even ridiculed by others, by intellect and reason. "He who is always listening to the voices of others remains ignorant of his own. He who is always going to others will never come to himself." (id. pg. 507) I ask each student to participate in a way that is unfamiliar to them; to challenge what they know; to test the boundaries of what is tolerable. At times, it is humbling. Most times it reveals something about the internal process of making — a repetition or pattern emerges, or an avoidance or resistance is discerned. Design as Experience class has become a foundation course in training students to respond spontaneously on impulse and to not worry about details. In broad terms, it asks that students come face-to-face with their feelings, fears, anxieties and parts of their process they have not been called to answer to professionally.

For example, when asked to create a visual response to granular white substance in a plastic bag (the substance given to the students was salt) along with the hand-lettered word adrift, Dennis Ludvino (MFA 2010) created an animation made up of all the readings he had received during that week of classes. Thousands of words bombarded his senses. How could he cope? Perhaps by destroying them in order to recreate something new might solve the dilemma. It did. It solved the immediate purpose of creating a visual response. However, as he stated in class, it also opened a door that he had closed off. This door was his writing past, the past that he had embraced since an undergraduate studying English. He loves to write and was faced with the requirement of visualizing responses. A small paper boat floating in a sea of words convinced him that he didn't have to give it all up nor leave it behind. The small boat surrounded by a sea of words carried a lot of meaning for him; he had paid attention.

In the same way, Agata Stadnick (MFA 2009), faced the limitation of creating visual responses from a rope. The restrictions require that each student work with a rope made of sisal every day for 15 minutes. At the start of the daily project, students documented what they were beginning with; at the end of the 15 minutes they again documented what they had made. The same procedure is repeated daily. Agata's work ranged from threads to sculptures, from objects to mobiles. The range of her work was explosive in detail and energy. Each day presented something new as she challenged herself: Could she make something completely different with each 15-minute chunk of time? While her classmates stayed within a certain comfort range, Agata overwhelmed all of us with her brazen departure. This courage followed her throughout her studies at DMI.

In relation to Agata's connection with body and motion (for she was in motion even though sitting still) I brought Merry Conway (performer and acting coach in NYC) to spend some workshop time with the students. Merry challenged all of us to be aware of our bodies in space. She brought a different awareness of gesture, interaction, and reaction. During the two evening workshops, we as a group became more aware of levels of engagement and

Words adrift by Dennis Ludvino (MFA 2010)

levels of discomfort. She challenged us to extend ourselves into sensory areas previously unfamiliar to us.

Merry's workshop allowed us to feel more confident about body in space. The movement combinations passed around a circle from one person to another focused our attention on how we perceive movement and how we attach meaning to it. Mark Solms and Oliver Turnbull in *The Brain and the Inner World* codify this type of movement as procedural memory." It is a kind of 'bodily' memory. It is memory for habitual motor skills.... It allows us to learn skills and know how to do things." Did this help us become actors? No, but it made us feel completely silly in a safe environment, where all we had to do was what was instructed of us. Paired up, we engaged in exchanges where one participant is leader the other a follower; then we changed roles. For us, who are not trained in observing physical cues, this was a new and daring experience. Some students discovered that they felt more comfortable in larger group participatory experiences, while others preferred a smaller pairing of partners.

In another instance students were assigned literary excerpts. They were asked to create a tool to serve the main character in the story. One of the stories was Nikolai Gogol's "Diary of a Madman." Briefly, the story follows the main character's slide into madness where he is sure, as king of Spain, that he is being mistreated by authorities. Audrey Fu (MFA 2010), analyzed the story and presented a visualization of a 'tail' to assist the madman. This 'tail' protected him from hostility in the environment by serving as camouflage; as a robe, it provided warmth and kingly comfort when he felt neglected, and it functioned as a weapon if necessary. Audrey had unconsciously joined the madman's defenses. Joining is a term used to describe a way of relating to a patient. Psychoanalyst Dr. Mara Wagner visited our class during the fall semester of 2009, and focused discussion around psychoanalytic concepts that facilitated a curiosity about emotional communication as it applies to characters in literature. She enlightened us with diagnoses and treatment disorders. Mara described the difference between the conscious and the unconscious as a beam of light which illuminates a small portion of a large, dark room.

Unconscious motivations played out in a very interesting way during that semester. Upon reading the three assigned short stories students were asked to choose one to bring to a visual form. I had wanted to pair up students, to continue exploring their visual responses, but how should I pair them? Upon presenting their visual responses to class, it was obvious that students had paired themselves (unconsciously) by thematic choices they had made. This was the first time this had happened in class. It was also the first time I had 'team' taught this particular project, in this case with Dr. Wagner.

Reflecting, as a process of inquiry. is a vital component to what we do in the Design as Experience class. Students are asked to write about their process and work through articulate verbal responses to inquiry. This method of reflection is inspired by my mentor and friend Anne West (professor and curator), who when I was in graduate school stated it this way: "How do I know what I think until I see what I say." Inquiry leads the way to discover core concepts unique to each student's experience. It is a private process, but one that offers a critical evaluation and thoughtful approach to understand why we do what we do. The reflective process of writing gives us the opportunity to discern our successes and failures and helps us understand where we are in the balance between frustration and gratification.

Questions we consciously (and unconsciously) explore are: What brings us to understand ourselves in relation to each other? In relation to our audience? At the same time, what distances us? What separates us from this kind of understanding? Distance can cause misunderstandings and conflicts, and can eventually tear apart the fabric that shapes us in a civilized world. Each workshop, each classroom discussion that brings to light the recognition of 'the other' facilitates empathy, awareness, and a responsibility to the participant, the audience. Awareness of message and meaning, empathy and emotion, user, participant, and context identify our role as communicators, as facilitators of interactions that examine new dynamic territories.

Gunta Kaza is Professor at Massachusetts College of Art and Design

Thinking Inside the Box

Using System Logic as a Conceptual Tool

EVAN KARATZAS

System logic lies at the center of interaction design. It establishes the operating principles of the experience and serves as a governing body that connects the actions of participants with the how, when, what, and why of the system's computation and output.

Logic can and should play a central role in the conceptual development of virtually all interaction design. It is as essential to effective interactive experience design as aesthetic choices, interface, and content and can be used as a conceptual tool to push interaction and experience to new levels.

Complex formulas and flow charts often come to mind when we think about system logic and these forms can play an important role in expressing logic. But we're talking about something else — a different way of looking at interaction and computation. To think of interaction design in terms of observable events and data is to see them as dynamic and interconnected elements which are in a constant state of change but which can be harnessed and exploited with intent.

INTERACTION AS COMPUTATION

While system logic is generally expressed independent of the visual treatment of the work, it is impossible to consider it completely divorced from specific content, treatment, and method of interaction. In fact, the conceptual possibilities multiply when we explore our work with a sense of flexibility. Committing to a particular method of interaction or aesthetic too early can severely limit the true potential of the experience — as can indecision.

The designer is always challenged to make smart choices throughout the design phases of a project — to operate in that narrow, and sometimes uncomfortable, space between specificity and openness to radical revision. But too often, relationships between users and the system are not fully considered.

As designers, we're accustomed to modulating between multiple perspectives as we shape our work. At a minimum we move between our perspective as an artist,

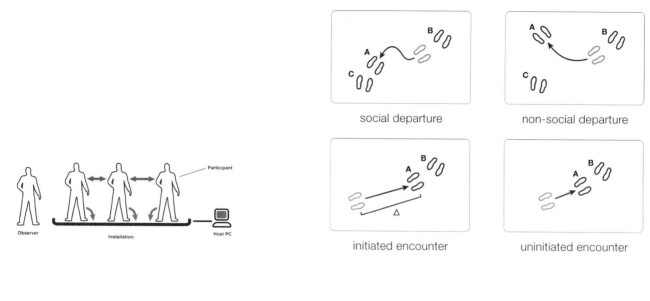

social departure · non-social departure

initiated encounter · uninitiated encounter

Previous page, participants interacting with *Proximity Lab*. This page, diagrams showing system components and different types of social interactions on the *Proximity Lab* platform. Opposite page, visualization of participant interaction.

documentarian, communicator or mediator, and an envisioned empathetic view of our users. These perspectives are fundamental, critical, and irreplaceable. But new conceptual opportunities appear when we augment these perspectives with a data-oriented, system-level view of the experience.

WHEN VISUAL EXPLORATION IS NOT ENOUGH

The *Proximity Lab* installation developed as the centerpiece of my thesis provides one example. From the beginning I had a strong sense of the type of experience I wanted participants to have — the installation would be human scale and the interface would be transparent, based on natural human interaction.

I had figured out a few important aspects of the installation; (a) the sole interface would be the real-time positions of participants as they moved around on the floor, and (b) the system would respond by way of projected image down onto the walking surface as well as with sound. But I struggled to understand what content would occupy the visual and auditory channels of the installation. Was this pre-recorded video footage, real-time footage from the gallery, or a collection of shapes painted by participants as they moved about?

Months of visual studies, sketches, and animated simulations ensued. Literally hundreds of hours of exploration later I was no closer to answering these questions than when I started. Something was missing and the solution would not come without looking at the problem from an entirely new perspective.

Frustrated by an inability to answer these content and aesthetic questions, I returned to the structural aspects of the project. Having clarified the experiential goal as visualizing social interaction, I was forced to consider and articulate precisely how various degrees of socialization would be recognized by the system. There would be no observer present to make these judgments and key them into the computer. The system would have to be able to make this determination on the fly.

LOGIC PROVIDES THE ANSWER

When I began expressing the conditions by which the system would rate the socialization of participants, the content, and eventually the visual language, came into focus. Proximity, or the amount of distance users create between each other, became the critical data point. I developed a formula for this socialization rating based on a set of detectable conditions including the time spent in close proximity to others and the choices individual users made. Terms like initiated, uninitiated encounter, and non-social departure — as well as a series of diagrams resembling dance step instruction — became ways of thinking about the system logic.

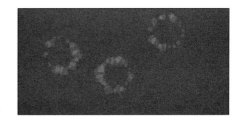

As these formulas and observable conditions were established, I started work on a screen-based prototype to demonstrate how the socialization rating would change as users moved. This prototype work included experimenting with a simplified calculation by representing personal space as a circle surrounding each user. It was easy to detect when these objects intersected and for how long and this provided another method of detecting close proximity and calculating socialization level.

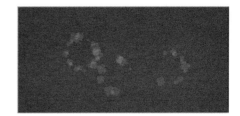

The circles — an invention of necessity while developing the system logic, provided much more than a practical method for measuring social interaction. It forced me to view the experience from an entirely different perspective, from the view of the computational system if you will. This, combined with sound experiments I had been doing for another project, lead to a breakthrough. I discovered the visual and auditory language for the experience — modulating floral shapes as molecules that form a ring around users and which react and exchange when two or more users are in close proximity.

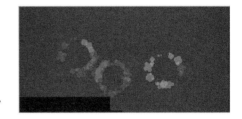

With further development, I realized that the content I was looking for — this prerecorded or real-time footage — was not necessary. Each participant would be assigned a unique color. The resulting distribution of colored shapes, based on the exchange of these molecules, provided a kinetic portrait of social interaction. This was the content and it spoke directly to the subject matter of the experiment.

PUTTING IT INTO PRACTICE

This alternate view of experience and interaction can introduce new conceptual possibilities, perhaps even shift the trajectory of your work. Consider the following techniques designed to jump-start this process.

1. Think of interaction in terms of the data it produces.

Your existing understanding of the work likely already includes some concrete interface elements and content. You probably have some idea of how this material will be delivered. The point of this exercise is not to discard or replace these components. The idea is to look beneath them at the structure of the system needed to facilitate the interaction. How are the various forms of user interaction recognized and recorded by the system? Do different interactions involve different sets of data?

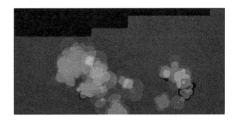

2. Consider every component as a range of values.

Reconsider your current understanding of how users can interact with the system. Broaden your view of how they might choose to participate. Do the same with your understanding of how the system will respond visually, audibly, or with new opportunities for participation.

Develop a matrix with a specific form of user interaction along one axis and specific system response along the other. Explore the extremes of user interaction and participation as well as system response. What values represent the highest and most active levels of participation? Is the absence of interaction accounted for in the system? If so, how is that represented and how will the system respond when this condition is observed?

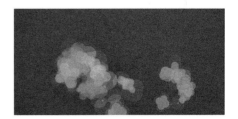

If the interaction is designed to support multiple users, how might the system respond to a variety of interactions and participation levels? Return to your original concept and motivation. How can the system logic advance those goals? Should certain responses or participation levels be rewarded? Will you choose to illuminate the different types of user behavior or highlight their commonalities? Or is your goal to change their behavior, to nudge them toward a certain form of participation? Can they unlock a new level of system response or experience new content only available to users whose participation meets certain criteria?

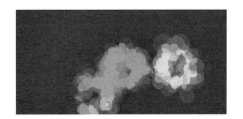

3. Think of your system as event-driven.

Consider the various ways participants can interact with each other and with the system within the construct of your designed experience. Abstract these as conditions and think about them as events that define a higher order of relationship between participants and the system.

Instead of looking at individual actions and a correlating system response, put the granular user actions aside. Think about the experience in much broader, goal-oriented terms. Return again to your original concept and motivation. Define very broad levels of user achievement. Can certain combinations of user choices or patterns of behavior be defined and linked to more elaborate system responses?

That is to say, can the totality of a user's interaction be recognized by the system? Perhaps this could alter or extend the relationship between users and the system? Think of this as an event that the system is watching for. What are the major events — separate from but connected to individual interaction — that the system is prepared to identify and respond to?

4. Consider and exploit the visibility of system logic.

Think about how the disclosure of system rules to participants may affect the way they interact. Explore a variety of approaches and consider how they align with the experiential goals of your work. What happens if you withhold all instruction and prompting? How might this affect the way participants choose to interact as they investigate the system and try to understand its rules? Will it give users more opportunity to shape their own experience with the system? With other participants? How will it affect approachability and usability? Will users be more or less likely to participate in the absence of clear instruction and details about how the system works?

Explore the other end of the spectrum where everything is explained. How might this affect participation and the opportunity for users to experiment and explore? Is the disclosure of these rules a dynamic element that is revealed as user interaction unfolds? What is the proper balance between ambiguity and disclosure that will encourage and enable the type of experience that you seek and that participants will find fulfilling?

IN CONCLUSION

Not all of the techniques discussed here will be applicable. Some will be more effective than others depending on the nature of your work, specific goals, and motivation. Most importantly, these techniques cannot replace experimentation, user testing, and direct observation. Prototyping your work early and often is critical to testing your assumptions and learning how users will really behave.

There is no substitute for thoughtful research, an iterative approach to development, and a constant critical examination of your assumptions. But combine these best practices with a multifaceted approach to interaction design — as an artist or communicator, from the vantage point of end users, and by adopting a personified view of the system — and there is no question that the conceptual and experiential possibilities of your work will expand.

There are many more questions to ask. The exploration of shared authorship and relinquished control are critical considerations. And of course, there is never a formula that leads predictably to creative solution. You must pose questions specific to your interests about your intellectual investigation and expressive goals, then explore them and allow them to branch into new directions and possibilities.

Evan Karatzas is founder of Proximity Lab and visiting faculty
at the Dynamic Media Institute

Love Child of Art and Engineering Makes Good

TOBY BOTTORF

The original attraction was probably based as much in mutual suspicion as anything else: the allure of the other. Computation and aesthetics hooked up and we are the bastard offspring, equally at home (and equally alien) at technical schools and art schools. But this fledgling discipline, dynamic media, is growing up self-assured and outgoing. Our field has helped improve the relationship between engineering and aesthetics by building a way to work, and a way to talk about the work, that includes them both.

From the outset, we have had to navigate irreconcilable differences in how to talk about this stuff. The early days of dynamic media (or interaction design) were governed by an engineering mindset, with little room for an arts vocabulary. While the basics of interaction design were being invented, usability was far more important than expressiveness. The most accessible entry point to interface design from the usability perspective remains Steve Krug's *Don't Make Me Think*. And yet, that represents only one valuable perspective or a phase our field has had to go through. Because what if we actually do want to make people think? What if we want people to engage with the interface consciously? These are legitimate artistic intentions.

Happily, engineering made space for art through its own achievements. Interfaces quickly became predictable in essential ways, and we developed a process of standardizing the rules of interaction into design patterns. Good. We have settled on a number of consistent approaches that cast in clearer relief the gestures and interactions that deliberately break the rules. The things that are unexpected can be assumed to be intentional now, not mistakes. In general, we can do more things wrong because what's right has become agreed upon and familiar.

THE INAPPROPRIATENESS OF ART IN INTERFACES

> *No matter how cool your interface, it would
> be better if there were less of it.*
> — **Alan Cooper,** 1995

Compare this quotation to the feeling expressed in Beatrice Warde's 1955 lecture (famous to graphic design students) arguing that typography should be a perfectly transparent vessel for content, a crystal goblet:

...it is mischievous to call any printed piece a work of art, especially fine art: because that would imply that its first purpose was to exist as an expression of beauty for its own sake and for the delectation of the senses.

Years apart, Warde and Cooper are worried about the same thing, that the medium might have some intrinsic message in it, that the designer might be the author of something. I find it reassuring to see old precedent for more recent anxieties. It suggests our concerns aren't new nor bound tightly in a specific field of work. The fact that we consider these sentiments dated and only sometimes appropriate reflects how far we've come. Rules are for novices, whether novice people or entire disciplines, and we can confidently say that in much recent and ambitious work they don't apply. They don't apply to work that is mainly a kind of storytelling, though they still matter to the design of tools. But even there, the tools that we make out of dynamic media are increasingly a new kind of tool — they are services, not products. A well-designed service has to be more than just functional, it has to have an emotional component to it. User goals are not just behavioral, but affective too. As Donald Norman, stalwart of the usability perspective, puts it — attractive things work better.

I would go further and say challenging things are more interesting. Art is not user-abuse. The audience for art isn't a "user." Artists can and should summon the power of dislocation and disorientation as some of the most potent ways of focusing attention. These are ways of making people mindful of aesthetics, aware that they are looking. More challenging and startling experiences are called for.

These days user-abuse isn't about interfaces anyway, it's about EULAs (End-User License Agreement) and the legal terms of our relationships with digital services. Design is free to be challenging to the audience because we have a general consensus of interface patterns. Art was only ever a problem while the engineering was still unresolved.

I think this family squabble between art and engineering is over. It's over because we realized there never was a conflict in the first place. The false Either-Or choice is answered with Both. We shouldn't abuse the user, but we shouldn't stop at just mitigating UI harm either. We are now as a field able to talk like architects about both the programmatic needs and the expressive intent. We trust that the stuff we build will stand. Now that we have an established set of interaction patterns, our ambitions move to emotional content and storytelling. We have mostly solved the engineering challenges — until we create new ones. Although, ask an architect, and they'll admit that all great buildings leak.

So, on to creating new engineering challenges. We have tools and technologies at our disposal that seem to be capable of more than we have the imagination to invent. More art is desperately needed.

One way to aim for more surprising work is to include more disciplines as influences and sources of inspiration. Not to be dismissive, but we are not satisfied with just a revived Renaissance unity between art and science (no offense, Leonardo). We have not brought together something that was split in two. Rather, we've come to recognize hybridity as a defining quality of our discipline. We're not a stable hybrid of different fields; we are all about the ongoing mixture of ideas. We stole from architecture when we sought models for navigable information structures, we enlisted anthropology to help us get better at contextual research and understanding users and cultures, and as long ago as 1991 Brenda Laurel proposed that we think of computers as theatre. Come on in. It seems we'll welcome anyone.

DESIGN AND EVERYTHING ELSE

As the boundaries between different disciplines blur and dissolve, how do we resolve their different work methods and sometimes incompatible criteria for critique? I would bet on more and more disciplines becoming relevant to design, because ours is a restless and promiscuous discipline. Design-thinking values research and synthesis. It is outward-looking. But we need some limits. We need to be able to study and practice a field that doesn't aspire to be about everything.

This calls for a curriculum that is both more fundamental — based in things of enduring value — and more modular and flexible. The fundamental is a basis in practice and craft, though not all craft is analog. We need craftsmanship in any number of specific areas. The flexibility calls on design-thinking, frameworks for work and critique across these different areas. Our domain easily includes animation and video, lighting and sound design, products and environments. Not only can we make stuff out of more and more responsive and dynamic materials, we can also make stuff about more personal and social experiences.

In 2005, the first year I was a critic at the Dynamic Media Institute, I was disoriented by the thesis project demonstrated by Lynn Faitelson (MFA 2005). Her project combined video, audio, and light effects mediated by the actions of the audience, and projected onto semantically loaded objects and materials. I asked whether I ought to approach this as a piece of interactive art or as a sculptural installation. The answer to that question told me how to handle my disorientation.

This challenging work also revealed to me a perennial difficulty in this field: it is hard to make deeply personal work, because the "person" in the art is the user-audience-participant and not the artist. In that regard maybe Warde and Cooper are not as wrong as they often seem to me, so long as we update what we think transparency means. Not necessarily something we see through, but something we can see into deeply. We need to design for open, unintended uses — paradoxical as that seems.

As the work gets more expressive, social and multi-sensory, its need to be self-exemplifying doesn't go away. There is still a need for it to behave as an interface and tell you how to operate it. Through more artful means, this work still must direct the user's attention toward their role and agency in the experience. If one axiom of software design is to build things under the assumption that nobody reads the manual, for more artistic work we should ensure that the audience's experience includes their own process of writing the manual.

For the audience, discerning the relationship between cause and effect and understanding the feedback loops in the system are often a large part of the experience of interactive art. That offers an opportunity for deep engagement and self-reflection. It also highlights perhaps the greatest pitfall in our discipline: It is never enough for this work to just be a puzzle that the audience needs to solve. The most common trait of mediocre work is that the experience of it proceeds like this: mysterious, challenging, mysterious, inviting, mysterious, a sudden *aha!* and then banal. It cannot be like a punch line, dependent on the shock, and effective only once.

Good work maintains a level of elusiveness and invitation. It can succeed by never fully giving away its rules. If it does that in a way that isn't arbitrary or hostile, it isn't user abuse. Even better, it can continue to stimulate and delight (or challenge and disorient) after its rules for operation have been understood. There are abundant ways to achieve this. Sensory and social experiences are their own rewards, and games offer the pleasures of play and increasing mastery. More and more, we see these sensory, social, and playful experiences as being what our work is *about*.

CRITERIA FOR CRITIQUE

From engineering we get one of the rules of critique for this kind of work: can the audience/ user discern the feedback loop? That is, can I tell what is the relationship between input and output, between causes and effects? In simple interfaces, the feedback loop is usually one action, one effect, to confirm that the user action has been detected. For dynamic media, the loop is larger and often based on many input variables, like social behaviors.

A similarly analytic lens for critique is to evaluate projects as they are, giving little weight to intention. An art critique allows for investigation into motive, but I believe that is mainly useful as critical and formative feedback, driving the next phase of work. Final critique, such as I've enjoyed at many thesis defenses, should not be influenced much by motive. The work is finished. WYSYWYG. It either works or doesn't.

If critique allows the question "does it work?" then the critic must approach the work as a user. Ideas and historical references (designing for designers) have to be evident in form, or they're irrelevant. To some extent, we have to momentarily not know about the historical precedents in form and ideas. In effect, critique is a little like testing. That makes a form of research.

What do we mean by research in academic work, in art, and in professional practice? These are three different perspectives that come together at DMI, and each recommends different and complementary things as worthy of research.

- The academy wants us understand our history well, place our work in a historical context, and advance the knowledge base for the field.
- An art program wants our research to generate many experiments with materials and our own selves, our motivations and personal mythologies.
- Professional practice wants us to research the context of use, and to test the usefulness and fit of prototypes with users.

All three encourage us to turn our research into something: to invent new things as well as new methods and tools for making things. The quality of research, and its value to the field depends on our documentation of process: our research into aspects of a problem and the tying together of many explorations into a coherent subject or approach. Admirably (and dauntingly) DMI asks that students defend their work in a written dissertation. They need to be able to tell a story about the entire body of their work. It reveals the methods taken, the personal applications of design-thinking to the craft of making stuff out of a broad range of different kinds of media. The collected dissertations capture DMI's state and evolution of the art. This body of work suggests a way to address the relationship between design-thinking and practical craft, and engages the crucial question: What is the right level of media-specificity in a curriculum?

This question is proxy for another scary one: Do designers need to know code? My answer, simplified, is that design students definitely do. Know how it works, know what it does well and easily, know how to get help. We need to know how to make the things we design, or at least how they are made. There is nothing particular to dynamic media in this. I believe generally for all design disciplines that a deep grounding in craft, in how things are made, is essential. It leads to richer, more controlled, and more imaginative work. Before design was a profession, it was the quality of invention in a number of different professions: type designers were people who cut metal or stone, graphic designers were printers. Bradbury Thompson, one of my favorite designers, did work that was inseparable from the ink-and-paper potential of CMYK printing. Good design is not just expression of ideas: it's made of materials, whether they be physical or digital, time based or space based. The same connection between ideas and craft that you find in the analog world of print is evident in projects where the material is code. Carolin Horn's project from 2007, *Anymails* shows the same clear connection between ideas and the means of production. In this great project, emails are manifested as microbes, with a rich vocabulary of behaviors. The work expresses well what the medium affords and outlines its constraints. (And, yes, Carolin got help with the Flash and Processing code).

Art made out of code can be abstract, symbolic, or representational. Purely abstract art plots curves and shapes from algorithm. It is usually static, and not derived from any data set. More interesting and recent experiments take advantage of data sets that are large and dynamic. More and more data are becoming available as sensors grow in capability and ubiquity. The process of data-capture and display (the simple input/output model, still) leads to an incredible array of possible investigations. Colin Owens' *Shape Mix*, from 2009, presents a focused investigation into the visual display of captured audio. This project goes beyond visualizing sound, investigating the uses of metaphor and the development of an extensible visual and behavioral language.

We judge this work on how well it shows us something new, or helps us see other things in new ways. In being about ideas and based in sensory experience, it aims, as design always must, to be smart in its beauty and beautiful in its intelligence.

Toby Bottorf is Principal of Digital Design, at Continuum
and visiting faculty at the Dynamic Media Institute

Some Reflections on Cross-Disciplinary Dialogue and Dynamic Media

RONALD BRUCE SMITH

In September 2005, I attended a gallery event at the Massachusetts College of Art and Design where work of both current students and recent graduates of the Dynamic Media Institute program was being shown. While the work was often very inventive and striking, some also contained certain problems that were similar, in a somewhat reversed way, to ones I had been encountering in works by audio artists. Recent advances in technology at the time had allowed artists whose primary area was in music to attempt to create their own time-based visuals to accompany their work. The results were often dilettantish on the visual end, which ultimately compromised the quality of the work as a whole. In the DMI show, several of the works, while extremely accomplished visually, were significantly reduced in their impact by audio that was poorly conceived and executed. While the accessibility of all sorts of software made such things possible, there are only so many Leonardo's in any given millennium who are able to do everything at a high level. I was introduced to Jan Kubasiewicz, coordinator of the DMI program, later that evening. When he asked me what I thought of the work, I expressed my concern about the audio in some pieces. Without pause, Jan responsded, "Do you think you can help us?" I was both interested and frightened. The former because I had been thinking that it was time, due to technology trends, to develop some way for visual thinkers to better understand audio and to communicate their ideas to someone who works in the audio domain. I also wanted audio artists to be more visually literate. It frightened me because it meant having to teach some very basic, and some not so basic, things about an art form that is rather complex. After several conversations, Jan arranged for me to give seven lectures to the graduate design symposium during the spring 2006 semester.

The students in DMI are largely concerned with time-based work. I built my lectures around this common denominator as all time-based art attempts to engage people in an experience that unfolds over a period of time. In a general sense, the most common way to do this is to create a goal-oriented structure from a succession of periods of tension-and-release in which the release is understood as a goal. Building hierarchies from short-term and long-term

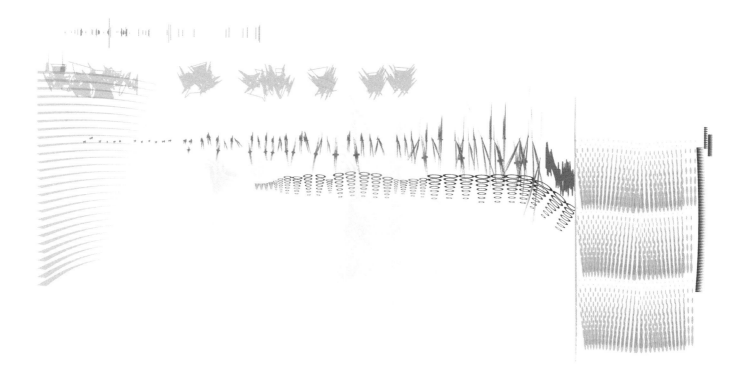

Visualization of Trevor
Wishart's music by Colin
Owens (MFA 2010)

goals in turn creates a structure. And so I began by playing recordings of the music of Gyorgy Ligeti, Igor Stravinsky, and a few plunderphonics works of John Oswald (some rather extreme examples) in order to demonstrate some basic principles of how time can be structured in music to create form. In the first lecture I also went over some basic music terminology such as texture, color (or timbre), register, melody, and so on. The terms color and texture, taken from the visual arts vocabulary, caused some understandable confusion initially.

Following a lecture in which I discussed Karlheinz Stockhausen's five parameters of sound, (frequency, duration, loudness, timbre, and spatial location) as well as symmetrical versus asymmetrical phrase rhythms using Beatles' songs as examples (asymmetrical phrase rhythms are why one might find it difficult to dance to "A Day in the Life," for example), the students started their first assignment. They were asked to visually represent an excerpt of experimental electronic music by the British composer Trevor Wishart. The assignment, in one sense, is an information design problem. However, in order to fully represent the music, the designer had to listen to the piece in ways they had never listened before.

For their final assignment, students had to compose a short piece, about two minutes long, of musique concrète and then create a video for it. Musique concrète is a genre of music that uses found sounds — trains, doors creaking, footsteps on the floor — as its basic material. Founded in the late 1940s at Radio France in Paris, composers there would record sounds onto tape and then alter it by changing its speed, by playing the tape backward or by playing the tape backward at different speeds. Once the composer had created a library of sounds, they would then begin to assemble them into a composition. Musique concrète was an ideal genre for our project since it freed the students from having to read music or even play an instrument. While the class recorded and manipulated their sounds digitally, the processes they used were not terribly far removed from what the earlier French artists did a half-century earlier.

Initially, the project terrified many of the students. They had never experienced anything like it before. They were also challenged by the task of completing a musical work that held together as a piece of music, not simply an audio accompaniment to a video. The idea was that the student would focus completely on the musical work during its composition without the distraction of making the video.

The completed final projects were very impressive. The students even surprised themselves by their accomplishments. Katie Westgate, who had recorded sounds from an elevator, created a surrealistic soundscape that was tightly integrated with the video. Juan-Carlos Morales became very interested in using music as an integral part of his work through the experience in the symposium and continued to take independent studies with me the following year.

One semester was the tip of the iceberg. Continuing to find common ground between our disciplines helped the students understand my critiques. Wherever I could, I drew parallels between what one sees in a design or in a painting and what one hears in a piece of music. For example, seeing symmetries or asymmetries in a visual piece is not such a challenge. Most people can understand the effects such visual rhythms produce in a given work. While there are parallels in music, such things might not be so easy for a non-musician to discern even though most people can intuitively sense when something might be regular in its rhythm or a little off kilter, like "A Day in the Life." I actually counted through the meters and phrase lengths in a few songs in order to show students what was happening on a slightly larger structural level. I was then able to show how these larger rhythmic units are perceptible and how they affect how we understand music. From that, I was able to show in a certain sense that form is rhythm.

In 1991, while I was a graduate student at the University of California, Berkeley, I came across a copy of Paul Klee's *Pedagogical Sketchbook* in a used bookstore. I was immediately struck by how much of what he wrote could be applied to how one thinks about music composition. It was a truly revelatory moment for me. While I knew some of Klee's work at that time, I did not know that he had been a gifted musician before deciding to pursue a career in visual art. Of course, when I learned this a little later, it made perfect sense. Then in 1994, I came across Andrey Tarkovsky's *Sculpting in Time*. It is a book by a great film director that made a remarkable impression on me. Combined, these two remarkable books sparked my passion for sharing ideas across artistic disciplines. The opportunity to work with DMI over the last five years helped put my passion into practice. The interaction with students and faculty has been enormously rewarding. I now think about what I do from a different angle and, for that, I am deeply grateful.

*Ronald Bruce Smith is Professor of Music, Northeastern University
and visiting faculty at the Dynamic Media Institute*

Changing Worlds

COLIN OWENS

Over the past decade we have seen a magnificent convergence of media. Mobile phones can play music and display web pages. Computers are capable of crisp, legible text and high quality video — sometimes on the same page. Movies capitalize on advances in display technology with immersive 3D experiences.

The tools to build media have also evolved from the highly specialized toward the generalized. Thirty years ago the reproduction of text required a printing press. Music making needed at least a mixing console, some multitrack tape, and a microphone. Filmmaking necessitated at least half a dozen specialized skills and many distinct pieces of equipment.

Making and viewing can now happen on a computer almost instantaneously, changing the nature of the media and the tools that we use to create it. Genres of entertainment are colliding toward a total reality rather than as separate, static media. Moving pictures, text, and sound can be experienced simultaneously using a computer or mobile phone as an instant input and output device for multimedia platforms such as YouTube, Vimeo, Flickr, and others.

Gene Youngblood, in his 1983 essay "New Renaissance," described that a computer "in principle can become anything that can be precisely defined." His essay continued that the computer as the tool and feedback device would engender a "non-hierarchical structure of authority and reality."

The delineation between creator, viewer, and participant in non-hierarchical online platforms such as YouTube or Flickr is blurred. Members can comment or respond to content with their own content and can reorganize or reframe others' content using platforms such as web blogs or RSS feed aggregators.

These early platforms only scratch the surface of what we're capable of producing.

SENSE SYSTEMS

Building a platform requires knowledge of how we, as humans, work. Modern platforms are instantaneous feedback devices in which humans are the variability. What we see and hear as a result of what we change gives us clues as to what's happening in all stages of the platform's experience. All of our sense inputs, in effect, can be taken advantage of in creating dynamic media. Touch, sight, hearing, balance, temperature can be approximated by sense and sensors that interface computers with humans. The more sense we incorporate, as input and output in dynamic media, the closer we get to total reality.

Sound and image are two obvious collision points for creating a synaesthetic experience. Every day we are presented with audiovisual messages from our television, video games, neighbors, and the public address systems on the subway. Our analysis of how these commonly conveyed senses work together (or not) can give us clues about how traditional and dynamic media are similar or different from one another. We see what we touch and listen to the sound it makes.

A spoon hitting the side of a half-full glass of water will produce one sound and a spoon hitting another identical, but nearly full glass of water will produce another, higher pitched sound.

We can create this kind of variability using dynamic media rather than mixed media. Mixed media creates a multisensory experience by placing distinctly different media in the same space. Dynamic media marries the two as one in a repeatable, playable format that utilizes both senses as output to inform one input or action by the participant.

TEACHING WORLDS OF SENSE

In the Dynamic Media Institute course *Sound for Dynamic Media,* we turn the tables on visually minded students and ask them to look at the world through their ears. Sound can be visualized, images can be interpreted aurally, and finally computer manipulation can influence how both are perceived together.

What makes the interaction between light and sound most interesting is not what we think we may know, but what we don't know. We know that the spoon creates a sound against the glass. We know that pouring water out of the glass creates a different sound when we hit it again. We don't know exactly how much water to pour out right away, although we can repeat the experiment until we do know.

What cannot be explained through science or repeatability is what sound gives us pleasure (or not) when we hit the side of the glass. This method of exploration is encouraged in class. Equivalencies of light and sound have more subjective than scientific significance.

On the first day of class students are asked to find somewhere inside or outside of the school to sit, close their eyes, and listen to the world around them. They draw these sounds on paper in any method they wish, keeping in mind light and sound equivalencies such as location, height, depth, composition, and relative volume. Afterward, students are invited to share their findings with one another and to compare the visual output of their sound drawings. More often than not, we see more similarities between the drawings than differences. The most exciting part of these conversations is the discovery of these commonalities. The drawings help students gain a visual foothold in, and to create to a base perceptual pattern language for, a medium they may have never been exposed to previously.

EVERYTHING IS MUSIC

The next step is to break down the qualities of the audiovisual objects into repeatable signifiers that show a sound's influence on a visual object in time.

The exercise is named "Everything is Music" after John Cage, who once asked: "What is more musical: a truck passing by a factory or a truck passing by a music school?" This post-modern questioning of music helps frame the questioning of media from a wholly different angle.

Students record a series of sounds. The important part is that they own their material. Their sounds can be anything: their own voices, the sound of motors, the jiggling of keys, sound generated by a synthesizer, and so on. They are also asked to take notes about the quality of these sounds.

Guest John Owens leads
the class in an impromptu
musical ensemble

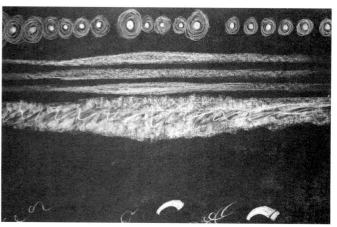

Sound drawing by
Kent Millard (MFA 2010)

Then they categorize distinct sounds according to metrics of their choosing and match them to their own created visual objects. This becomes the database.

TOOL TRANSFER

To test their theories they render each of the objects as time-based media and place them in a two dimensional environment (much like the historical works of Oskar Fischinger and Norm McClaren). The visual representations animate with the sounds. The objects have both visual and auditory relationships with one another and can illustrate properties like harmony, pattern, and rhythm that change over time.

My own experience with testing these parameters gave me the body of research that became the project *Shapemix,* but since it was based partly on my own empirical evidence, how many other possible permutations exist? It is the intersections and differences between people's perceptions that make this project personally interesting to me.

Difference in approach created different challenges. In one example, Jason Bailey (MFA 2010) made several moving three-dimensional timelines of his soundtrack. As the sounds came into prominent view, the eye matched the sound with the object according to its convergence with a static vertical sightline.

Bailey says, "I think the big thing there was trying to create a shape in 3D that would visually map to the sound regardless of what angle you are viewing it. That was really hard to do because as you move around the shape what you see changes dramatically."

Scott Murray's (MFA 2010) approach produced different results. His project presented each visual object randomly around a semicircle. As each object moved into view, its sound became more apparent and its size changed according to its volume.

Elaine Froelich's (MFA 2010) method presented visual appearance (and disappearance) choreographed with the timing of sounds. Each sound had its visual equivalent, with motion and repetition handled through visual patterning on-screen.

VARIABILITY & DIGITAL HARMONY

Once students establish a language of audiovisual equivalencies, they translate their work to dynamic sketches. These sketches serve as platforms for understanding how sound and image work together. The perceived objects have multiple states and those states have visual and audio outputs, and possibly inputs, that are controlled by participants. Variability and significance of change in sound and its visual representation(s) play a large role in what is perceived.

Sound drawing by
Kyoung (Emily) Lee (MFA 2010)

Dynamic interpretation of final
project for "Everything is Music" by
Scott Murray (MFA 2010)

Each approach is different and is selected by the student to test an idea or series of ideas, rather than moving toward a preconceived goal, and can range from musical instruments, random-yet-sequential proofs of audiovisual objects, or experiments in pure aural perception.

Kyoung (Emily) Lee (MFA 2010) created a video-chat program that used sound as input to produce an overlaid visual output to create perceptual significance for participants. Elaine's Froelich's timer experiments ranged from pure audio to audio-as-supplement. Murray's *Aural Data Plot* worked with pure sound:

> *If visualization was not an option, what about an auralization? I created the* Aural Data Plot, *which takes x/y values and plays through them like music. It's essentially just the audible version of a simple bar chart, with left/right panning indicating the x position and pitch indicating the y value.*

CONCLUSIONS

At the end of this course students have created their own pattern languages and have created platforms for sound and vision. Students take their experiments of sound and image and incorporate them in further studies beyond the class and in some cases explore sound as part of their thesis. At the very least they have devised ways of working with their material so that it reflects who they are and what they perceive combined with continual feedback from their peers and others.

Platforms create new realities. Creators of platforms would do well to learn the layers of programmatic abstraction in order to understand what the medium's potential. In the same way mechanical typographers must know the intricacies of manipulating press machinery in order to produce a useful printed design, designers of dynamic media must know how to incorporate logic and variability into platforms that appeal to as many of our senses as possible.

Colin Owens is visiting faculty at the Dynamic Media Institute

featured projects

RandStudio

LAUREN BESSEN

Class of 2006

OVERVIEW: Play With Your Form

All creative art is intuitive. So if it's intuitive, how do you know why you do something? You know why you do something after the fact, then you make up all kinds of stories about it.

— Paul Rand

In a sense, *RandStudio* is a project about those stories and how we use them. More specifically, *RandStudio* is a set of visual analytical tools that lets the design student explore the intuitive formal decisions of Paul Rand. It is an investigation of how the use of motion and interactivity can complement traditional approaches to teaching by demonstrating the vocabulary of visual literacy in a time-based context. Conceived as a system that would eventually cover 10 classic Rand works, ranging from logos to posters to book jackets, this demonstration version examines in depth only one work — the Tokyo Communication Arts poster from 1991.

The prototype version deeply examines a series of formal considerations behind the poster. Users can explore the work within ten specific categories of elementary visual vocabulary: form, counter-form, grayscale, color, hue, opacity, rotation, spatial relationships, scale, and direction. Each examination allows the user to selectively modify the property in question in the composition through the use of a simple draggable slider. For instance, in the scale category, the user can drag a slider to examine how enlarging or shrinking individual forms, from 25 percent to 150 percent of the original size, affects the composition.

Throughout the categories of examination, the range of possible modification is intentionally limited in order to demonstrate opposing formal states — small versus big, geometric and symbolic versus biomorphic and literal, opaque versus transparent. Unlike a commercial design application, creative manipulation is curtailed — only one property is editable at a time and only within a set range — to clearly emphasize the nature of a particular aspect of the visual vocabulary. These ranges help users see Rand's decisions as points on a series of spectra applicable to all form — colors can be more vibrant or alternately grayed-out, tonal value can be darker or lighter, spatial relationships can be tighter or looser.

Each interactive examination is, in essence, an interactive animation. Dragging the slider is equivalent to scrubbing through the playhead of a short timeline. Wildly jogging the slider back and forth or cautiously pulling the bar across the stage produces different results. The quality of temporal sensations rests in the hands of the user.

What do these interactive examinations do beyond encouraging playful formal exploration? Playing with form, users witness the dynamic transformation on screen while becoming more aware of the communicative potential of formal decisions — the dynamic correlation between form and communication. The potential number of alternate compositions that could result from each examination is finite but enormous. The potential for alternative communicative interpretations is possibly infinite though the potential number of clearly articulated visual messages is more difficult to ascertain. Between the polar states of each slider's animation lies a range of communicatively "fuzzy" points. When does the square stop being a square and become a circle? When does the circle suggest an organic form and not a geometric form? The system offers no answers but simply raises the users awareness of the range of possible meanings.

Viewing what Rand didn't do, we acquire a greater appreciation for what he did do. Quite frankly, *RandStudio* allows the user to create any number of horrifically awkward interpretations that communicate radically different ideas. By dynamically altering and re-altering the work, we understand the communicative potential of formal decisions. Short movies, featuring informative animations and voice-over, provide greater context for the communicative role of various formal selections accompanying the interactive features. Quotes from Rand's own articulate writings about the nature of visual form combined with these short features provide a framework for the analytical "stories" which users gain from the experience. Coupled with the interactive explorations, these contemplative encounters with form provide a bigger story. They encourage a deeper visual consciousness that is intended to aid students, whether they are beginners or already experienced designers, in developing a greater intuitive awareness of how to manipulate form to communicate meaning.

FRAMING THE EXPERIENCE: Connecting the Visual to the Verbal

My intention in creating *RandStudio* was to foster an experience in which a student-user could connect the terminology of visual form to examples of form in a manner that emphasized the complexity of these concepts. I wanted a learner to see "color" not merely as question of selecting a particular value, but to understand the symbolism

DESIGN + CONCEPT | Lauren Bessen

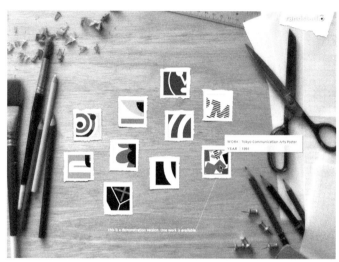

A pedagogical interface to
explore the work of Paul Rand.

inherent in hue, to see various colors as interrelated and dependent, and to recognize quality of chroma as dependent on the degree of saturation and brightness. That said, most of these lessons are implicit and take place through interactive explorations. In order to group these complicated concepts the student must be prepared intellectually. This is a question of framing the student's mind for the coming demonstration or visual lesson through the targeted delivery of sequential text-based information presenting the terminology of visual form in depth. This verbal component illuminates the workings of the visual.

The text-based information is introduced successively. Increasingly more advanced concepts build on those previously presented. The information is arranged, in order of experience or appearance, from the visual term to a more specific definition, to a broad question that frames the interactive exploration, and finally to an insightful animated commentary presented in audio- and text-based form, that offers deeper intellectual explanation. Each successive bit brings you deeper into a discussion of the formal concept at hand. For example, rolling over "form" reveals the further definition "shape and representation." Clicking on the term reveals the questions: "How does the use of geometric forms affect the composition? Could more realistic forms be used instead?" while loading a voice-over animated commentary that can be viewed by the user.

DESIGN METHODOLOGY

What is it that enables this cohesive progression of ideas? Motion, or animation, was used throughout *RandStudio* both to sequence text-based information smoothly and as a means to illustrate visual concepts dynamically. Motion can be found at different levels — in the most simple rollover animations on the individual visual terms, as broader definitions glide in and out, to the way in which the poster animates to represent the concept under investigation when new "design elements" load. Motion as a design methodology was a guiding principle in the project. This motion can be further distinguished into two categories, passive and active. On the one hand, the user watches the short animated commentary segments accompanying each "design element" section. Here, in these brief movies, animated graphics combined with voice-over remarks provide explanations through motion of the primary visual concepts. On the other hand, each interactive design exploration is effectively made up of single or multiple animations. As the user drags the slider forward or backward, he or she drives the playback of the animated sequence forward or backward in time. Guiding the progression of the animated sequence ahead or behind, the user actively controls the motion and correspondingly the transformation of the visual property.

Form communicates meaning and motion is only one significant aspect of the project's design. The design of several interface elements was carefully considered to aid in framing the mind of the user for the experience. The primary goal of the experience is to provide an environment for playfully examining and manipulating formal elements of a poster. As such, the metaphor of a studio — a setting in which designers are consciously engaged in process of creation — was used for the interface. From the outset of the piece a studio tabletop, a symbol for a sort of laboratory of formal play, serves as a backdrop setting for the interface. In the animated introduction pieces of torn paper arrange and rearrange themselves on this tabletop, as if controlled by the unseen hand of the designer, to form the title of the project emphasizing a theme of formal experimentation and creation. With the conclusion of this sequence, a set of square, torn pieces of white paper arrange themselves in the center of the tabletop and a single piece bounces excitedly up and down in place as if asking for our attention until it is selected by the user. When selected, it triggers the appearance and animated formation of highly recognizable graphic elements drawn from Paul Rand's work, carefully masked, inside the squares. The animated development of these works inside the paper squares underscores the purpose of the project: the analysis of composition. Rolling over these individual squares, reveals tooltips with information on the title and date of the framed work adjacent to the square. These square pieces form the menu of works available for examination. Clicking and selecting a square transforms the interface. The paper squares fall away, the chosen work loads and a menu of design elements, terms drawn from visual vocabulary, appears. Now the process of interactive exploration can begin. These animations and design decisions set the tone of the experience, emphasizing playful and creative formal examination.

THEORY: Critical Perspectives on Dynamic Form

Shifting to a more critical perspective, there are two key observations to be made regarding the broader theoretical design concerns at play in *RandStudio*. First, the project makes unique use of dynamic media as a means to visualize analytical formal decisions and, accordingly, it fulfills a critical pedagogical role. Second, the examination of the work of a key modernist designer within an interactive environment offers new perspectives on both the legacy of modernism today as well as the aesthetic issues inherent in 21st century software tools.

A PEDAGOGICAL ROLE

If, as Ellen Lupton posits, the role of formalism in design education has waned to a critical nadir, a current dilemma for design educators is to refashion formalism for a generation of designers weaned on the instant creative ease of drop-down menus, filters, plug-ins, and templates. While Lupton's *Manifesto for a New Formalism* encourages educators to find self-critical approaches to using software in the classroom, how can we think outside the boundaries of commercial applications but still use digital media to talk about form? This thesis takes up that challenge. Why talk about form through dynamic form?

Design is a dynamic act. Form undergoing the process of design exists in a state of perpetual change: when we design, we are continually and constantly manipulating it, whether in pixel or on paper, moving and shaping the elements of a composition until it has reached that particular point where it speaks the intended meaning. A little bit more or a little bit less of a particular formal element, until it reaches a particular sweet spot — often an appropriate intersection of the conceptual and the formal. Only then does it become fixed.

It is precisely because design decisions are inherently conceived within a spectrum of formal choices that using dynamic visualizations to analyze form succeeds as a pedagogical tool. While one could argue that in this sense all commercial design applications enable dynamic visualizations of form — that their various filters and menus offer numerous instant algorithmic manipulations — these applications are primarily design-creation tools, not design-education tools. As a pedagogical visualization tool, the crucial difference between *RandStudio* and commercial design applications are the limitations of control in the former.

In *RandStudio* the extent of dynamic analysis is intentionally curtailed to limited pairs of oppositions for the purposes of demonstration and learning. In a design application you can manipulate a form, controlling various properties successively, to your heart's content. But how much of that process of manipulation will inform you about the structural conditions and the formal potential of the object in question? In *RandStudio*, witnessing the limits of dynamic change enables greater learning potential: you see a form as existing within a spectrum of structural conditions, you recognize the endpoints of the slider as representing more or less extreme manifestations of formal properties, and you ultimately attain greater insight into the nature of formal decision-making process. The ability to perceive these ranges of the formal potential and to attain greater analytical insight into the design process is valuable pedagogically and uniquely realized through dynamic visual form.

The use of limited parameters for formal manipulation shares the pedagogical approach that came to characterize Paul Rand's philosophy as a design educator. During more than 35 years as a professor of design at Yale University, Rand came to articulate a pedagogical style that emphasized the use of restricted problem solving in classroom assignments. In her essay, "Paul Rand: The Modern Professor," Jessica Helfand succinctly summarized Rand's intellectual outlook in the classroom as guided by "the study of limited means — a pedagogical celebration of the modernist ideal."(Helfand, 157) Helfand argues that under this guiding philosophy, "the success of a given problem lay largely in the way it was articulated — and the limitations within which it was given." (Helfand, 156) This educational ethos was encapsulated by Rand's landmark essay, "Design and the Play Instinct." Here, Rand lays out the rationale for structuring assignments as a kind of rule-based play.

I believe that if undue emphasis is placed on freedom and self-expression in the statement of a problem, the result is apt to be an indifferent student and a meaningless solution. Conversely, a problem with defined limits with an implied or stated discipline (system

Users are able to examine Rand's posters through a series of formal categories such as, space, symbol, movement, and typography

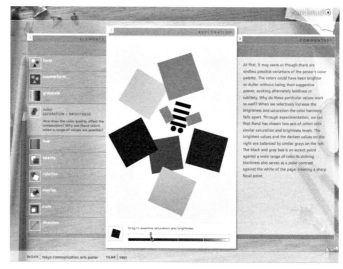

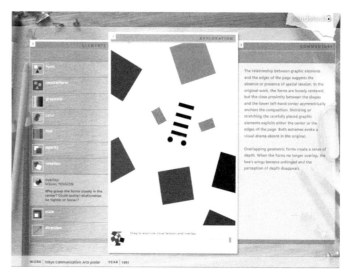

of rules) that in turn is conducive to the instinct of play, will most likely yield an interested student and, very often, a meaningful and novel solution. (189)

What Rand deemed effective about the "play principle," an exercise of playful exploration framed by a set of structured rules, was that it provided an opportunity for observation, analysis, curiosity, and enjoyment — a diversity of "psychological and intellectual factors" fostered by the pursuit of variations within specific limitations. Inspired by the effectiveness of the "play principle" and Rand's pedagogical philosophy, the use of sliders and limited interactivity in *RandStudio* similarly enables playful formal exploration while spurring formal analysis and insight.

MODERNIST IN THE MACHINE: Aesthetic Decisions

Dealing with the polished work of a modernist master requires a certain degree of delicacy in design. An interface in which to examine the work of Paul Rand had to reflect a reverence for his aesthetic sensibility and at the same time provide some form of stylistic commentary on his body of work. The appearance of the interface could not be too graphically transparent but at the same time should enable the work to remain hierarchically prominent. Accordingly, alpha transparency figures heavily in the interface elements such as the "design elements" and "commentary" panels. Furthermore, an outline display version of the typeface Frutiger was used to suggest a similar graphic lightness and transparency.

The graphic "look" needed to be stylistically consistent with Rand's work but not to the point of mimicry — visually it needed to be modernism, remixed and remastered for 21st century viewing. The project identity draws upon the typographic and graphic treatments from two important Rand works — the TK book jacket and the "eye-bee-M" rebus poster. The logo also incorporated the typeface Avenir — a not so completely geometric interpretation of Futura. While drawn within the lineage of Paul Renner's modernist masterpiece, Avenir can be viewed as an updated vision of this classic, one that offers an appropriate and divergent commentary on modernism reinterpreted within an interactive context.

But, the design decisions were not solely informed shaped by trying to fit a modernist-shaped peg into a Flash shape hole. Rather, they exploited what Lev Manovitch eloquently termed the "soft modernism" of Flash — the vector graphics native to the application. Utilizing Flash's vector-based drawing tools made replicating the cut-paper graphic shapes of the original works easily possible. The vector-based versions also served to be easily malleable with the controlled use of shape tweens.

PROCESS: Making RandStudio

RandStudio was the end product of a semester-long process. My two initial concepts were attempts to organize the vocabulary of visual literacy into an interactive dictionary. Both attempts shared a similar approach to mapping the vocabulary around a circle. Inspired by Jessica Helfand's survey of circular information diagrams, I was drawn to this kind of organization as means to visualize the information in a non-hierarchical format.

The first sketch organized visual vocabulary using the definition of the word "design." Classifying the terminology into parts of speech — noun, verb, adverb — I placed the words inside rectangles and grouped them with related terms around the edges of a central circle. In this concept, mousing over the groups of terms would force them to align, while additional, more specific terminology would appear inside the circle. Clicking on a given term would bring up a dictionary-style definition in the corner of the interface.

Critical of what I deemed to be an overly verbal approach, I began to revise the circular concept towards a more visual presentation. Seeking to create a visual metaphor that would be loosely evocative of a color palette, I was additionally inspired by 2x4's Design Classics kaleidoscope movie for Vitra. Incorporating the metaphors of a color palette and a kaleidoscope, as well as a desire to create a symbolic visual language for the terminology, I created a spare, mandala-like diagram for the terms. Next, I developed an animated explanation of the diagram in Flash that heavily incorporated the use of abstract sounds synchronized to the appearance of words on the screen.

Yet, this second attempt eventually seemed too conceptual visually and still overly biased toward a verbal representation of the terminololgy. How could I create a visualization that balanced the visual and verbal representations and was also a compelling interactive experience?

Reading an essay by Tibor Kalman on teaching design through the study of design history, I was struck by his insightful comment on the role of context in understanding visual design concepts. Intrigued by Kalman's challenge, I sought to devise an interactive experience that would teach the visual concepts using key design works. Who would provide these examples? My initial inclination was to focus on Kalman's work, but after a quick survey of his work I deemed it too difficult to draw connections between a coherent set of pieces using the visual concepts. I sought a designer who was both an articulate critic of design, and who possessed a catalog of work that would illustrate the visual terminology well — the most obvious candidate was Paul Rand.

Rand, the consummate design professional, professor, and intellectual, was not only a prolific creator but through his polished writings offered a wealth of pointed commentary on the terminology I sought to elucidate. Moreover, Rand's writing on design drew upon his exceptional body of work to provide insight by example into his complex design decisions. In examining Rand's work, I developed a diagram that mapped the highlights of career, from his early covers for *Direction* magazine to his last corporate logos, against series of design concepts grouped by aesthetic considerations, formal techniques, and typographic selections; this organizational structure was drawn directly from his writings. Using Rand's concepts as a system for analysis, the diagram indicates which formal categories each piece exemplifies.

Mapping Rand, I discovered a pattern of consistency in his use of design concepts throughout his long career. Impressed by the repetition and newly informed about the breadth of Rand's work, I decided to shift my inquiry to a few key pieces — a total of ten logo, poster, and book jacket designs — for my interactive explorations.

With a set database of works, I then began to develop what was to become the first complete interface for the project. A preliminary version was presented at the end of the fall semester. This version incorporated animation to demonstrate several topics of visual literacy yet differed in its approach from the final version in two significant ways. First, users were offered the ability to watch an animation that composed the poster from the basic formal elements of colored squares and circles. Second, users were only able to examine the poster through a series of formal categories, such as space, symbol, movement, form, and typography. Users were offered a list of terms within the categories, and clicking on a word would trigger the poster to animate and illustrate a particular concept. For example, to illustrate "weight" the poster animated so that all of the graphic elements existed in a small pile form at the bottom of the poster rather than harmoniously balanced in the center of the composition. The second and final version incorporated much of the design elements of the first version, including the animated intro and interface elements, but the emphasis of the interactive explorations was revised to enable greater playful exploration with the use of dynamic sliders.

Shifting my focus to in-depth coverage of one work, the Tokyo Communication Arts poster, I restructured the areas of explorations into ten categories and added the short movies and voice-over commentary. *RandStudio* was presented publicly for the first time at the CAA Regional MFA design exhibit during February 2006. Observing users interact with the project in a gallery setting was an invaluably rewarding experience. Over the course of a week, a number of MassArt faculty and students, as well as participants from the CAA conference came through the space. As a graduate student teaching assistant, I had the opportunity to bring 15 students from my sophomore level Form and Communication class to the gallery and watch them interact with the project. Seeing my students interact with *RandStudio* was the most personally meaningful experience of the entire week. Having previously only presented the project to my professors and graduate student peers, witnessing my intended audience's reactions was an incredibly helpful experience. Having thus far developed the project without the benefit of repeated testing, witnessing my students use in the gallery confirmed that the interactive explorations were both engaging and robust demonstrations of formal properties. One student "drove" the project as the rest looked on attentively. As she began the first category of formal exploration, "form," slowly dragging the slider and transforming the shapes into biomorphic forms, a collective excited exclamation swept through the group. For my students, it was a perfect demonstration of the elementary formal vocabulary they were just starting to deal with in graphic design. For me, it was the perfect reinforcement that dynamic visualization held tremendous potential for teaching design principles.

Teaching Typography as Visual Form

Dynamic Visualization for the Letterform

LAUREN BESSEN

Class of 2006

OVERVIEW

Rolling with the momentum of the positive response to *RandStudio*, I turned my attention to developing a second case study. During the process of creating *RandStudio*, I discovered a methodology of using interactive animation and motion to demonstrate the principles of visual vocabulary. Now, with this newly formed knowledge in my grasp, I shifted using dynamic visualization to another indispensable body of formal vocabulary: typography.

Type, the visual record of spoken language, is a formal language unto itself. For the design student, applying and mastering this abstract "language" is no easy task. The terminology used to describe the anatomy of letterforms, the formal attributes of typefaces, and various historical classifications can seem obtuse and sometimes arbitrary to the beginner. Typography is a visual form, yet it is one with a host of associated concepts and specific vocabulary. Learning to "speak" articulately within typographic form is in part a matter of gaining a keen sensitivity to the rules and inner workings of the letterform and a passionate appreciation of this form.

FOR THE LOVE OF THE LETTERFORM

It is probably safe to say that no one loves typography more than designers. No one. The particular stylistic nuances native to typographic form are a favorite hot-button topic among astute designers. Typographic form is design dogma. Do you worship at the house of rational functionalism or expressive delight? Serial typographic monogamists stick to a precious few typefaces, fearful of picking up something distasteful, while the polyamorous throw classical caution aside and need to sample the wares of thousands of foundries.

When I began to develop an interactive educational project based around typography, a wise professor cautioned me that I was entering into an arena of designer turf war. Every design professor has a particular take on the most insightful way to approach teaching typography. Begin with the single character, move to groups of letterforms that build lines and then paragraphs that create pages. Start with a survey of the tools used to make strokes and explain typographic classification as the evolution of mark making. Approach typographic form as a series of contrasts including form, space, direction, color, and texture.

These perspectives and many others have roots within the wellspring of typographic writing past and present. Within design literature, there is a long, established tradition of esteemed writing on typography. It is a genre that continues to evolve with shifting tastes and technological developments, and revise the trusted tomes of the past. Accordingly, most designers can name their single most favorite dog-eared manual of typography, if not two or three.

Given the vast offering of revered writing on type, I chose to create an interactive project on typographic principles not out of the desire to add another work to the genre, but to examine how dynamic visualization can help to communicate in an even more visually and intellectually stimulating manner what has already been set forth in so many books. It is not an investigation based on presenting a novel academic take on the subject but rather on presenting newer ways to see, interact, and experience existing scholarship on typography with new media. That said, in this enterprise I have chosen to take on in my breadth of subject matter a very small slice of the "typographic" pie. I am concerned with the formal qualities of the humble, individual letterform: the most basic element of typography.

In this presentation of the absolute atomic unit of typography

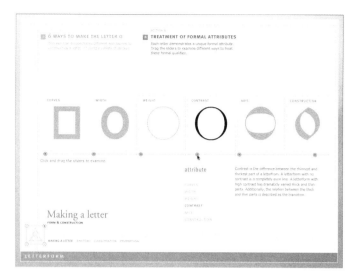

This exercise allows users to explore
several formal nuances of typography.

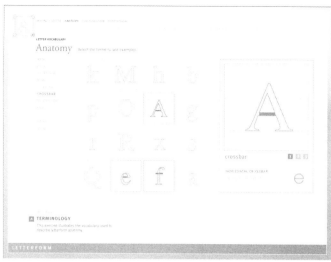

Typographic anatomy
and vocabulary

I am interested in conveying, on a magnified scale, the formal attributes of the letterform. My intention is to render the abstract language of typography — which seems so foreign to the beginner — comprehensible through a dynamic visual demonstration highlighting subtle formal differences to convey several key concepts. *Letterform: An Interactive Typographic Workshop* covers four basic areas of typographic form. 1. The first section, entitled "Making A Letter," covers approaches to formal construction. Through nine different strokes this interactive exercise demonstrates ways to create a letter "o" using modular elements, geometric strokes, and calligraphic strokes. Additionally, this exercise allows the user to explore several formal nuances of typographic attributes such as the treatment of curves, line weight, broken or continuous construction, contrast, and axis of contrast. 2. The second section covers typographic anatomy and a brief survey of the vocabulary used to describe the structure of letterforms. 3. The third section covers typographic classification, presenting an animated timeline of the formal evolution of serif and sans serif typefaces, and enables the user to examine each category in-depth through interactive examinations. 4. The fourth and final section investigates the concepts of point size, x-height, and proportion. In applying such a strictly formal lens to the subject area, it is my contention that starting with the most micro-typographic elements, drawing attention to tiny distinguishing formal characteristics, facilitates a macro-typographic formal appreciation.

MAKING *LETTERFORM*

In creating *LetterForm*, I once again sought to incorporate the use of animation to both "frame the mind" of the user and to create interactive sequences to demonstrate formal potential. Yet I wanted to continue to hone in on the most successful visualization elements from *RandStudio* and draw them out further in *LetterForm*. Watching users interact with the Rand project, I noticed that the most intriguing and visually engaging exercise was the first formal exploration. In this exploration, moving the sliders forwards transforms the

geometric squares into biomorphic shapes. The dynamic contrast of form, accomplished through shape tweening in Flash, received the most positive attention among users. My suspicion was that the illustrative use of shape morphing was more visually arresting, and perhaps entertaining, than the color transformations or spatial rearrangements of forms. I decided to capitalize on this observation and similarly make use of shape tweening to accomplish the visual demonstrations of typographic form. For example, in the "Making A Letter" section a single character "o" morphs nine times in total, through animation, from modularly constructed typefaces, through geometric approaches to letter construction, and finally to calligraphically rooted fonts.

Demonstrating subtle formal differences through animated transformations applies to the topic of typography well because motion accentuates the existence of formal nuance — the most difficult appreciation to gain for novice typographers. Existing contrasts of form in structure, shape, and weight, are made dramatically visible through the use of motion as forms morph into other forms. For example, in the "Classification" section the letters "Aa" transform from one example of a classification to another — such as transitional to modern. The key frames of each are individual examples of typographic terms fused together seamlessly through animation. This conversion illustrates not only differences in form but is used to point out specific typographic terminology, such as the placement of crossbars or the axis of contrast, in a fluid evolution of shape.

In *LetterForm* interactive explorations use dynamic visualization to enable students to better "see" typography and gain a greater "feel" of typographic form. Learning to design with type in a fully digital age — where the acquisition of software skills can seem paramount — sometimes enable student designers to initially bypass composing with type directly on the physical page. Developing a physical relationship with the letterform through setting metal type, copiously drawing or tracing letterforms, or photocopying, cutting and pasting found specimens, is an invaluable component of design

An animated timeline of the formal evolution
of serif and sans serif typefaces

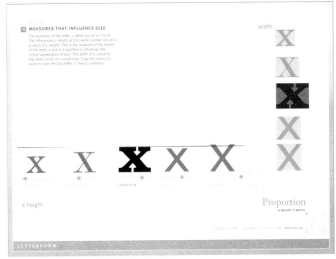

Exploring concepts of point size,
x-height, and proportion

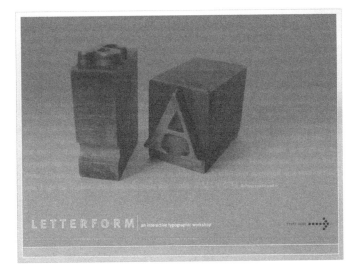

Opening animation for
the teaching typography
interface

education. In the expanded technological toolkit of the contemporary designer, students must be able to transfer this working comfort
with the letterform from the physical to the pixel and vice versa.
With commercial design software applications, the ease of using
drop-down presets allows students to not think out the minutiae
of tracking, kerning, leading, and point size of their typographic
intentions as they effortlessly set type. Complex decisions of color,
contrast, and legibility can be overlooked with the "presto" design
ease of picking numbers and coordinates. It is then imperative that
teachers push students to conceive of typography beyond the preset
limitations and impart a consciousness of the mutability, plasticity,
and sensitivity of typographic form as pure form. The ultimate aim
of *LetterForm* is to encourage this sense of type as a flexible medium
within the realm of the pixel.

MetaLingua

KAROLINA NOVITSKA

Class of 2006

In *MetaLingua*, a human character becomes a teaching aid as well as a conversational partner.

In the fall of 2006, I experienced a major breakthrough in my work. I was fortunate enough to be part of a class called "Design for Motion + Sound" at Dynamic Media Institute taught by Jan Kubasiewicz. I was introduced to cinematic language for the first time in my career. I completed my first short film, "Mashed," in this class. The film depicts the last moments of a dying potato which is being boiled for a Thanksgiving dinner. In this tragic but humorous exploration, we witness the potato's life flash in front of its "eyes" from its perspective. My second short film was even more playful and experimental in nature. In a cinematic adventure titled "PhonOpera," I create a phone conversation between a violin and a piano.

The connection to my case study is clear; I was so inspired by the creative freedom I experienced while working with film that I decided to incorporate this medium into the next stage of the project. Integrating a cinematic vocabulary into the project simultaneously allowed me to address a troublesome shortcoming of the last iteration, a lack of human and emotional involvement. One way to integrate cinematic language into the realm of interactive media is through using real people in video. "This new medium needs cinematography that can satisfy both the emotional and the interactive aspects that arise from the interplay of human participants and virtual characters." (Tomlinson, 1999) How does cinema contribute to the learning experience? Cinematography visually guides the viewer. This allows me to design a fictional reality which leads the learner through the complexity of educational content. By experimenting with the expressive qualities of cinematography, I open the door for an immersive learning experience.

Cinematography calls for an emotional investment from the viewer — the camera, lights, frame, shot, editing, acting, and soundtrack make up a dynamically flowing platform which guides the viewer's emotions throughout the experience. A carefully orchestrated cinematic sequence of images may alter how the viewer perceives a particular event. Manipulation of the learner's perception contributes to the emotional investment in the learning experience.

Editing in cinematography becomes an invaluable tool in guiding the user experience. As Alfred Hitchcock points out, "movies are life with the bad bits cut out." Juxtapositions of interrupted cinematic imagery allow the creator to evoke viewer emotion, change the viewer's perception, transcend time and geographic location, show parallel action time in multiple locations, and dramatically emphasize critical events or downplay non-significant ones, among others. If used correctly, these powerful exploitations can strongly influence the learner's experience within an educational environment.

In an interactive environment, cinematography may also help drive the narrative which in turn helps to sustain the learner's interest and curiosity. However, a major challenge surfaces when the interactive medium is combined with cinematography, particularly as it relates to storytelling.

In a digital learning environment users want to interact, not simply watch the action. Cinematic flow of imagery needs to interweave itself into the interaction rather than cover it up in an artificial way. The experience, in order to become immersive, cannot be interrupted or switched from interactive to cinematic abruptly. Instead, cinematography should enhance and guide interactivity.

THE NEW APPROACH

Interactive video is a natural extension of the visual and contextual responses from which we learned the language in the second iteration of the case study. Aside from verbal and grammatical matter, we are now part of a social setting.

In MetaLingua, I use a human character, named Roza, as our major source of feedback. She responds to all of the interactions with words, objects, and our verbal input. She may gesture a response, display emotion, speak to us, or transform her state or location depending upon the cues that the user provides. Via these responses, Roza becomes a teaching aid as well as a conversational partner. Being able to have actual conversations brings a social meaning to our interaction with the material, unlike the more abstract interactions we experienced in the last phases of my case study. As a human character, she also helps to bridge

the gap between the user, new linguistic concepts, and the unusual interface. It is through her social and emotive responsiveness performed in a personal and almost intimate manner, the student can establish a deeper emotional investment with the material. Furthermore, her physical responses captured in a series of subtle and intriguing motion sequences help this investment on both — cognitive and sensory levels.

My choice to employ Roza as a lead character of MetaLingua is far from accidental. When I thought of the concept of using a human character in my system, she immediately came to mind. Her energy, positive aura, and bright personality, coupled with an enormous talent for acting made her the perfect candidate for the role. I also owe her credit for some of the hilarity that ensued in particular scenes due to her improvisational skills. Her liveliness and her sense of humor, her powerful stage presence, her gracious movement and natural ability to entertain were not necessarily planned in my storyboards. Rather, these elements were born out of her individuality and the actual process. I was constantly filming and re-filming, editing the video and using accidents to my advantage. Some of these accidents worked well within the scope of the project, while others became the perfect material for an outtake section on the final DVD.

In one particular scene, we were filming her pronunciations of the alphabet at MassArt's blue screen studio when suddenly a person dressed in a goblin suit walked onto the set, directly into my frame. To everyone's surprise (there were at least five students in the room at the time), Roza got up and gave the goblin creature a big hug. Apparently, it was Halloween.

In another instance, we were filming the sports section for one of the language activities when I asked her to kick a soccer ball as a future response to user interaction with the word for "soccer." She kicked the ball and inevitably knocked over the lighting post that I had meticulously positioned on the set.

During the process Roza has stoically endured many of my, as she described them, "crazy ideas" — having water poured all over her for the "rain" reference, letters projected on her face for the alphabet section, having to dance sporadically in the presence of a large group of students, even performing a mild form of striptease meant to help the learner understand the meaning of the word "hot" within the weather activity.

Unforgettable situations like these were some of the most enjoyable experiences during the process of developing *MetaLingua*. Overall, I think Roza became an invaluable asset to the project and added so much life both to the process of creating this project as well as to the actual learning experience students encounter. I will conclude my tribute to Roza with the famous MasterCard format: Renting a video camera, $0; renting a lighting kit, $100; seeing Roza perform... absolutely priceless.

THE NEW LANGUAGE

Because the last two versions of my case study suffered from my lack of Spanish language and culture, I switched from Spanish to my native tongue, Russian. The goal is to use my knowledge of the language supported by personal experiences with Russian culture in creating a meaningful educational environment.

PLAYFUL LEARNING EXPERIENCE

We start our experience in an empty room. Roza, our main character, is standing motionless in the middle of the room. Her pose is somewhat of an awkward one as if she is paused in the midst of motion. We move our mouse and she walks in the same direction as our cursor. Noticing the correlation, we are intrigued. We move the mouse back and forth, Roza moves with it. As we realize that we are affecting the environment, the relationship between ourselves and the interface begins to build. However, the interface seems too simple; it now only consists of Roza in front of an empty wall. Moving our mouse to the left of the room suddenly causes a flower tree to grow. We move the mouse away from the tree and it returns to the ground. Should we click on it? We listen to our curiosity and we click. The tree bursts out a series of words, and these words are now part of the interface. What are these words? What can we do with them? We click on the word "ЗЕЛЕНЫЙ" and Roza pronounces it. Since the flower tree is the object that seemed to spawn these

words, we try dragging that word on top of it. Suddenly, the closest flower to where we dropped the word becomes green. We make a mental note that the word "ЗЕЛЕНЫЙ" must mean "green." We are pleased; we just manipulated the elements within this environment and caused the interface to change. Soon, we find ourselves playing with the other words and causing the flowers to change color. As we interact with the words Roza pronounces them, smiling. What if we gave her a flower? Would she react? We drag one of the flowers towards her. "СПАСИБО," she says, as she takes it with a smile and a nod. "You're welcome," immediately comes to mind.

We try moving the mouse to the right of Roza. A large clock face starts to reveal itself in a similar, almost secretive, way. It is apparent that the clock has no numbers on it. Clicking on the clock produces more words that are now mingled together with the first series. As we can see, the level of interaction, while fairly simplistic in the beginning, becomes increasingly complex.

What is our next possible choice of action? Judging from the previous visual responses we received from the flower tree, we try to drag the new words on top of the clock. Do these words stand for numbers? We drop the word "ОДИН" onto the clock and it eases back to its original location. We continue to play, and suddenly one of the words snaps onto the clock reflects the number "1." We realize that matching each word to its appropriate location on the clock face will produce a similar result.

As a supportive mechanism to our learning by association, all words and objects within the space are related. For example, when we drag the word "ОДИН" onto the flower tree, we witness that all the flowers, but one, disappear. Similarly, by dragging the word "ЗЕЛЕНЫЙ" onto the clock we cause it to change its color to green. These dynamic transformations encourage us to experiment more. Our choices of interaction are motivated by our curiosity as well the positive reinforcement we receive when we perform certain actions. Sooner or later we begin to associate the words with what they represent. Through continuous interactive play, intuitive or random guessing transforms into conscious choice. We

make subsequent choices of action based on previous visual, emotional, and contextual responses from the system.

INTERACTIVITY

The interactivity present in *MetaLingua* goes beyond pointing, clicking, and observing. Rather, each scene is a unique interactive engagement that draws us into the environment. Interactive discovery takes place on many levels, from the formal interaction of the system's objects and pieces, to the social interaction of users and fictional characters, to the cultural implications that objects and characters have. The user links unfamiliar words with visual elements and reveals their meaning. In some cases, we sit back and watch a story unfold. Playing with *MetaLingua*, we often find ourselves surprised at what is taking place. For example, when we accidentally drag the mouse over one wall, it rips as if it were delicate paper. The digital transforms into the tactile, appealing to our natural senses. Layer by layer, we rip the interface and reveal new objects that we can interact with. The active process of revelation of the new material stimulates the active construction of new knowledge. An interesting transformation happens at this point of interaction — our curiosity subconsciously changes from sensory (desire to rip the interface) to cognitive (desire to reveal new information).

MetaLingua supplements our curiosity to interact with the many mysteries embedded within the system. For example, a live parrot is present in almost every scene and serves as a metaphor for repetition. Interacting with the parrot causes Roza to repeat her pronunciations, and helps us comprehend unfamiliar sounds.

In some cases, when we are slow to respond, the cursor transforms into a hint. A good example of this is the introductory scene. By rolling over the walking Roza, we notice the cursor change into a miniature version of her sitting, indicating the action that will take place once we click on her. Occasionally, we have to resist our impulse to click and instead try to comprehend the scene, utilizing our newfound knowledge and language skills.

Throughout *MetaLingua*, learners constantly influence the interface. They see it grow and evolve into something different, something that they have a part in creating. Most interactive media experiences train the user to act immediately and expect instantaneous responses. There is rarely time to observe, experience, and reflect. We are a twitch-speed generation that absorbs and discards digital information instantly. An experience with a surreal environment like *MetaLingua* helps us put aside our preconceived notions about interactivity. Rather than utilizing interactivity as a mere tool meant to transform us from one scene to another, *MetaLingua* uses interactivity to allow for experimentation and play. Via experimentation and play we discover new relationships between words and objects, and construct meaning from seemingly abstract concepts. Interactivity allows us to learn by association.

VISUAL FORM

The interface of *MetaLingua* is far from traditional language software, lacking the typical menu bars, drop downs, input fields, and buttons that link to linear content usually titled Chapter 1, Chapter 2, etc. The visual form of *MetaLingua* is a careful juxtaposition of photographic objects, handwritten and digital typography, film, animation, sound effects, and spoken word. These representations of real-life entities exist within a digitally drawn surrealistic environment. Supporting the way real linguistic content appears in surreal situations, the visual interface plays upon this dichotomy.

Visually and conceptually, the interface of *MetaLingua* resembles a theater stage where nothing is constrained but the width and height dimensions. Flexible and visibly unstructured, the interface flows in line with our explorations of the environment. Through interactive play we discover the visual elements hidden within *MetaLingua*. These elements resemble theater props — they are communicative devices that help our understanding of the material; they exist backstage [the database] and are brought in only when needed for a particular purpose. In *MetaLingua*, the learner becomes the director of the play [pun intended] — responsible for affecting, manipulating, and rearranging the visual form of each scene. These are the interactive responses.

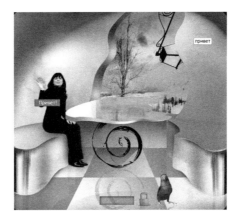

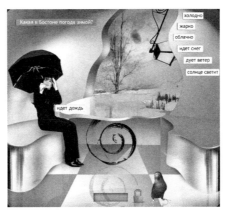

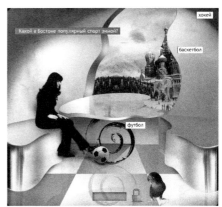
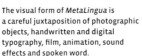

The visual form of *MetaLingua* is a careful juxtaposition of photographic objects, handwritten and digital typography, film, animation, sound effects and spoken word.

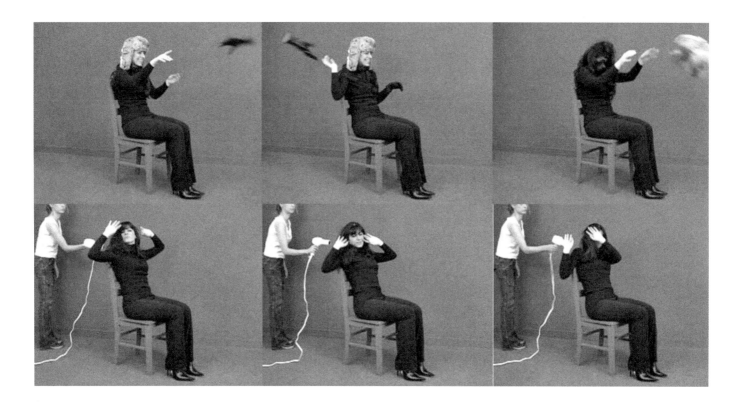

I was constantly filming and re-filming, editing the video and using accidents to my advantage.

So what is the role of the visual responses in *MetaLingua*? As a result of our interaction, the visual responses we receive from the environment directly shape our construction of knowledge. They help the learner draw meaning from both abstract and literal forms. The learner forms these new ideas based on previous life experiences. The cinematic language aids the formation in multiple ways — through gesture of the human character, through emotion exuded in the video, and through the human behavior of Roza evoked by the interaction. For instance, in the introductory scene when we drag the word "ПРИВЕТ" onto Roza, she raises her hand and waves at us. Drawing from previous experiences of what the gesture of waving means to us, we come to a realization that she is saying "Hello." To continue our association of word-to-concept we can drag the same word onto a book. It responds by opening up its pages. While this associative concept is more abstract than the action of waving, the combination of responses from abstract and literal visual form aids our construction of meaning.

What is not immediately obvious to the learner is that at any given moment of playing with *MetaLingua*, the available visual elements directly correspond to the underlying curriculum, changing dynamically according to what linguistic topic is currently covered. The secretive manner in which the objects appear on stage carries its own magic powers — it appeals to our sensory curiosity, encouraging us to continuously play. The objects themselves are metaphorical representations of the current topic that help us learn by association.

The surreal nature of the visual form is perhaps one of the most important characteristics of the interface as it stimulates the learner's curiosity to interact with the environment. What is it about surrealism that affects our perception and evokes our curiosity for continuous exploration? Surrealism is often described as "an ironic transcendence of multiple realities through their juxtapositioning." (Bennington, 2000) Even if we disregard the visibly surrealist style of the interface, the mere conceptual integration of the cinematic language which depicts real human form, a digitally composed synthetic environment, and embedded photographs of real objects and locations exemplifies this definition of surrealism. The *MetaLingua* environment expresses this juxtaposition, and plays with multiple realities, mixed media, visual contradiction, ambiguity, and time/space alteration. The environment also reflects a fundamental element of surrealism — "the rediscovery of hidden and suppressed, but very real, worlds." (Aitken, 1998) Moreover, in surrealism, the process of discovery is incredibly visual, entailing complex relationships between the perceiving "eye" and the perceiving "I." (Bennington, 2000) Unique juxtapositions of multiple realities in *MetaLingua* intentionally elicit an active response from the learner, engaging him/her in the experience.

CULTURAL FORM

The fluid structure of the transparent interface correlates to the notion of Russia as a somewhat unstructured entity. I designed the interface to behave like Russia. My decision reflects the notion of cultural references as an aid to our learning of a new language. A supportive factor to this decision is my desire to add another layer of playfulness to *MetaLingua*.

How does the interface behave like Russia? At first glance it seems unpredictable, obscure, and cold, but through the user's interactions it becomes responsive and human. "Russians respond with a human approach, and they can be kind and helpful once a good interpersonal relationship has been established. This is the key to understanding the Russians." (Richmond, 2003) While there are no specific instructions embedded within *MetaLingua* that clearly describe the relationship between the interface and the nature of Russia as a culture, by prolonged interaction with the system learners begin to understand the cultural connections on a subconscious level. In order for learners to take away conscious knowledge of these connections, the cultural nuances are woven into the dialogues with Roza.

A METAPHORICAL JOURNEY THROUGH RUSSIA

Being able to communicate in a foreign language is a far more complex task than familiarizing yourself with a range of vocabulary words. Breaking the language barrier in the context of a human conversation is one of the most significant milestones in the process of learning a foreign language. What became a major challenge for me as the designer of *MetaLingua*, was figuring out a way to teach complex linguistic content by association. I wanted to create a new module that accomplishes this goal.

MAKING ROOM FOR CONVERSATION

One specific idea for this module — a train ride through Russia — seemed to offer the most potential to support my approach to teach a language by association via playful interactions within a culturally based environment. This ride goes beyond traveling through Russia as a geographic landscape; it is also a metaphorical ride through Russia's language, its rich culture and extensive history. The "locations" we visit range from major metropolitan cities like Moscow and St. Petersburg to destitute rural areas; the train might visit cultural subjects such as the Russian Constructivism; on occasion we can even travel inside someone's home to deal with the linguistic and cultural topic of a Russian family. Such concrete and sometimes abstract locations are visible through the window of our train cabin.

Our journey also becomes a social experiment; throughout the ride we have conversations with Roza, our fellow passenger. This concept opens up a wide variety of linguistic opportunities; the conversations can cover a multitude of themes — ranging from basic greetings, nationalities, family, occupations, sports, weather, and clothing to topics like history, art, and theater. Each conversation correlates to the curriculum while its complexity increases in tune with the learner's ability. *MetaLingua* observes and evaluates the learners' responses and guides them in the right direction, whether presenting the same material in an alternative way or increasing the depth of conversation.

This module incorporates micro-level goals that help to sustain our interest in play. During the train ride, we choose the destinations of our interest. Our question-and-answer dialogue with Roza, allows us to advance from stop to stop until we reach that destination.

EMOTIONAL INVOLVEMENT

A particular layer of interaction, only partially explored in previous renditions of my case study, is the emotional aspect of social interaction. During the conversations, we influence the emotional state of Roza. What becomes interesting is how with each scene our relationship with the screen changes. By having control over the environment, particularly Roza's mood, we often feel personally accountable and responsible for what is happening.

Constant control over the environment, however, is not always required for visual, spatial, temporal, or even contextual transformations in *MetaLingua*. By halting interaction, there is still room for emotional expression of our character. Roza may be surprised that we stopped interacting with the elements in her world. On occasion she might try interacting with words and objects by herself, subtly clueing the learner in.

Emotions, however, are variable and impulsive psychological properties. A simple definition of an emotion states that it is "a mental state that arises spontaneously rather than through conscious effort and is often accompanied by physiological changes; a feeling: the emotions of joy, sorrow, reverence, hate, and love." (Dictionary.com) If we try to avoid conscious effort, then how do we design an emotional system? Design implies a conscious effort that cannot be avoided. Let's restate the question. How can our character truly feel something in a pre-set environment? While Roza's individual emotions are true and human, they are not spontaneous; rather, they exist in a set of recorded clips that reside in a database of *MetaLingua*. The timing and order in which we see her emotional responses, is pre programmed based on each specific interaction. Does the artificiality of Roza's responses impede our experience? Because we have a direct influence over her emotions through our actions, such reciprocal form of communication mimics a real human relationship. While each action causes a particular reaction, the emerging relationship is not fixed in a nonlinear system like *MetaLingua*. Our choices of actions, coupled with the underlying curriculum, guide the direction and the scope of this relationship. The unpredictability of the relationship that results from interactive play adds a layer of surprise to our experience. It is through this collaborative effort that the spontaneity of human emotion takes place.

PLAY AS EXPERIENCE

Essentially, to play with *MetaLingua* is to experience it — to see the environment, to touch the objects, to hear the sounds, to feel multilayered emotions about the emerging outcome, to communicate with the onscreen character, to bend time and space, and to alter one's thinking. Unlike the clear mathematical algorithms that make up the architecture of *MetaLingua*, the experience of play is more ambiguous and difficult to pinpoint. The nuances of the actual experience will vary for each individual learner. They might even change each time the same person plays with the environment.

When these experiences are relevant to the curriculum they become another supporting device that helps our learning by association. For example, at one point on our train ride through Russia, we have a conversation with Roza on the topic of weather. In one instance, when we drag the word "ХОЛОДНО" on top of her she begins to shiver. The longer we hold it, the more dramatic her shivering becomes. Soon the word "ОЧЕНЬ" appears next to "ХОЛОДНО." What does it mean? Is that an adjective to describe the degree of how cold Roza feels? If we continue to hold these words, we might eventually see a hint of frosting on her hair. We soon realize that through these words we affect her physical state, causing her to experience extremely cold conditions. Inevitably, this influences our own experience of play. Since we made her uncomfortable, are we uncomfortable? Perhaps the feeling of coldness will reach us on a subconscious level. In this example we associate our sensory experience with related linguistic content. Participating in a memorable experience helps us remember the educational material that is associated with this activity. Next time we come across the word "ХОЛОДНО," we will remember Roza's shivers.

Identifying the qualities of play learners might experience in each scene becomes a useful method to explore learning by association to its fullest potential. The challenge for me, as the designer, is that the experience of play is not something I directly create. Rather, play is an emergent property that arises when a learner engages with *MetaLingua*. What I create are the rules and the structure, the environment and the internal system behaviors, which learners will inhabit, explore, and manipulate. It is through these actions that the learner will experience play. By directly designing the elements that make up *MetaLingua*, I indirectly shape the learner's experience.

PLAY AS SIMULATION

A quick and effective method of learning a foreign language is complete immersion in the environment where the target language is spoken and the cultural setting serves as a stage for this immersion. Often such direct experience is not feasible, possibly due to high cost, danger, inaccessibility, or lack of time. As an alternative, achieving similar results may be viable through a simulation.

What is a simulation? A simulation is any attempt to mimic a real or imaginary environment or system. (Alessi & Trollip, 1991) Educational simulations are designed to teach someone about the system by observing the result of actions or decisions through feedback generated by the simulation in real-time, accelerated time, or slowed time. (Rieber, 1996) *MetaLingua* simulates real human conversations in a culturally based environment. It is designed so that the scope of the dialogue expands as the learner is ready for it. Continuous play with the elements allows the learner to test their newly acquired ideas and linguistic concepts in a safe and easily accessible way.

PLAY FOR LEARNING

Current language software assumes that the system should guide the learner as the software becomes an electronic teacher. My approach in *MetaLingua* emphasizes learning more so than teaching. What is it that makes an effective learning environment? Rieber defines it as a space where the resources, time, and reasons are available for students to nurture, support, and value their learning of a limited set of information and ideas. (Rieber, 2001) *MetaLingua* is a model of experimentation, distributed control, and conversational exchange rather than a system guided by a sequential curriculum fully controlled by the teacher. Learning in *MetaLingua* is based on curiosity and interest as opposed to relying on specific rewards and threats. The learner shares control with the system, through dialogue rather than conquest — a dialogue that the learner initiates.

MetaLingua does not impose a prescriptive sequence of activities or topic. Rather, it responds to the learner's interactions with specific, consistent, context-sensitive functionality. It allows the learner to initiate a dialogue and responds by generating unpredictable emerging effects and provides suggestions for further experimentation. *MetaLingua* is a learning environment that gives students autonomy, responsibility, and flexible choices for their learning.

The constructivist principles are seamlessly woven into this iteration of my case study. By exploring linguistic content based on association and avoiding direct translation, the students construct their own knowledge, testing new hypotheses against real-world situations. By focusing on the experience of the user/character interaction, the system emphasizes process rather than product. By providing a nonlinear, user-driven access to a wide curriculum it promotes student-directed, student-centered learning. Through multiple representations of linguistic content allowed by the digital medium, *MetaLingua* accommodates different learner styles and strategies.

MetaLingua also encourages users to try new learning styles by recognizing their interactive behavior, their successes, as well as the mistakes they make. If the learner is experiencing difficulty in understanding the material, the system introduces supplementary visual and audio clues as well as customizing the interactive behaviors to reflect a particular learning style.

One of the most important principles of learning in an interactive system is co-construction where learners feel like active agents (producers) and not just passive recipients of information (consumers). In a digital learning environment it is crucial for the student to feel that their actions and decisions are not just the designer's actions and decisions. Rather, they should feel they are co-creating the world they are in and the experiences they are having. *MetaLingua* exemplifies this principle in a way that students feel empowered to reveal new information, to induce emotive and behavioral responses from the character, to experiment and play with the material interactively, and finally, to manipulate, affect and change the visual form of the environment. Thus, the experience of play becomes different for each student; learning becomes an active process of constant participation.

Deep learning in an interactive environment requires an extended commitment which is powerfully invoked when learners are able to take on a new identity. This allows them to reveal new information coupled with opportunities to become heavily invested in the experience. In *MetaLingua*, particularly reflected in the Train module — the learner takes upon the social role of a train passenger, in increasingly complex dialogues with the virtual human character. The character herself is so intriguing that she becomes a magnet for curiosity-driven continuous interaction that triggers deep investment in the learning experience.

In order for learning to occur, the challenges within the system should be pleasantly frustrating in a way that a learner feels at the outer edge of their competence. Thus, new challenges always seem difficult but approachable. *MetaLingua* adjusts the challenges and gives feedback via the visual and emotional responses which indicate whether or not the learner is on the path to success. Moreover, *MetaLingua* provides

well-ordered problems to learners; the initial challenges within the system seem relatively easy but are used to demonstrate the "rules of behavior" of the system in order for the learner to apply the same rules to harder problems in the future.

MetaLingua is a system of exploration, discovery, and most importantly play. It is an experimental approach designed to challenge traditional language teaching methods by utilizing playful interactivity for educational purposes. Perhaps this method is not meant to work for everybody. Those, however, who are willing to experiment with *MetaLingua*, might begin to view language learning with a child-like attitude and become more receptive to the new language. Willingness to experiment requires intriguing targets of experimentation. *MetaLingua* offers a multitude of uniquely responsive elements to interact with in order to reveal new information coupled with opportunities to affect, manipulate, and change the unusual environment. Curiosity, driven interaction causes these alterations to the system which in turn promote student interest and willingness to continue the process of meaningful experimentation and play.

We were filming at MassArt's blue screen studio when suddenly a person dressed in a goblin suit walked into my frame.

Karolina Novitska
Class of 2006

Adobe Design Achievement Award winner, avid traveler, aspiring linguist, and student of the salsa dance

Advice to incoming students: *Don't get intimidated by open-ended projects. Use these opportunities to explore a subject you are passionate about. Get inspired by the tremendous intellectual resources the professors provide. Don't lose focus and embrace failure and confusion and you will be surprised at the creative thinking that can transpire when your mind is most uncomfortable.*

Before moving to the United States in 1996, Karolina Novitska and her family traveled from Ukraine to England where she began learning English. While she eventually succeeded in her primary goal and speaks fluent English, the experience left a strong impression on her. Something from the stale and rigid classroom environment inspired her, nearly a decade later, to begin thinking about the intersection of new media and languages. In her thesis, *forWordPlay: Experiential Learning of a Foreign Language via Interactive Play*, Karolina explores the nature of playful activity and how it applies to learning new languages.

From the beginning of her thesis it is abundantly clear that Karolina takes play seriously. Within the first page of her introduction, in an attempt to outline a definition of the word play, she sites the work numerous theorists, psychologists, and academics. Later in the book she notes John Dewey and Jerome Bruner's role in shaping her understanding of thought processes and how individuals learn. This backdrop of theoretical discourse allows her work to gracefully straddle two worlds: the playful and the serious.

In 2006, during her final year at the Dynamic Media Institute, Karolina won an Adobe Design Achievement Award in the Live Action Category for her project, *Crossword*. The short film is a series of over 2,000 still images exploring Alzheimer's disease. The experience of watching her film is jarring: she quickly cuts from sequence to sequence, the camera frantically shakes as it zooms and pans, and at some points the soundtrack runs in reverse. Each visual element frames the emotional content of Karolina's exploration of what it might feel like to have this disease.

It is this level of detail and curiosity that makes her work as a designer so poignant. Speaking about her creative influences, Karolina discusses how her ideas begin to take shape. "I usually get inspired by seeing and feeling new and unfamiliar perspectives. One of my favorite questions that sparks my imagination is 'What if?'" In some sense, her decision to return to school was based partly on this question.

After graduating from Emanuel College, she became a designer for ReadyAbout Interactive, an agency specializing in corporate website design. Graduate school was an opportunity for Karolina to move outside the constraints of commercial design and to push herself to do more playful and experimental work. Her experience at the DMI program played a pivotal role in her development as a designer. "DMI was truly the hardest, but most impacting, educational experience of my life. Through working with the brilliant team of professors and advisors I have grown as a designer, as a thinker, and as a person."

This growth can still be seen in her work as a Senior Designer at Boston Interactive, in her own freelance work at studioekara.com, and as an adjunct faculty member at MassArt. Whether she is playing the role of designer, consultant, or educator Karolina continues to ask "What if?"

Written by Dennis Ludvino

Julia Griffey

Class of 2005

Dancer, educator, entrepreneur, machine embroiderer, mother of three, and sustainable housing enthusiast

Advice to incoming students: *Produce, reflect, write, produce, reflect, write, produce, reflect, write, and pursue only projects that speak to you.*

After graduating from the Dynamic Media Institute, Julia Griffey did what most students only dream of — developed her thesis into a successful business model. *Animocation* delivers interactive games that encourage learning through movement, socialization, and play. In Julia's world the experiences of barn owls, giaraffes, and flamencos are transformed into engaging educational games that users navigate with their bodies. *Animocation*'s work has been exhibited across the country at places like the Amelia Park Children's Museum in Westfield, Massachusetts, the Santa Maria Discovery Museum in Santa Maria, California, and the Winston-Salem Children's Museum in Winston-Salem, North Carolina.

Motion was nothing new to Julia. As an undergraduate student at the University of California at Berkeley studying Civil Engineering, Julia was heavily involved in Modern Dance and its influence began to trickle into her graduate work. "After my first year at DMI," Julia said, "I knew I wanted to do a project that integrated human movement and interactive media. I was also interested in traditional animation and expanding my skills in this area. I toyed around with a lot of serious ideas like developing a movement analysis tool. Then I discovered Dance, Dance, Revolution and that changed everything for me. I allowed myself to focus on something that was fun and this allowed me to integrate the animation component."

Although this enthusiasm propelled her to create an engaging, original body of work, it did not come without a spectacular effort. "I really credit the faculty at DMI for making me dig, dig, dig and evolve my ideas. I knew that animation could be a great teaching tool. I also knew that movement-driven interactive experiences were fun and engaging. So why not create an interactive, movement-driven experience that was educational?"

Education lured Julia into the DMI program. While she was looking forward to pushing her thinking as a designer, she mostly wanted an MFA to pursue teaching opportunities. It just so happened that while working on her thesis she was teaching full-time in the department of Interactive Media at the New England Institute of Art. And currently, Julia is a full-time tenure-track Assistant Professor in Interactive Media at Webster University in St. Louis.

Her passion for education and animation was something not easily given up, "My thesis was a project I was deeply invested in for three years. After I graduated I couldn't just abandon the idea." While teaching and her family take up most of her time, Julia continues to produce pieces for children's museums and sees plenty of potential to develop the business.

She is an active member of the Association of Children's Museums and the Association of Science and Technology Centers. *Animocation* is a work in progress and Julia has plans to expand the experiences, content, and technology currently in use. The desire to continue pushing her professional life as an educator and business owner is summed up best by her graduate school experience, "DMI encouraged me to think bigger, experiment more, and let the solution evolve."

Written by Dennis Ludvino

Evan Karatzas

Class of 2005

Philanthropist, Big Brother, successful entrepreneur, educator, and fearless designer

Advice to incoming students: *I think the most important thing is to find an area that you feel strongly about — something personal that can serve as a foundation for your thesis work either as an underlying content area or that can translate more directly into your thesis investigation. Without this, your thesis work will be a chore and you won't approach it with a sense of purpose or passion and it will make it all but impossible to claim a topic or territory as your own.*

It is not surprising that one of the most frequently cited projects at the Dynamic Media Institute is *Proximity Lab*, Evan Karatzas' major thesis project. Comprised of an 8 foot-by-16 foot platform complete with custom-built RFID sensors, hundreds of antennas, a high-power projector, and special shoes that feed location data, *Proximity Lab* is perhaps the most ambitious thesis offering in the DMI program's 10-year history. To execute this idea, most students, inhibited by a lack of resources, would combine some creative green screen work with a touch of AfterEffects trickery and *voila*, out comes an interesting project. Evan, on the other hand, meticulously designed and built each element resulting in a workable prototype installed in the Stephen D. Paine Gallery at MassArt.

Speaking about his experience developing *Proximity Lab*, Evan discusses his desire to think beyond the limitations of the screen. "My interest in developing human scale installations grew from having spent nearly two decades as a screen-based interaction designer. I felt extremely limited by this small screen and desktop orientation, which, when you think about it, is one of the most constrained and unnatural settings for an immersive experience to take place. I was anxious to explore work that was not bound by these conventions."

This level of innovation was nothing new for Evan. As an undergrad at Syracuse University, he first majored in computer science, but quickly realized his interest was in multimedia development and interface design. After hopping from one fruitless major to another, Evan ended up developing his own concentration in interactive design through a series of independent studies. In 1997, after graduating, he went on to co-found Flywire, a web design and development firm based in Portsmouth, NH. The firm grew quickly during the dotcom bubble and reached 35 employees in less than two years.

This experience left a clear impression on him. "I was in my late 20s and not terribly qualified to be running a company. I was pretty overwhelmed and learned some painful lessons about running a business. Many of my failures as a manager and team leader shaped the direction of my thesis work. The role that technology played in my personal failures — notably my tendency to hide behind email and Instant Messaging rather than engage my team directly — was the impetus behind my interest in proximity, social interaction, and technology."

Proximity Lab has achieved a vibrant life beyond graduate school. It is the name of Evan's successful design firm touting clients like Bose, Adobe, and PBS. He looks at his current success as an extension of what he learned while studying at the DMI program. "I see my professional work as an opportunity to engage people, to give them a chance to be creative and expressive, and make them think about their relationship to others and how their actions affect a larger system or community."

Most recently, *Proximity Lab* became an integral philanthropic partner to the DMI program. After numerous discussions with Jan Kubasiewicz, coordinator of the program, Evan recently announced the *Proximity Lab Fund*, an annual scholarship designed to help DMI students realize innovative and ambitious dynamic media projects that would be difficult to achieve without financial support. The fund will provide access to the necessary materials and resources that students need to build their thesis projects. The fund will include grants totaling $6,000 per academic year with $3,000 awarded at the beginning of the Fall and Spring semesters. Awards will be distributed to one or more students each semester with variable award amounts determined by an advisory panel.

Evan has a long history of generosity. He has been a Big Brother for over fifteen years, helped built greenhouses for Friends of Boston's Homeless, and volunteers whenever he has free time. His decision to give back to the DMI program resulted from his overwhelmingly positive experience. "It was certainly one of the most rewarding, creative, and productive periods of my life. I found a true mentor and advisor in Jan and the opportunity to do highly creative, self-directed work that is virtually unrestricted in scope and scale has been incredibly gratifying … it seemed natural to do something to help students realize their work at a larger scale where financial limitations would otherwise prevent them from going big."

Beyond helping students financially, Evan remains active on the academic side of the DMI program. As a guest lecturer, professor, and critic he continues to influence and shape the direction of the program. While he undoubtedly will be successful in this phase of his career, it is not something that he takes lightly. "This is a fairly new role for me and in many ways I feel inexperienced as I did in my early years of learning how to run a business. I have quite a lot to learn."

Written by Dennis Ludvino

Samsara

ELIZABETH LAWRENCE
Class of 2006

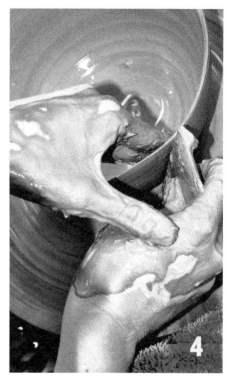

INTENT

As my final Dynamic Media Institute project, my original intent was to create a divination deck for artists and designers. A bit like *Oblique Strategies*, but with imagery and an internal system. It would be well-suited to mirror aspects of consideration in art-making contexts, yet retain a flexibility that also allows for general-purpose readings.

Exploration of change is at the heart of divination practice. Changing the system of tarot to create this deck was odd for me, at first. I had always wished for a deck that contained more contemporary imagery, but as a system, tarot had always seemed to me to be quite flawless.

Yet as I moved past understanding of the structure into genuine analysis of it, I also moved past paranoia that tarot fanatics would burn me at the stake for altering things. In fact, purists would not call this system 'tarot' at all, but I've decided to label it as such because it was inspired by and draws so deeply from tarot that I feel it is a genetic alteration of the same species.

Tarot has always had the potential to mirror creative process, but in *Samsara* this attribute is foregrounded. The imagery of the (4) form card, for example, depicts a ceramics artist shaping a bowl on the wheel. In the context of a simple question like, "what aspect of my project needs the most work right now?" this card might indicate an emphasis on formal considerations, whereas in the context of a question like "what pattern am I stuck in with Mr. X," maybe there's an imbalance of emphasis on the physical.

IMAGERY

All *Samsara* imagery is original; no stock or professional photography was used. Happily, too, the project became a little bit collaborative. The following cards are based on photos submitted by:
  – Nicole Meinhardt: Rebellion, Death, Strength, Mend and Sensuality:
  – Christine Biegert: Idealism
  – JonVan: Generosity:
  – Sally Lawrence (my mom!): Pedagogy:
  – Matt Samolis: Patience
  – Katya Popova: Tone

Very traditional tarot decks depict in the allegorical major arcana figures from antiquity. Adrian Frutiger defines visual allegory in *Signs and Symbols, Their Design and Meaning*:

> *The allegory consists of a purely figurative representation, usually a personification of an abstract concept, with the objective of providing a naturalistic illustration of some extraordinary deed, exceptional situation, or outstanding quality. Most of the allegorical figures of Western culture are derived from the mythology of Greece and Rome and given attributes in a manner that generally dates back to the Middle Ages or the Renaissance.*

Much of *Samsara's* imagery is allegorical, but has broken with the Grecian/Roman tradition. *Samsara's* imagery is less esoteric than any deck I've seen, with the exception of "spoof" decks like The Housewives Tarot. The imagery always references familiar objects

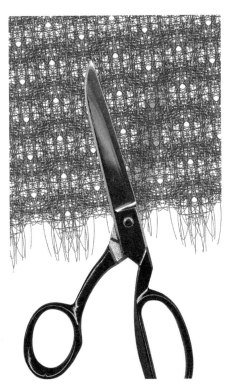

from contemporary experience, for there is a wealth of metaphor in everyday objects. For most people, employing familiar imagery is more approachable than the attempt to contextualize imagery based on life in the fourteenth century. It also encourages more flexibility in its application; for example, use in the classroom.

SUITS

In the 1300s, the suit imagery of tarot was contemporary. The tools of the minor arcana were a part of daily life. Swords, for example, are a lovely, apt metaphor for intellect but it's the rare individual today who will ever see a sword in real life, let alone use one.

It was tempting to simply "update" the imagery of tarot, keeping the system and themes intact. An update for the suit of swords, for example, could be knives. One problem with such a switch, however, is evidenced in the quasi-contemporary Victoria Regina Tarot, which "updates" swords to guns. Although in the fourteenth century swords were somewhat commonplace, they retained connotations of ritual, ceremony, and service. What guns have to do with this today won't be debated here. Knives, when employed past the practical, also hold connotations of violence, and I sure wouldn't characterize cutting food as an intellectual pursuit. I could have transformed swords to pens or the like. I didn't. I have not designated suits at all. This is not to say I don't find them relevant in the old system. It is that, with imagery that is less obscure and more contemporary, the designation of suits is not necessary, and may even be counterproductive.

Because the imagery in *Samsara* is in many ways more direct, I believe that a delineation of experiential realms (physical,

A divination deck for artists and designers with imagery and an internal system based on tarot cards.

One challenge in creating imagery for these cards was straddling the line between specificity and abstraction, between revealing too much information or not enough.

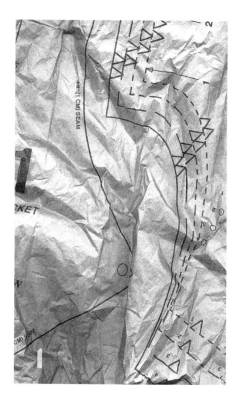

emotional, intellectual, spiritual) through suits (pentacles, chalices, swords, wands, or some variation of these symbols) would be unnecessarily restrictive. If you draw the (9) humor card, for example, who is to say how that quality is being, or shall be, manifested? In general analysis, humor does relate most dominantly to the intellect. But in this context, how does that matter? There is physical humor, humor that relieves stressful emotions, and humor based on spiritual concerns. In other words, because humor is manifested in each of the four realms according to circumstance, pigeonholing it as "intellectual" would be at best superfluous and at worst obscuring of personalized circumstance. Such directives would interrupt the fluid nature of the system.

NUMBER

Numerological aspects, however, reveal relevant information without, I feel, being unnecessarily restrictive. As stages of process, number clarifies an additional level of qualitative meaning in the cards without restricting experiential domains that are fluid and interconnected. As described in the chapter "The Minor Arcana and Qualitative Number," the numbers 1–10 represent a linear process of development. Of course, we don't always experience these stages in perfect archetypal order. For instance, if you are 'at 5' in a project or situation — experiencing instability or crisis — you might not proceed directly to the adjustment of 6. You might choose to almost abandon the situation altogether and revise it so radically that you are back at the 1 of raw potential. This, of course, is the non-linear aspect of creative process that is mirrored by processes of shuffling and drawing.

HIERARCHY

In card games, higher numbers are usually worth more points. But numbers in tarot represent qualities, not quantities. Higher numbers in tarot can't be seen as better or worse than lower numbers. Sometimes the most challenging, frustrating, "negative" phases of creative work are experienced in the middle or toward the end of a project. But a structural hierarchy manifests in the major versus minor arcana. Some situations or aspects of situations demand more attention and consideration than others. The major arcana point to strong archetypes, constellations of energy that may have been based on spiritual concerns. Of course, this is not to say that major arcana cards are "better" than the minor cards. They're just more intense.

THE MINOR ARCANA

Samsara's minor arcana contains forty cards: four of each number, 1–10. As mentioned, there are no suits. If each grouping by number is considered a set (the set of 1s, the 2s, and so on), the variations among the cards in a set represent varying aspects of the quality of that number. For example, geometrically, 2 is a line between two points. And so qualitative aspects, or principles of creative development, of the number 2 include duality, connection, affirmation, and initial understanding, whether these principles manifest physically, spiritually, emotionally, or physically in the querant. Card themes (names) for 2s in this deck include intimacy, mirror, balance, and reveal.

Because there are no suits, the cards do not depict 4 objects in the imagery of a 4 card, but rather an archetypal image that more directly conveys the 'essence' of 4.

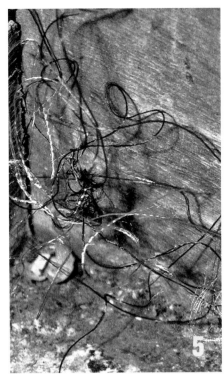

THE MAJOR ARCANA

In homage to tarot tradition *Samsara* includes a major arcana, but the themes of almost all the cards have changed. The major arcana can be considered "trump cards;" they carry more intensity and more weight in a reading. In a spread, the presence of a major arcana card often becomes the focal point of a reading, like a sun with minor cards in orbit.

Like the minor arcana, the major arcana includes a linear progression. Here the progression begins with 0 The Portal, and develops through to XXI Birth. As a linear narrative, this is a story of development and maturation.

The traditional tarot's major arcana is of a political nature; one starts out as The Fool or the court jester, and progresses through political stages like the Empress, the Emperor, and the Hierophant (Pope). I have included one card called Politics, as that maze is a great archetype to contend with in any creative process, but have done away with any obvious reference to political rank or station.

In changing many of the themes, I have also tried to keep a consistency with the minor arcana regarding qualitative number. Traditional tarot doesn't always do this. In a standard deck, for example, card V in the major arcana is The Hierophant (philosophies and teaching/learning) but numerologically, V is instability and great change, usually crisis. A hierophant (an ancient Greek priest), does not exemplify this principle nearly as well as would card like traditional XVI, The Tower (destruction) for example. I've retained teaching as an archetype in my deck, but I call it Pedagogy, because that word contains both teaching and learning. And I place it at IX: understanding, strengthening and attainment. At V I've placed

Oppression, of which the closest correspondence in a standard deck would be The Devil.

Some major arcana cards in *Samsara* reinterpret familiar traditional themes while placing them at different points along the spectrum; IX Pedagogy in place of V The Hierophant and VIII Discretion in place of VI The Lovers (customarily about choice), for instance. Others, like XII Rebellion, XIV Distance, and XV The Mulch, for instance, have no direct parallel to a traditional deck. Cards that reinterpret familiar traditional themes while placing them at the same points along the traditional spectrum are: 0 The Portal (0 The Fool), II The Sensor (II The High Priestess) III Compassion (III The Empress) X Luck (X The Wheel of Fortune) XIII Death (XIII Death) and XXI Birth (XXI The World).

DUALITY

Every card contains duality. Any card can be interpreted as positive, negative, or neutral. Depending on the context, VI enable might portend focusing on the aspect of a project that stresses user experience, or in another context, it could be about complicity in a negative pattern. The image on this card shows feet stepping through a path. If you look closely, you see that the objects in the path aren't flowers (as some first thought) but eggshells. One challenge in creating imagery for these cards was straddling the line between specificity and abstraction, between revealing too much information (being too literal) and not revealing enough information (being obtuse). Sixes embody aspects of adjustment, solution, and harmony. Here the image of walking on eggshells might be easy to interpret negatively, but depending on the mind-set of the reader, it may not be seen in its negative aspect at all. Maybe she's tiptoeing through tulips. In each reading, it's the initial feeling response to the card that will determine its general meaning. The more time spent contemplating a card, the more nuanced, and yet more specific, this meaning will become.

REVERSALS

A card that's turned upside down (a very common occurrence) in a spread is called a reversal. Many people use this random occurrence as another level of informational directive regarding duality in their readings. Customarily there are five methods for dealing with reversals; people tend to choose the method that feels right to them and stick with it.

1. Inverse. Some folks interpret upside-down cards inversely. For example, a right-side-up Death card would mean "change," whereas a reversal would mean "stagnation."

2. Negative. Others interpret a reversed card more negatively than an upright card.

3. Negation. Some see reversals as negating the relevance of the card altogether.

4. Inner/Outer. Many interpret reversals as more relevant to one's inner life, and upright cards as more relevant to outer manifestation.

5. Ignore it. My favorite.

A POINT, BEGINNINGS, INCEPTION

1s: Raw energy, Opportunity, Potential A line, Duality, Connection

2s: Affirmation, Initial Understanding A Plane, Perspective

3s: Fertility, Manifestation Volume, Solid, Stability

4s: Stubbornness, Stagnation, Instability, Crisis, Change

5s: Loss, Uneasiness Adjustment, Solution

6s: Centeredness, Harmony Feeling, Deepening

7s: Introspection, Mystery Order, Repose

8s: Contraction, Retreat Integration, Understanding

9s: Fruition, Strengthening, The challenge of moving to a new level

10s: The end of a cycle, Transition

The traditional tarot's major arcana is of a quite political nature; one starts out as the Fool or the Court Jester, and progresses through political stages like the Empress, the Emperor, and the Hierophant.

The Fool

The Empress

The Emperor

The Chariot

The Moon

The Sun

Strength

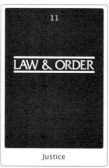

Justice

The Devil

The Star

Judgement

The Universe

InsideOut

KATE NAZEMI

Class of 2006

Digital information in tangible form puts knowledge transfer into the receiver's hand by forming a direct relationship with the receiver. This method also appeals to multiple senses. *InsideOut* is a prototype for an installation that investigates language through simultaneous engagement with textural objects and associated sounds.

OVERVIEW

Completed in December 2003, *InsideOut* is a preliminary case study investigating language, in the form of texture, sound, and interactivity, by using a physical object as an interface. This piece aims to talk about the gap between internal and external language through interactions where participants wade through sound by pulling out textured materials from a series of larger than life-size heads. The action of pulling is a metaphor for forcefully stimulating the externalization of an internal language. The texture of materials signifies the tone of internal content.

The project began in response to the word "tropos" (a Greek word that means: to bring out from within). Initially, several three-dimensional small-scale models of heads with a variety of materials coming out of their mouths were made. These initial small-scale models evolved into two final representations of life-size heads, which were sewn, stuffed, sanded, and mounted on to armatures. Two nonverbal expressions were chosen (squeak and mumble) with corresponding textures (soft, sprightly branches and course rope, respectively). Manipulation of these materials, through the action of

pulling initiated sounds and allowed participants to experience language through the body.

OBJECT

Many physical materials have an emotional value due in part to our organic similarity to them — we are both taken from matter — and, to the personal life experiences we bring to them. They also have an aesthetic value, in the sense that we make use of the fundamental properties of materials. And, of course, materials also have a useful value. *InsideOut* examines this phenomenon through poetic form: the inherent qualities of leather used to make the heads — protective, tough, opaque — make reference to our own skin. The raw, twisted, and course qualities inherent in rope felt in our hands connects us to the rough and course quality of sounds heard. The focus of this type of interface is on forming an emotional relationship between the object, media, and the user, where the user's action stimulates an esoteric response of sound. The form of the object is so vague and fragmented — mounting only the head on white armatures that blend into the background, the heads are disembodied, suggesting a disconnect in the content that follows — that interaction with them allows for a great number of individual interpretations. The heads and sounds heard are meant to let the user's mind fill in the gaps. This not only determines the level of interactivity but the degree to which the experience is received or understood.

InsideOut is a prototype for an installation that investigates language through simultaneous engagement with textural objects and associated sounds.

SOUND

Connecting the physical to the digital through sound was a great discovery. Sound is integrated with texture to communicate the abstract and emotional tone of each head. Here, fragments of speech rather than intelligible speech convey the abstract and complicated nature of a premature language. Human voice was digitally recorded and paired with the action of pulling out materials from the heads. In theory, pitch and tone corresponded to rate of pulling and could be manipulated according to the user's interactions over time. In this context, the user's interaction with sound creates an explorative environment for individual interpretation and personal reflection.

USER-EXPERIENCE

Experience is shaped by context, user interaction, and the user's ability to form an attachment to the object. Critical to creating an experience is the creator's ability to define what type of experience they wish others to have. In my work, this is shaped by (and it may not be until the making is well underway) the semiotics and poetics of an object: its material, form, aesthetic, symbolic, and emotional value and how those qualities relate to environment. For example, while I wanted the user's experience with the heads to convey a sense of conflict between an internal and external language, I wanted

to do so in a lighthearted and whimsical way. This is what led me to take parts of common things (rope, twigs, leather), stuff them into the mouth of a head, and juxtapose with unintelligible fragments of spoken word. These relationships are specifically designed to be unusual. By appealing to the user's curiosity (Why are twigs coming out of that head's mouth? What are the strange sounds I hear?) I hope to capture the user's imagination and bring a participant into the experience. Once there, the user must be curious and comfortable enough to interact with the objects. In order to have a simultaneous engagement with textural objects and sound, users must pull out the contents found in the heads. Depending on how fast and hard the forceful action of pulling occurred, alterations in pitch and tone of grumbles and groans were heard.

Code Performs

KATE NAZEMI

Class of 2006

Who are the makers in the digital world, and what is their form? Since physical objects are more likely to reveal the process of making done by the hand, I wanted to investigate the process of making in a digital environment to find visual clues of making. The question — where does this take place? — led me to investigate the programmer's role in making. What happens in the process of programming and its visual result, code, is quite interesting. Take for example the programmer's process of making a change. When the programmer changes something, it is usually an act of replacement — substituting one word for another that works — and commenting, a process of inserting notes only to be interpreted by another programmer. These changes are a part of the creative process, yet have no visual residue in the final outcome. Thus users are confronted with the results, such as an interface to a software program, that bear little human evidence of the process of making that went into it. It is this kind of thinking that led me to consider ways of revealing the humanity behind the code.

I am not a programmer, so for me the programming language is esoteric, it feels cold, and it is a silent language. But the language is composed of words, and in the world of poetry words have a voice. I looked at a variety of programming languages and began reading (sometimes performing) lines of code: int SUBU arg! (treated typographically in book). Line after line I read these strange words out loud: loud, low, excited, slow, high, quiet. I was enamored with how expressive (and funny) the words were. It was this expressive

potential found right in the language of code that began my journey of transforming code from a silent fixed language into one that is tactile, sculptural, phonetic, dynamic, and performative.

OVERVIEW

Expressive Code is a gesture-driven, object-based interface and printed book. It is my largest case study contributing to the development of my final thesis project: *Code Performs*. With *Expressive Code,* both print and interactive domains are examined: the interface allows participants to explore the visual and aural elements of code though a touch-screen, while the book provides a historical foundation for learning various interpretations of the programming language C. The book is an analytical examination of the transformation of the scientific language of code to the poetic interpretation of code. The interface was developed in flash and runs on a touch-screen monitor. Participants, presented with a continuous left-to-right flow of code, are encouraged to explore the poetry through touch. Interactive specifics are discussed later under the heading "Relationships." Together, these methods blend the nonlinear, dynamic, and unique explorative attributes of interactive media with the linear, static, and analytic properties of the printed book for a complete multisensory experience.

Each method of representation rigorously investigates various levels in, and representations of, a programming language in order to relate it to the broader context of human experience and learning.

This is observed in the following ways: 1. Translation – code to computer, fixed language of science to the fluid language of poetry, visual to sound; 2. Relationships – size, weight, value, contrast, rhythm, space; and 3. User-Experience.

CONCEPT: TRANSLATION

Digital code is the requisite material used by scientists to process information and produce results, and now by artists who use it as a creative tool. Here, we find a link between two seemingly disparate disciplines. But the connection goes deeper than shared material and the challenge is how to communicate it across the linguistic divide. Where artists and scientists differ in unique forms of language, they are alike in their approaches to creativity. For example, the artist and the scientist are curious investigators of the unknown. As Leonard Shlain states, "while the scientist demonstrates that A equals B or that X is the same as Y, artists often choose signs, symbols, and allegories to equate a painterly image with a feature of experience. Both of these techniques reveal previously hidden relationships." (20, Shlain, *Art and Physics*)

To translate is to transform. This process is one of conversion for the purposes of learning and understanding, and takes on many forms. In one sense, to translate is to express in another language precisely the original sense. In another, to translate is to "convey from one form or style to another." (*American Heritage Dictionary*) In accordance with this definition, *Expressive Code* uses the processes of translation to identify and communicate unique connections between the diverse languages of science and art.

CODE TO COMPUTER

What do the many expressions of code look like (or even sound like)? What connects the process of translation from human thought down to the interpretation of binary code by the microprocessor? Where does one expression begin and another end?

Given the relative secrecy that code operates in (its activity is invisible to most computer users), the search for answers suggests both an analytical and creative approach.

Beginning analytically, code is expressed in several distinct forms before being interpreted by the microprocessor. Take for example the following line from the highest-level language of code:

sum.c #include int main (int argc, char *argv [])

These characters represent the first step in transforming the programmer's instructions into specific tasks the computer can perform — in this case, to count from 0 to 100. Curiously, high-level language is considered closest in relationship to human linguistic communication.

Before high-level language can be interpreted by the microprocessor though, it is reduced to assembly language through the substitution of mnemonics and operational commands:

sum.s .text .align 2 .globl main .ent main 2 main: subu $sp, 32 sw $31, 20($sp)

This translation is silent, private and exact. Finally, assembly language is reduced to binary code called machine language. This lowest level language has the smallest vocabulary, yet is largest in volume:

of analysis. Code in its new context is freed from a silent and fixed form, and transformed into a rhythmic array of visual language:

*sum.c #include int main (int argc, char *argv [])*

The parameters that govern this visual language originate with the avant-garde artists of the 1920s who pioneered the reduction and restructuring of language to form new relationships to space and time, and thus new ways to perceive and create meaning. Of particular influence are the concrete poets "who reduced words to their elements of letters (to see) syllables (to hear)." (*Concrete Poetry: A World View*) This approach to language came from a belief that accepted grammatical-syntactical standards were inadequate to express certain ideas of the time. It is in this sense that the transformation of code from a scientific to a poetic language makes a historical connection to the avant-garde artists.

VISUAL TO SOUND

When we read we give voice to the world of words. Tapping into multiple layers of perception, phonetic poetry (a subcategory of concrete poetry) explores this combination of sound and visuals through the juxtaposition of sound and typography. Here, it is the expressive aural and visual communication channels that transform the scientific language of code into its new poetic form: int SUBU arg! (treated typographically in book). This new poetic form not only takes on the properties of phonetic poetry (letters are seen and syllables are heard), it also transforms code from 2D to 3D by considering each word as an immediate and tactile object that responds to human interaction. It is this union between sight, sound, object, and touch that creates an explorative environment to experience the emotive qualities found in the poetics of code.

CONCEPT: RELATIONSHIPS

To relate is to connect. *Expressive Code* fuses traditional formal elements in design (scale, contrast, rhythm, and space) with properties of dynamic media (modularity, variability, and time) to make clear visual and aural connections between content and form. In unison with the poetic language of code, this creates an environment to explore and experience these unique relationships through physical manipulation. In keeping with the properties of an explorative environment, *Expressive Code* has no explicit rules, allows users multiple paths for interaction, and is generally ambiguous.

Integral to *Expressive Code* is the typographic scale of code. Here, distinctions in typographic size distinguish inactive typography — small type flowing from left to right — from active typography that, when touched, scales in relation to the volume of the word heard. Here, the following relationship between scale and sound are formed: the larger the word, the louder the pronunciation. Another relationship between scale and sound is found in the rate of word flow: the larger the word, the slower it moves from left to right. These variations in typographic scale and sound create contrast and rhythm in the interactive environment. It is within this environment that poetry is created and new expressive relationships are realized.

Adding to this sense of contrast and rhythm are the vocal expressions of the two typefaces chosen: Mrs. Eaves and Franklin Gothic.

A visual language offers countless creative ways to express complex information, and is where the transformation of code from a language of science to a language of poetry begins.

0010011110111101111111111111000001010111110111111 0000000000010100101011111010010000000000000100 0001010111110100101000000000010010010101111101

And to think that this three-step transformation takes place in the blink of an eye and in complete silence! (code courtesy of Professor James Larus, The University of Wisconsin)

Perhaps well understood by the computer programmer, the degrees of abstraction apparent in the translation of code make this language difficult to understand. Therefore, code remains elusive to the many who depend on it for creative work. It is with this assumption that the search to convey code in more approachable forms begins.

LANGUAGE OF SCIENCE TO LANGUAGE OF POETRY

One of the best ways to understand something better is by breaking it down into smaller, more manageable parts. A visual language offers countless creative ways to express complex information, and is where the transformation of code from a language of science to a language of poetry starts.

The expressive and communicative potential of this traditionally silent and purely computational material begins with the isolation of unique letter combinations from each line of code:

*sum.c #include int main (int argc, char *argv [])*
*sum.c #include int main (int argc, char *argv [])*

This process of isolation, when applied to the entire programming language, detaches code from its original sense and creates a reduced vocabulary subject to a new set of parameters and a different kind

The interface allows participants to explore the visual and aural elements of code through a touchscreen.

Participants, presented with a continuous left-to-right flow of code, are encouraged to explore poetry through touch.

The voice of words set in Mrs. Eaves (a feminine typeface) is female, while Franklin Gothic (a masculine typeface) is male. Within each voice, alterations in volume range from high to low depending on speed. Here, relationships between dynamism and sound are how the poetry is created. Assigning voice to code is paramount to what brought me to this piece in the first place: my need to reveal the humanity behind code. While typography is a great visual expression of voice, it is only in combination with the human voice that gives rise to a phonetic performance.

Space and time are also explored through the developing user-relationship within the interactive environment. Through the touch of a hand, changes in size, content organization, and time are investigated. The fluid gestures of a hand allow participants the freedom of isolating certain words and re-organizing them within the given space. Although typography streams across the composition continuously, the system can also be paused to allow a more thorough investigation of the poetry.

THE USER-EXPERIENCE

Allowing participants to intuitively examine code as poetry through interactions leading not to specific results, but rather to individual explorations is the interactive objective of *Expressive Code*. Interacting with programming code through touch directly relates to expressing the humanity of code. Here, guiding principals of intuition and nuance lead the way to investigating the poetic representation of code as natural physiologic considerations like touch, pressure and object manipulation work in creating poetry.

REFLECTION

Expressive Code was a featured exhibition in the Boston 2005 CyberArts Festival and the 2005 Language of Dynamic Media Show. These two shows provided me with great feedback which influenced my final project, a revised version of *Expressive Code*, called *Code Performs*.

At first, I was ill-prepared for the feelings I had while observing others interact with my work. It was incredibly intimidating. All could think about was how terrible the project must be. But, the warm reception I received helped mitigate my unease.

Overall people seemed to understand the conceptual thinking behind the project, which was rewarding. I think people found the transformation of a programming language into sound poetry to be intriguing. Many people found humor in the project (the way the strange words were pronounced), which made me feel good.

Right away, though, I recognized people struggling to interact with the streaming words. It was clear I really confused people by not revealing any interactive tips. Only through individual demonstration did interaction make sense. Therefore, one of my goals in developing *Code Performs* was to create a transparent interface — one that encourages self-directed exploration — one that could be easily understood and explored through independent interaction.

Although I kept the interface physical by using a touch screen, I still felt that the project did not fully reflect the high degree of humanity I sought in my previous work. I think this had mostly to do with the screen-based environment the project was in. Thus, another goal of *Code Performs* was to better integrate materiality into the interface.

The overall exhibit lacked cohesiveness. The environment was not designed to evoke the kind of poetic response I was hoping for. The code words needed to sing, yet, they were drowned out by competing noise and such a small visual in which field to interact. By placing the book next to the screen, rather than integrating it interestingly it into the space, I did little to entice people to read it. Another goal of *Code Performs* then is to make better use of the book form by transforming it into a sculptural object that communicates content more openly and clearly while fully occupying the exhibit space.

The essence of sound poetry is found through live performance. I was left wanting to further explore this through the expressive qualities of speech and more sophisticated typography and interaction. These are the primary investigations in *Code Performs*.

The expressive qualities of speech that foster a direct and unmediated sensorial experience of voice experienced through touch is something I explored in one of my first projects, *InsideOut*. It seems fitting to conclude my thesis with a project that takes this idea further. *Code Performs* further explores my interest in nonrepresentational language by investigating the visual, acoustic, and dynamic properties of words derived from the same programming language in *Expressive Code*. This time, consideration is given to code's phonetic performance as playful interaction with words collide on screen and create unexpected juxtapositions of words and sound. This exhibition is set in the context of a large gallery space at MassArt (the Bakalar Gallery) where three interactive exhibits allow participants to explore all aspects of *Code Performs*: Book and Performance.

BOOK

There is a new book form associated with *Code Performs*. The content is drawn directly from the book designed for *Expressive Code*. This book gives a macro view of how certain words used in the performance piece emerged from programming language. The new form and layout reflect the need to communicate this. This book is printed on translucent rice paper. Each page is 8.5 inches square and individually glued at a 90 angle to the wall in descending order. The pages take on a sculptural form as they protrude from the wall. The pages run horizontally along the wall in a long row. They are arranged on the first long wall that gallery patrons encounter. As a result, patrons are able to glance at all of the pages to quickly observe the transformation of programming code to poetry. Due to it's open form, this arrangement also allows for a more intimate look at the content.

PERFORMANCE

From small screen to big screen.
Screen as discrete object "floating" in space
Material effect of curtain
Choice to use my voice
Aural Form: variations in emotion, tone, repetition, achieving phonetic poetry through visual-verbal patterns

INTERACTION

Collision of words

Transformation of words on screen: scale, sound, visual morphing, change in velocity and direction, compositional changes

Result: new sound and visual patterns of poetry

Addition of individual characters

Input object: ironic use of optical mouse, simple transformation found through change in color. Dramatic change in scale and space between mouse and screen places user in uncertain environment.

VISUAL FORM

Typography dynamic notes on dynamic page, more visual contrast

Use of constraints: choice of white type on black background

SCREEN

Impact of materiality on projection: from 2D to 3D typography, typographic transformation, fluid movement, gritty, expressionistic style of black and white, theatrical use of curtain.

Expressive Code was included in the American Institute of Graphic Arts, Boston 2005 Best of New England Juried Show, the American Institute of Graphic Arts Best of New England On the Road Show, and exhibited at the American Institute of Graphic Arts 2005 National Design Conference.

Anymails

CAROLIN HORN

Class of 2007

MY EMAIL INBOX

Anymails was developed with the help of my advisor Professor Brian Lucid in Fall 2006 and Spring 2007. Florian Jenett coded the prototype in Processing, an open source language based on the Java programming language.

Anymails is a visualization of my received emails. This visualization is not a new email application but an experiment. I have investigated how I can use natural metaphors to visualize my inbox, its structure, and attributes. The metaphor of microbes is used. My objective is to offer the user another experience of his email world.

VISUAL SYSTEM

One Email = One Animal

One animal represents one received email.

One Category = One Species

The emails are categorized in six groups: family and friends, school, job, e-commerce, unclassified, and spam. For example, all the emails I have received from my advisors and fellow students are in the category school. These categories are represented by six species, which are different in color and form. For instance, all received emails from school are blue and look a bit like croissants.

Status and Age of an Email = Appearance and Motion of an Animal

How an animal looks and moves depends on the condition of the represented email. The age of an email (when it was received) is shown by the size and opacity of the animal. For instance, a new email is big and opaque, an old email small and transparent. The age is defined in relation to other emails of a certain time period. The status of an email (unread, read, responded) is shown by two animal attributes: the number of hair/feet and velocity. An unread email is hairy and swims fast; a read email has less hair and does not swim so fast anymore; a responded email is hairless and barely moves.

ANYMAILS

On the opening screen of my interface, all animals are swimming freely. Only animals (emails) of a certain time period are visible at once, such as received emails from today. The user can modify this period in the time line in the menu Time. He can decide if he wants to see emails from today, from the last week or month. The animals represent the following information about the email inbox: The user can see the amount of received emails by the amount of animals. He can see how many emails he has received from which category by the different colored and formed animals. Are there more spam (brown animals) or more emails from family and friends (light green animals)? He can see the status of emails — which animals move fast or slow, which animals are hairy or hairless. For instance, if there are many unread emails from different species (categories), then the screen will be full of different colored and fast-swimming, hairy animals. If there are only a few responded emails, then only a few barely moving and hairless animals will be visible.

FILTER

The user can filter emails by species and status in the *Anymails* menu. There are buttons for each species and kind of status. He can fade in or fade out certain species like spam. Or he can make all unread emails visible or invisible. For instance, he can combine these filters to see only emails from school, which are unread.

The impression of the inbox can be really different depending on which species or which status is visible or not. For instance, I receive a lot of spam emails every day so my screen is full of brown worms. My other animals seem to be attacked by this superiority. If I fade out the species spam, everything seems to be calmer and less aggressive.

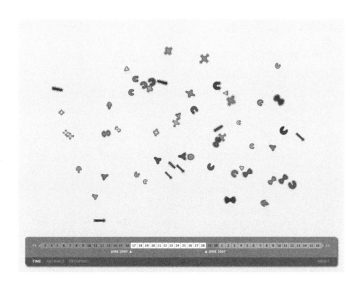

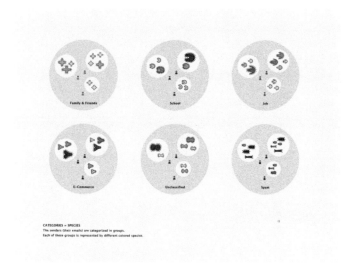

CATEGORIES = SPECIES
The senders (their emails) are categorized in groups.
Each of these groups is represented by different colored species.

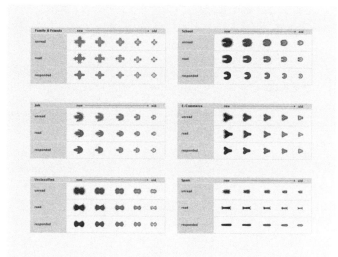

How an animal looks and moves
depends on the condition of the
represented email. The age of
an email (when it was received)
is shown by the size and opacity
of the animal.

TIME TRAVEL

The user can go back in time to see emails received during previous
months or years. In the menu Time, he can scroll through the time
line to previous inbox conditions. The user can compare different
times; he can recognize patterns. When has he received more or
fewer emails? When have more relatives and friends sent emails,
or people from school? When has he responded to these emails? Is
there a relation between these patterns and personal circumstances?
For instance, I can recognize certain patterns which I can connect
to personal circumstances. I received a lot of emails from my family
and friends in the first weeks after leaving Germany to study in the
USA. In this time period my screen is filled with light green animals. At the time I worked as a freelancer, the screen is filled with
job emails as orange animals. These patterns reflect certain circumstances in my life.

ROLLOVER AND GROUPING BEHAVIOR

Selecting one animal, triggers different things at once. First, a text
field appears, containing information about the email (name of
sender, status, delivery day and time, subject line). In addition, related animals swim next to the chosen one and group in the form of
a string. The other animals do not group and move away from the
string. The user can define which emails are related in the Grouping
menu. He has the choice between emails from the same sender,
from the same species, with the same status, or from similar delivery times. For instance, the user decides that emails from the same
sender are related. When he selects one email, all emails from the
same sender swim next to the chosen one and group. Emails from
other people move away and do not group. The user can also decide

how the emails are arranged in a string. He is able to sort the emails
by status, time, size, person, or species. For instance, the user can
arrange the emails from the same person inside the string by time.
Then newer emails (bigger and opaque) are in the beginning and
older emails (smaller and transparent) are at the end of the string.
This grouping behavior offers the user additional information, such
as the amount of emails he has received from one certain person.
The position of the animal, the spatial relation to other animals,
acquires meaning. Animals, which are related, are close together;
they are bonded together. Other animals, which do not belong to this
group, avoid it. The user becomes an explorer through this interactivity. He becomes curious about what will happen when he catches
one animal. Will other animals come, which and how many?

GROUPING CONTINUOUSLY

The user can group emails continuously. In this mode all emails
are grouped in the form of strings. As in the rollover mode, the user
can define which emails are grouped and how they are arranged in
the groups. Depending on which emails should group, the animals
form a few longer strings or a lot of shorter strings. For instance, if
the user decides to group the emails by status, the animals will form
three strings. One contains all responded emails, one all read emails,
and one all unread. If the user decides to group emails by the same
person, the animals will form several strings, each containing emails
from one person. How many strings will be formed, depends on the
user's email traffic. For instance, if he received many emails from
only a few people, only a few, long strings would form. If he received
only a few emails from many different people, many different but
short strings would form. This grouping mode is not visible at once;
it evolves. The animals swim toward each other, arrange themselves
and form a string. It offers a completely different view. The screen
full of freely swimming animals becomes a screen full of animal
strings. These strings move fast or slow depending on their members. For example, a string containing a lot of unread emails moves
faster than a string containing answered emails.

In this mode the user can quickly recognize the structure of his inbox in a certain time period. He can see how many emails he has received from certain people, how many different people have sent emails, how many emails he has received from certain species, and so on. For example, the user can see how the email string of a certain sender is changing during a period of time. The string becomes bigger, smaller, bigger again depending on the continuousness of email traffic.

UNCOMPRESSING

The user can uncompress strings. The more he stretches a string the more information he gets about the contained emails. Small text labels become visible showing, for instance, where unread, read, and responded emails are located.

OTHER CONCEPTS

Other concepts emerged during my work on *Anymails*. They are not included in the prototype, but show how the case study could be further developed. Are there other grouping methods to arrange emails? What are the interactivities to customize the visualization?

CUSTOMIZED *ANYMAILS*: PREFERENCES

Right now *Anymails* is a visualization of my emails. The user should be able to customize the visualization to his inbox. For instance, the user could arrange his emails by his own categories. Not everyone would like to have the current categories; maybe someone wants to have fewer or more. The user could also decide which species represent categories or what color a certain species is. Maybe users could create their own species. One idea is that the user creates species by giving information about certain person groups. How formal or informal are the emails from this group? How much does the user like or dislike these emails? How aggressive (demanding) or shy are these emails? For instance, my family and friends species is very informal, I like them very much. They are shy because my family and friends understand and accept when I do not respond immediately. This is only a concept; this kind of tool would require further investigation. How much freedom does the user have in this creative process? Which rules have to be developed to ensure that created species can be differentiated at the end?

Changing categories, modifying, or creating species offers a customized visualization. Then *Anymails* enables the user to draw conclusions about his personal inbox, to uncover personal patterns inside his emails. It also supports his understanding about the different species. For instance, when he defines the color of certain species, he can give them a certain personal meaning. He loves blue and because of this his family species is blue. Then he can easily remember the color-coding during the running application.

SPACIAL GROUPING: STATUS

The user can group emails spatially. The emails are forced to swim in certain areas according to their status. Unread emails are only allowed to move inside the inner cycle. Read emails are only allowed to swim in the middle cycle. Replied emails are only allowed to swim in the outer cycle. The size of these cycles can be changed to give, for instance, unread emails more space to move.

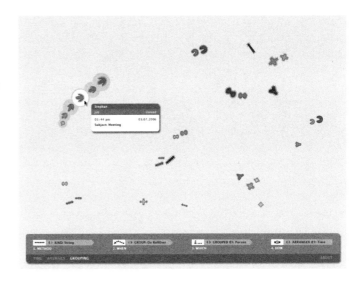

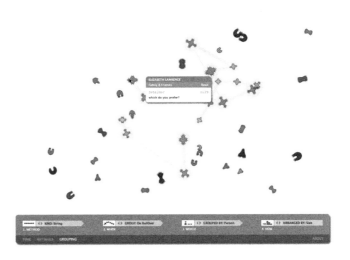

When a user selects one email, all emails from the same sender swim next to the chosen one and group. Emails from other people move away and do not group together.

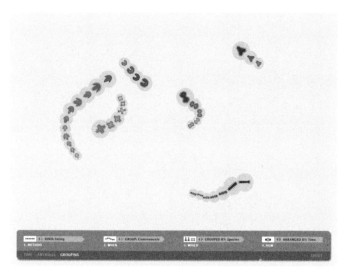

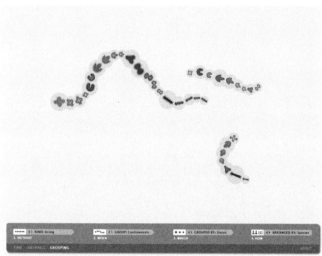

The user can define which emails are related in the menu "Grouping." Related animals then swim together in the form of a string.

SPACIAL GROUPING: SIZE

A coordinate system is used to arrange emails by their size in bytes. In this mode emails can only move horizontally. Their horizontal position indicates their size — emails with less kilobytes (Kb) swim at the bottom, emails with more kilobytes swim above.

When I look at my emails, I notice that 99 per cent of them are between 0.1 and 5 Kb big. Only a few are bigger than 5 Mb (1 Mb is 1000 Kb). Because of this, a huge crowd of emails swims at the bottom of the coordinate system. The coordinate system is flexible to resolve this crowding. The user can change the scale; he can stretch the coordinate system. For example, he can define that two-thirds of the screen show emails between 0.1 and 10 kb and only one-third emails between 10 kb and 15 Mb. This allows users to see detailed size differences between smaller emails.

FOOD

Another concept is to integrate the metaphor of feeding. The user can place food sources, which attract only certain animals. These animals swim close to the food. This could work like a search option. For example, the food attracts only emails from certain persons, or with certain subject lines.

DELETE

People have often asked me if they could also kill animals. The visualization could become more like a game. The user has to show certain skills to delete an email. Only if he hits an animal with a weapon, it will be deleted. Moral concerns may be disregarded.

TRACKS

The metaphor of tracks can be used to indicate the email history of certain senders. For example, emails from people who have written me constantly in the past leave tracks. The length of the tracks indicates the consistency of email traffic.

MOUSE ATTRACTION

The user and his cursor could increasingly influence the behavior of animals. For example, the user can define that emails from one friend are more attracted to the cursor. When he travels through different time periods, he can quickly see how often his friend has written. These emails will try to follow the cursor.

GENETICS

Right now, each sender is an exclusive member of a species. But sometimes I have worked with a person who is also a friend. Do his emails belong to the species of family and friends or my job? The concept of genetics can be integrated to solve this problem. The animal, which represents the email of this person, is a mixture between job and family & friends animal. For instance, it has the color of job animals and the form of family & friends animals. Of course, this needs further investigation. Which visual attributes are integrated? Is there a dominant attribute of one of the parent animals? How easy it is to identify the parent animals?

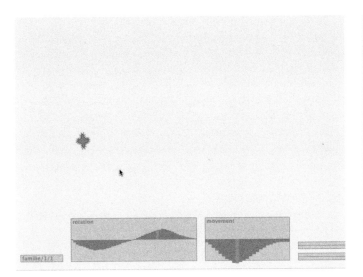

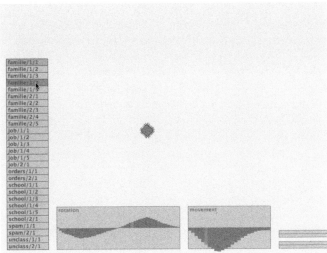

Users can easliy customize the
range of motion of each animal.

DEVELOPMENT

My work on *Anymails* is characterized by the development from
abstract to more concrete forms, from mechanical to natural motions,
from complex to simpler visual code.

(1) In the beginning of the project, the age of an email was indicated by smoothness of form: a new email was smooth; when it
became older it got more and more wrinkles. The created forms were
very abstract. The code, the meaning of certain forms, was hard to
memorize. I did not organize the emails by person groups. I created three levels of importance: very important, less important, and
unimportant. These levels were indicated by a symmetry of form:
a very important email was symmetric like a cycle; an unimportant
email was asymmetric. I had problems including motion as an attribute. It was difficult to move these forms without losing their form
and its connected meaning. The result was a very mechanic motion
such as pulsation. This was not only stressful to watch, but the motions could not be easily differentiated. For instance, unread emails
moved on a zigzag path and pulsed strongly. Emails that had been
read moved on a smooth path and pulsed lightly. Answered emails
did not move.

(2) There was definitely the need to create formal and motion
attributes, which could be easily recognized. I decided to organize
my emails by person groups and to represent these by species. I created simpler coded forms, which are still the basis of some current
animals of my visualization. The age of an email was represented
by the opacity; the status was represented by size and velocity. For
instance, a new unread email was big and opaque and swam fast, an
old responded email was small and transparent and did not move. I

also started to experiment more with motion. I wanted to create the
impression that these forms are swimming. Overall I was not satisfied. The forms were not animals; they were still too abstract, as was
the code. They seemed to be bubbles, which swam different in colors
and motion over the screen.

(3) I noticed, that code becomes easier to understand when one
email attribute like age is shown by more than one visual attribute.
Age is represented by size and opacity. Status is represented by the
amount of hairs and motion. Category (person group) is represented
by form and color. This was also a further step toward natural
metaphors; the abstract forms became animals. The motion of these
animals also changed according to their form. The spam started to
crawl, the job animal to push itself forward, and so on. For the first
time, I got the impression I observed something alive.

METAPHOR

I intended to use natural metaphors from the beginning of *Anymails*.
But the particular metaphor and its use evolved in the process as
it did during my work on *Jellyfish*. In contrast to *Jellyfish*, where I
only use metaphors to visualize structures, I additionally use metaphors to visualize attributes like the age of emails in *Anymails*. For
the inbox visualization I needed the metaphor of an animal, which
appears in large numbers, like received emails. The idea emerged
to use microbes as representatives. Some people associate viruses
with the animals, but that metaphor works too. One can believe that
microbes or viruses appear in bigger swarms. Motion and certain
behavior patterns can be integrated as well. We can imagine that
microbes or viruses move and form groups. My intent was to create
a micro-world through which the user can explore his email world,
like watching small animals through a microscope.

VISUALIZATION

When people watch *Anymails* for the first time they often miss the
clarity, which common email applications offer. For instance, in
common applications the user can quickly find a wished email by
using rearrangements of lists or using the search option. Everything

is in order, which gives us the feeling of control. We want to have control. Emails are important for us. We do not want to miss one. I can understand this; *Anymails* is not an alternative for such email applications; the user cannot find a certain email in such speed. I made this on purpose. I have dissolved the common clarity to experiment. Can I offer a richer experience by doing so? I did not want to create a new email application but a visualization of my emails, which offers a different point of view.

In common email applications, the user gets information about the amount of received emails in the form of exact numbers. The emails are arranged in a list; the length of the list additionally indicates the amount of emails. But the user cannot really understand what 100 or 200 emails mean. The amount is often not visible at once; he has to scroll through the list. In *Anymails* the amount of emails is represented by the amount of animals. Thereby it offers a completely different view if someone has received 5, 100, or 200 emails. It can become an experience for the user. A certain view can trigger feelings. I play with and amplify feelings, which the user already connects to his emails. For example, he feels overextended when he has to respond to many emails, he feels overrun when he gets too many spam emails, he feels disregarded when no friend or relative writes an email, and he is happy when he gets one. These experiences are exemplified partly by the animals. For instance, when I receive only five spams one day these animals seem to be nice and funny as they swim around the screen.

When I receive 200 spams one day, these animals lose their friendly impression. In bigger swarms they seem to be aggressive, and I feel overrun by them. When I only receive a few family emails, these animals seem to be lonely. Other animals, like spam, visually push them away. Another important aspect is the comparison of different sender groups. For example, how many emails are sent by schools or companies? In common email applications the user can arrange the email list by person but this option does not offer a real comparison. He can organize the emails by sender groups in different folders. Then the user clicks on one folder and get its email list, then he clicks on another folder and gets another one. But still he cannot really compare the amounts. In *Anymails* the user sees the amount of emails of different sender groups in relation to each other. Each sender group has its own color and all groups are displayed at once.

A colored pattern emerges which the user can interpret easily. Is one group more dominant or another one? Is the screen colorful or only two-colored? Are there more job or school emails? The user understands information not by numbers but by visual patterns. These patterns are not static; the status of an email is represented by its motion. It is a dynamic colored pattern that shows how much attention the user has given to emails of certain sender groups. Has he answered more family or school emails? Are there more replied, read ,or unread emails? For instance, when the user has not read or answered many emails, he sees many fast swimming animals. He can panic like his animals when he thinks about how many emails he must reply to. When he already has read and answered many emails, the animals are calm; they swim slow or barely. Depending on his attention he sees an accordant moving pattern.

In common email applications the user cannot experience time. He can arrange emails by time but he cannot experience time differences between emails. Emails are only arranged one after another. In *Anymails* the user can travel through different time periods in his inbox; the visual patterns are changing according to past conditions. He can see how far emails are separated temporally; he can understand the amount of emails in context of time. The user can set these patterns in context to actual life circumstances. The patterns get personal meaning. For instance, I can recognize when I had semester break (fewer school emails), when I was working (many job emails), when I had a stressful time (many unanswered emails), when I was abroad (many family emails).

Anymails allows the user to uncover patterns within the body of data, which are normally hidden within a list display. The missing static arrangement of emails takes its toll. The user cannot quickly find a certain email in *Anymails*. But the user can discover a new email world. His inbox becomes, through natural metaphor, a microworld, one that he has to observe and interact with before he can interpret certain conditions.

Carolin Horn

Class of 2007

Adobe Achievement Award Finalist,
Designer for Deutsche Telekom, and
Tireless Experimenter

Advice to incoming students: *Be curious.*

Germany has a history of great artists and designers renowned for experimentation: Gutenberg and printing; Kurt Schwitters and Dada; Walter Gropius and Bauhaus. Carolin Horn, originally from Würzburg, Germany, a small town near Frankfurt, gracefully follows this tradition. Her thesis, *Natural Metaphors for Information Visualization,* is 231 pages of experimentation into the world of information design. In short, her work at the Dynamic Media Institute set the standard for every student who followed.

Carolin's development as a designer, specifically an information designer, began early in life. In her thesis she writes, "When I was preparing for tests at high school, I restructured and remodeled the learning material to study. I designed digests in the form of tree structures to visualize connections and the order of events." Information visualization helped her process information more efficiently. Her thesis is an extension of this desire. Carolin wants to help us understand better.

Her project *Jellyfish* (2005), for example, is a visual encyclopedia of the arts using jellyfish as a metaphor to explore the connections between media, time, and space. While her vehicles for visualization are derived from nature, she does not use them simply at surface level. "I didn't analyze a jellyfish to imitate a biological mechanism, I investigated how we as humans perceive our environment to find metaphors from nature to utilize our interpretation ability. It is more a matter of identifying what non-human biology can be said to parallel metaphorically existent human behavior."

Anymails (2006-07), one of her major thesis projects, is an alternative visualization of email. Imagine if your inbox were a Petri dish and each kind of message — spam, family and friends, school, and work — were all different microorganisms that looked and behaved in unique ways. Her goal for development, as she puts it, is simple, "My objective is to offer the user another experience of their email world." But the project is so complex, thoughtful, and flawlessly executed that after seeing it for only a moment you understand why it was a finalist for an Adobe Achievement Award. What is surprising, however, is that somehow it didn't win.

Experimentation is in Carolin's DNA. Even returning to school was an experiment. She grew up in the same town where she attended college and needed to explore new places. "After receiving my diploma," she said, "I had wanderlust; there was a strong need to see something else." Before coming to the DMI program, Carolin worked as a freelance web designer and taught classes mostly on interactive media at her local University. Her growing interest in interactive media led her to travel the 3,735 miles to study at the DMI. "I was looking for open space to experiment and learn more about interactive design. DMI offered this possibility for me."

Currently Carolin is a designer for Deutsche Telekom, the mother company of T-Mobile. Her role at the company is to help centralize the design process and ensure that each product offers the same core experience. While she spends most of her time there working on web applications and websites, Carolin is happy to be in a position where her decisions affect things on a larger scale. And she always looks at projects with the same level of curiosity that she did while at the DMI program. "I don't have the total freedom to experiment as much anymore, but I try to question every project in order to find the best solution. This attitude comes from my experience at DMI."

Written by Dennis Ludvino

Heather Shaw

Class of 2003

Passionate educator, Vice President of AIGA Boston, avid runner, and practitioner of yoga

Advice to incoming students: *Do what you enjoy, and allow yourself the time to pursue it wholeheartedly.*

Before making the decision to pursue a graduate degree at the Dynamic Media Institute, Heather Shaw was a seasoned design professional. She spent most of her seven-year career as an Art Director for White Rhino Productions, a design firm that worked on everything from print and motion design to websites and interactive CD-ROMs. For Heather, graduate school was an opportunity to provide herself with the knowledge and credentials to teach design at the college level but, more importantly, it redefined her to approach to design.

> *I had been working with motion and interactive media for several years already, but my work was very formally driven. I didn't have a clear grasp of information architecture, so most (if not all) of my work was designed from the outside-in. Visually the work was beautiful, but structurally very weak. I needed to expand my vocabulary and have a smarter approach to my process.*

While studying in the DMI program, Heather explored the art of storytelling and its intersection with dynamic media. Her thesis examined the nature of authorship and provided radical alternatives to the traditional theatre experience. She points to a desire to provide deeper relationships between the viewer and the story. "*A Journey Through India* [one of her major thesis projects] was designed to enlighten the user through narrative, and by tying behavioral aspects of the interface to physical and metaphysical experiences in India." Her thesis thoughtfully approached a new type of cinematic experience, where individuals had greater control over the outcome of the story.

Since graduating in 2003, Heather has taken on many roles within the design community. She began teaching at numerous colleges before becoming an Assistant Professor of Graphic Design at Curry College. The transition from student to professor, she notes, was not easy. "As design professionals, our role is to solve challenges associated with client work. As faculty, our role is to create challenges for our students. This is the difference between being a design practitioner and design educator. As a professor, my ongoing struggle is creating 'good problems' for the students to solve — meaning assignments that provide enough constraints, but that are balanced with enough flexibility for the students to learn and produce successful varied outcomes."

Aside from her role as an educator, Heather is a prominent design activist. As the Vice President of AIGA Boston, she is tasked with organizing and promoting events that continue to push the definition of design. In this respect, she has served as a bridge between the DMI program and the broader design community, helping to publicize several notable lectures such as John Maeda, David Small, and Hugh Dubberly. "These lectures," she says, "have allowed AIGA to promote events that extend beyond our traditional audience and fulfill an area of programming we currently did not offer. These events have prompted the Boston board toward developing a partnership with DMI, enabling both organizations to share resources and programming initiatives. More importantly, the Boston board is pursuing a partnership because we value the intellect within the DMI program."

Written by Dennis Ludvino

Carlos Lunetta
Class of 2005

Advice to incoming students: *Get uncomfortable.*

Brazilian national, code experimenter, advertising designer, and novice home builder

As an undergrad living in San Pao, Brazil, Carlos studied social communications (advertising) and went on to become an art director at a big advertising agency before venturing out on his own. After running his own one-man company for about one year, Carlos realized that his design education had some serious gaps. "It hadn't even skimmed the topics of interactive and motion design. I wanted to think more about what can be done with new media." And with his love for great American designers like Saul Bass, Milton Glazer, and Paul Rand, Carlos came to Boston to study at MassArt.

The Articulation of Visual Experiences Through Algorithm, Carlos Lunetta's thesis document, is in its own right a wonderful visual experience. By the second page of the book he lucidly describes what sounds like a complicated thesis topic. What is more impressive is that he succeeds without using a single word. Rich geometric shapes dance from margin to margin; Simple lines endlessly twirl into complicated shapes; A fibonacci sequence spirals infinitely across the page. The visuals peppered throughout the 128-page document set the groundwork for an energetic exposé of computational design — its history, definition, and practice.

Historically, most students at the Dynamic Media Institute only timidly venture into the world of programming. We delight when we make a box move across the screen only to sound the retreat once we hit the chapter covering math concepts. Carlos, on the other hand, dedicated his entire tenure at the DMI program to computational design and examining how it expands upon our current notions of the broader field of design. "Creating through a computational medium," Carlos says, "completely changes the boundaries of what and how ideas are translated from the inside to the outside; it's not meant as a replacement of traditional methods, but an addition."

Learning to program did not happen overnight. Carlos began dabbling in programming in the late '80s and picked it up again when Macromedia Director was released and then again when Flash was developed. In a time when the lines between developer and designer are more blurred than ever, Carlos views this as a good place for experimentation. "If there's the aspiration of creating work through code, go ahead and study programming, lose your fears. DMI students are in the right place and time to experiment and try the most they can with new media, and that may involve coding."

Currently, Carlos is an Associate Creative Director at Beam Interactive, an advertising agency in Boston, Massachusetts, specializing in web design, web applications, and games. With over 50 employees, Beam Interactive is a medium-sized design company with a client list that includes Mini, L.L. Bean, Virgin Mobile, and Puma. Most recently, Carlos is proud of his work on Puma's Africa World Cup website. His goal as an interactive designer is simple and honest. "I like to let people have fun online, advertisements must be entertaining."

Written by Dennis Ludvino

El Pistolon / Shooter and Narrative Sequencing

JUAN CARLOS MORALES

Class of 2007

  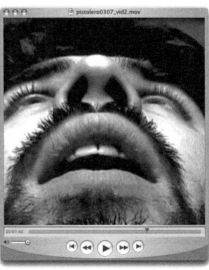

PURPOSE AND CONSTRUCT

The purpose of this case study was to explore how photography and sound could be used to create a limited sequence of images that tell a story. The story itself is then segmented into parts that can be triggered and resequenced by the user at a keyboard or MIDI device. This triggering of alternative paths in the plot allows the user to explore the narrative from the perspectives of the different characters. In the end, the narrative becomes potentially more immersive and provides a more dynamic storytelling experience.

The first step in the process was to build a reference movie of the narrative. The purpose for the reference movie was to tell the story uncut and expose the user to the basic plot of the narrative. This gives the user a beginning perspective from which to explore the content and points of view. To create the story, photographs were taken to depict the series of events that occurs. Various locations were selected for their ability to illustrate a very tangible sense of the character's cultural and economic station in life. The settings chosen reflect the blue-collar industrial backdrop of the story with an implied element of economic adversity that carries with it the grit and noise of starkly contrasted black and white imagery. Partly an exercise in conveying the character's less-than-hopeful sense of place, the imagery is at times dark, ominously lit and does nothing to conceal the urban plight of the industrial setting the main characters are rooted in.

The basic plotline of the story is a man seeking vengeance against another man that has wronged him but falls short of his convictions upon reaching the moment prior to taking the other man's life. The image sequences follow the man entering a building and confronting the victim and his own hesitations until the screen goes black and only a gunshot is heard. After the gunshot is heard a series of images flashes on screen that alludes to the second man's acts. It is only after the montage of images fades out that we see the second man opening his eyes in the realization that he is still alive. At that moment we realize that the pistolero (Spanish word for "shooter") turns the gun on himself realizing that the crime he was going to commit was far greater than the one committed against him. The variable story sections give the user the ability to swap out one montage for another. The differences in the montages depict the instant after the gunshot and the images that run through the minds of both men. The availability of variable sound accompaniments (essentially sound tracks) also provides more dramatic texturing to alter the feel of the piece as it is resequenced.

REFLECTION

As I worked through the various stages of the project one of the most difficult tasks was taking each picture with the intent of conveying a specific event in the story meaningfully and efficiently. Essentially, the most difficult challenge was telling a story with my photographs. Taking a photograph to show a particular event taking place between two characters at an exact moment in time — all in one frame — is not an easy task. After making several unsuccessful attempts at creating a mood (but not the actions that made up the events in the story) I turned to comic books and graphic novels to see how they did it. After flipping through a few pages of each it became clear to me that I needed to capture more than just the scenery or the mood it might imply. I needed to plan and stage the actions deliberately so that a clear series of events could be followed from one frame to the next.

I then changed my process. I had begun the project by going out and shooting raw material that I could then craft into my story. I had also created a scratch soundtrack to give the material I gathered the right mood and tonality. The result was underwhelming. While I had captured the mood and feel of the story and even given it added dimension with cinematic sounds and effects, no one could tell me what the story was about. I had made lush sounds and pretty pictures but had not yet told a story. I then decided I needed to storyboard the narrative and use my hands again to sketch the frames of my movie. Without worrying about where I was going to shoot or how, I began to sketch the characters and events. The story then began to take shape. I created one sketch after another and diagrammed my complex narrative into a series of drawings that I could map sounds to and then apply the proper mood and place treatments.

It worked. I brought my sketches into class and my classmates got it. They saw the actions, the change in scenery, and the change in events from one frame to the next. The other enlightening part of this process was what followed: the filtering and editing. Before even picking up the camera again I tossed more than half of my drawings and focused on the key scenes. I simplified and focused on reducing the number of shots to what was most necessary to get my point across. I was finally telling a story and now all I had to do was go out and shoot it. Having done that I picked up my camera, scouted new settings, and began shooting.

A user can explore alternative paths in the plot for a more dynamic storytelling experience.

Caras, the Totemic System

JUAN CARLOS MORALES

Class of 2007

PURPOSE AND CONSTRUCT

Caras is the Spanish word for faces. I chose this name because the range of emotions that can be expressed in a person's face is almost limitless. The purpose of this project was to combine a range of these facial expressions with sound, either ambient or composed, that is somehow telling of a person's background, personality, culture, or vocation. The goal is to learn something about them that begins to piece together elements of who they are beyond a name. The project at hand takes the user through the facial expressions of the members of my family, specifically my wife, my two daughters, and myself.

The "totem" element of the project is the arranging of the four characters into a totemic lineup that makes up a row or column of *caras*/faces. When appropriate, the actual arrangement uses spacial relationships to make a visual statement on that person(s) relationship, or lack thereof, with the rest of the totem. The images reveal only the face and part of the upper body and are shot on a clean field of black to minimize distraction from the characters and their gesturing.

The historical significance of totems and totem poles varies greatly worldwide. The use of totem poles to represent the lineage and historical events that mark the various cultures that have used them is what sparked my interest in the concept. Totem poles have often been used to memorialize the passing of life and mark the burial ground for cultural figures of great importance. Other totems have been carved to symbolize events and the legends that have shaped people and places throughout the ages. My totems simply celebrate people and the stories between them. The faces are not carved in wood but rather shaped by small gestures.

When the user approaches the totem they find that the faces are sleeping, at rest, while an ambient sound is playing as the background mood element. The user approaches a member of the totem initiating an "awakened" visual sequence of facial gestures. At the same time a sound layer is also triggered with the facial gestures (fading from one to the next) specifically chosen to personify the person.

The nature of these sound layers is meant to be suggestive of a personal trait or emotional quality that defines the character. Giving the sound an intimate quality is critical to how the audience responds to these *caras.* The intent is to draw interest beyond the surface level. The goal in combining these two elements is to suggest a connection between the tonality of the sounds playing and the emotions implied by the character's gesturing. The interesting question here is: which element (the visuals or the sounds) plays a greater role in creating a perspective or point of view of the *cara* the audience is faced with? Perhaps the greater question is whether or not this combined media makes for a more impactful experience. In this case, the intent is for the audience to get a deeper sense for each character's persona and how that might impact their collective life as a family.

For now the totems are made up of black and white photographs of the faces set on a black background. While this does provide a clean and uncluttered setting for the audience to focus on the change in facial expressions, color and real-life background settings might work as well. The goal is for the audience to gain insightful character impressions that will enhance the unfolding of narrative. Any implications made are articulated by character gestures and their accompanying sounds as the user interacts with the totems. The esthetic should remain clean so as not to detract from any gesturing or interaction between characters.

The combination of media is intended to make the process an engaging personal experience that draws on expression and doesn't become just another multimedia slideshow. In a slideshow there is a linear progression from one item to the next. In this totemic system, the user chooses which *cara* sequence is initiated causing a range of possibilities in how an embedded message or even story unfolds. In an interactive totem the sequence of *caras* selected by the user can, for example, determine the proceeding series of sounds and character gestures. As the designer, the ensuing formula of user choices could be used to lead the user through the experience to arrive at predetermined variable outcomes. These variable outcomes can be scripted to deliver different emotional experiences and messages. In the prototype I developed, high levels of interactions with the *caras* were not explored. A single linear stream of each *caras'* sounds and gestures were prompted by the user's selection of each character with the opportunity to repeat the sequence as desired.

The totemic system allows for a character's gesturing to be programmed in response to a point in another *cara* sequence. As it plays a particular visual and aural gesture along with that of another *cara*, the interaction can then suggest emotion and relationships between the characters. The fact that these types of expressions imply emotion allows them to change from literal to poetic devices throughout the course of the experience. This platform lends itself to conveying a point of view rather than simply presenting information.

REFLECTION

What originally drew me to the idea of combining mixed media elements in these totem sequences was the desire to put people together in an intimate context that provides emotional insights on the group and their relationships. In a practical sense, what better way is there to communicate that someone likes to sing than to actually hear that person singing? Going a step further, hearing them miss a high note or improvise when they forget the words lends a genuine

and intimate substance to the information being conveyed. That kind of information is more poignant and direct than being told that the person likes to sing and then being asked to believe that it's true. It also brings the audience into the moment by inviting them to identify with the characters on a more personal level. What is exciting about the totems is the potential they have to tell more complex stories. A more scripted approach could take better advantage of user interaction and make it an even more vital component in how the content is delivered. A deeper and more dynamic set of content could also be delivered that triggers different sets of gestures and sound by the order in which each *cara* is interacted with. That means that instead of one set of imagery and sound content being accessible per *cara*, the system could be expanded so that multiple interactions take place.

For instance, if the totem contains four people and the one farthest to the right is visually removed from the other three, that isolation or separation can be augmented by another person(s) 'waking up' and responding to that *cara's* gestures and sound bytes with a display of one or more telling gestures of their own. To tell a larger story, multiple totems can be combined to provide a cross-section of backgrounds and stories.

Imagines for example, the power and content that could be conveyed in a totem of social workers and prison inmates whose identities are revealed only over time? The possibilities for discovery become broader as you consider the different ways the system can be manipulated and expanded to accommodate more complex nonlinear narratives.

At the same time the system can be kept simple and poignant. Perhaps providing a discourse between only two *caras* that ends up providing a back-and-forth style timeline of gestures and sound bytes rewards the user/audience for their interaction with a continually unfolding narrative. The key is to keep the framework scalable and easy to navigate. This would allow the author to craft their content and messages to match the levels of storytelling and interactivity required to engage the audience to move toward the final resolution in the narrative.

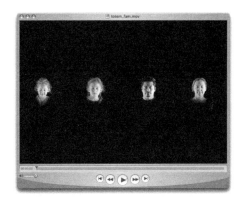
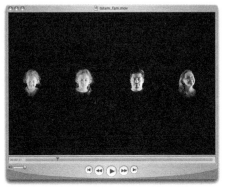
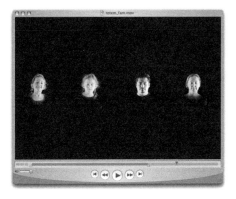
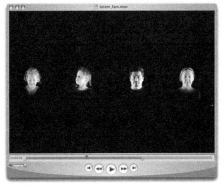

The user approaches a member of the totem initiating an "awakened" visual sequence of facial expressions.

Live Painting: Bamboo Garden

TING ZHI

Class of 2007

OVERVIEW

Imagine you enter a gallery with numerous paintings hanging on the wall. As you walk through, some works attract your attention. They make you stop and stare, while others do not. No matter how close you stand in front of the works physically, you always feel the distance mentally. They are flat and always quietly hanging there, never responding to any of your thoughts, emotions, or actions. This is the inadequacy of traditional art mediums; they only communicate with the audience in one way and the audience's role is relatively passive.

I created this case study *Live Painting: Bamboo Garden* with the provocative intention of bringing the prime ingredient of new media interaction into the traditional art domain of painting. By providing the audience with active roles, involving their physical movement and multi-sensory participation, I hoped to engage their concentration and immerse them in a poetic, illusive, and unpredictable experience. Instead of granting the author entire control of the context of paintings, the viewer now has the opportunity to affect or even manipulate the scenario that plays on the canvas independently.

As a metaphor for choosing the way we look at things, *Live Painting: Bamboo Garden* is a movement-driven, illusive, virtual painting installation. The visual and aural context the audience perceives is dependent on his/her body movement through tangible physical space. For instance, if the user looks in the middle of the painting, he/she perceives a static bamboo garden scene. As he/she moves toward either the left or right side, the scene is modified three-dimensionally. The audience surprisingly discovers that the bamboo garden is actually a reflection on the water and all the bamboo leaves are the tails of fish. In the end, the fish swim away and the water becomes still again.

In this project, I applied two visual approaches to create the immersive illusive experience: false perspective and ambiguous structure. The bamboo, rocks, and fish are virtual illusory sculptures that exist in three-dimensional space. When viewed from particular front perspective, the tails of the fish are at exactly the right position and angle to form the bamboo garden scene with the bamboo trunks. As the "truth" is revealed while the viewer moves his/her physical position, the ambiguous bamboo leaves switch to the alternative interpretations: the tails of the fish. Technically, each viewer's physical position corresponds to a certain frame of a video that plays on the canvas in real time. Ultimately, it is the viewer's role to control the perspectives of all the objects including the direction and speed at which the scenario plays.

PROCESS

The first challenge was to transform the way of thinking from graphical to three-dimensional with the z-axis. I started with several experiments by building simple three-dimensional forms in Maya to understand the multiple approaches of how to use perspective to create illusion, such as building distant illusions, ambiguous structure, and upside down images.

The next step was to decide the subject, one that met my objective of creating immersive and illusive experience while reflecting my own cultural background. I selected bamboo as the leading character because in Chinese culture, bamboo is a symbol of longevity and it is collectively referred to as one of the "Four noble ones" along with plum blossom, orchid, and chrysanthemum. In Confucian ideology, bamboo is admired for its perseverance under harsh environmental conditions and is known as one of the "Three friends in winter" along with the plum blossom and the pine tree. I was also

drawn to bamboo as a subject because I have observed and illustrated it for twenty years. I was inspired by two drawings I created at age five, "Panda and Bamboo" and "Gold Fish," to create an illusive experience by finding the alternative meaning between the bamboo garden and fish scene. Surprise could occur when the viewer perceives the juxtaposition of two distinctively different environments while they move their physical location. This unpredictable effect urges viewers to rethink their relationship to a painting, and also is a poetic metaphor exploring the way we look at things.

After deciding my subject, I built tangible bamboo, rocks, and fish by using modeling clay in the physical world. It was an invaluable experience to make, modify, and feel the texture of the models with my own hands. After that, I hand-drew all the textures with Chinese ink, built the models and animation in Maya, created the water effect in Adobe After Effects, and edited environmental water sound in Adobe Audition. By utilizing visual elements such as texture, tones, repetition, layering, transformation, speed, contrast, and sound elements such as volume and intensity I realized the initial goal of creating compelling, illusive, dynamic Chinese paintings in virtual three-dimensional space.

FINAL INSTALLATION AND REFLECTION

For the final installation, the "painting" was projected on framed vertical translucent vellum rice paper, which hung in a dark and quiet space to create the visual texture and an oriental atmosphere. The distance sensor, which sensed a viewer's physical location and recorded it as numerical data, was installed on the side of the path where the viewer was located. As the viewer interacted with the digital painting, data was sent to the Macintosh where it was analyzed in real-time through Adobe Flash ActionScript. Then Flash triggered the direction and speed of how the video played on the canvas and also controlled the sound correspondingly.

Visually, the transformation of the video and sounds worked tightly together; both bamboo garden and underwater scenes were successfully realized as I envisioned initially. The viewers quickly understood that it was their physical position which controlled the scenario that they perceived on the canvas. They also seemed to understand the conceptual thinking behind the project: a metaphor of the way we look at things. The viewer's experience was immersive, exploratory, and unexpected in a poetic way.

Overall, it has been a precious experience to devote and immerse myself in thinking, experimenting, testing, building, and finally creating a three-dimensional virtual painting successfully. I achieved the initial goal that encourages a viewer's physical movement, visual and aural engagement, while they enjoy the painting by granting them a certain degree of control. The convincing illusionary scenes captured the viewer's attention, broke their anticipation, and immersed them into the entire interactive process. I was eager to create more profound content in the next case study, one that would arouse an audience's deeper awareness by deceiving them more.

Live Painting: Bamboo Garden
is a movement-driven, illusive,
virtual painting installation.

Twelve Monkeys
+ *La Jetée*

A Learning Tool that Maps Narrative

JAE CHUL BAE

Class of 2010

PROJECT OVERVIEW

My goal for this project was to develop an interactive learning tool that could help compare two science fiction classics, namely: the 1962 French movie *La Jetée* by Chris Marker, and the 1995 american movie *Twelve Monkeys* by Terry Gilliam (which was inspired by *La Jetée*).

This interactive tool would help the user navigate through the past, present, and future of the narratives in each of the movies. By manipulating an interface that is of circular shape, the user explores meaningful connections within the complex visual content of both films. The target audiences for this project are people who have previously watched these films but are interested in furthering their knowledge of the narrative and storytelling aspects of the two films being analyzed.

ABOUT THE TWO MOVIES

La Jetée

La Jetée, meaning "the jetty" or "the pier" in English, is a 28-minute black and white science fiction film by Chris Marker. The film is about a post-nuclear war experiment in time travel. Earth lies ruined in the aftermath of a nuclear war. The few surviving humans begin researching time travel, in hopes of sending someone back to the pre-war world in search of food, supplies, and hopefully some sort of solution to mankind's imminent demise. The film is constructed almost entirely from still photos except for one short scene wherein the main character blinks and moves slightly. This film in turn inspired *Twelve Monkeys,* the other movie being analyzed in this interactive tool.

Twelve Monkeys

Twelve Monkeys is an American science fiction film directed by Terry Gilliam. The film depicts a world in 2035 — after a deadly virus has killed 99% of the human population forcing the survivors to flee beneath our planet's surface. This leaves the (other) animals topside, to rule the Earth once again. The scientists select James Cole, an imprisoned sociopath, to return to the past and gather information useful in the defense against this contagion. Once back in time, he is to investigate the mysterious "Army of the Twelve Monkeys" and report his findings. Scientific, social, and political themes like time travel (and its inherent paradoxes and nested loops), mental illness, the nature of reality, animal rights, and the Armageddon-potential of unchecked technological advances are artfully and cleverly explored.

EARLY RESEARCH

This project was assigned as part of the course, Design Studio I taught by Jan Kubasiewicz, as an exercise in "Mapping Narratives." The assignment was to map the complex narratives in the two films, *Twelve Monkeys* and *La Jetée*, with the goal of creating an interactive tool that would allow its users to find and make new and meaningful connections amongst their individual narratives.

In introducing this project, my professor described information designers as those who help people learn and comprehend complex information. This is achieved by organizing, mapping and representing information in an intuitively easy-to-use manner.

After I received the assignment I was nervous about the final deliverable format since I had difficulty imagining it. How does one possibly visualize a film? Professor Kubasiewicz had provided some initial suggestions on how to go about mapping complex information — such as to consider grouping, layering and filtering, clearly labeling content, and clarifying patterns that might emerge from within the information structure. With those suggestions in mind I began my research by first looking at contemporary examples that related to mapping narratives.

CONTEMPORARY EXAMPLE

"Similar Diversity" is an information graphic which opens up a new perspective on religion and faith by visualizing the holy books of five world religions. Commonalities and differences between Christianity, Islam, Hinduism, Buddhism, and Judaism are revealed in this data visualization.

The visual's basis is an objective text analysis of the Holy Scriptures, and works without any interpretations from the creators' side. Despite — or perhaps because of this abstraction — the artworks not only work at an informal level but also at an emotional level. The viewers are inspired to think about the current religious conflicts and their own prejudices.

For me, aspects such as using a simple word count and connecting words using lines to reveal deep relationships amongst the five world religions were touching and beautiful. It was interesting to think about the process that the creators of this project might have undergone to come up with ideas on how best to compare and explore such a massive and complex set of information. What I took away from this project was the importance of finding interesting ways to represent as well as enable an exploration of the information as critical to the success of a project such as mine.

DESIGN PROCESS AND FINAL PRODUCT

Analyzing and Mapping the Two Films

At first, I read the synopsis of both the films several times until I had a greater understanding of their respective plots. I also watched the two movies several times. Both movies portrayed their main character as one who traveled into the past, present, and future. The time changes were frequent and eventually climaxed at a moment that left viewers pondering whether the moment was in the past, present, or future.

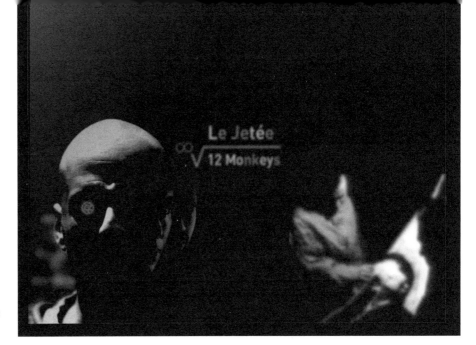

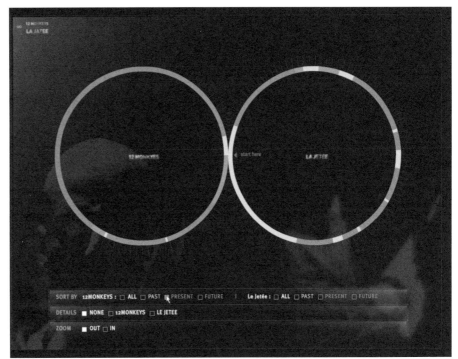

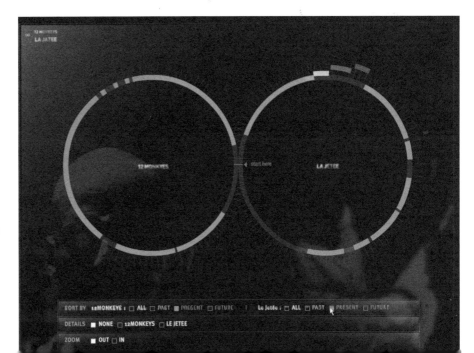

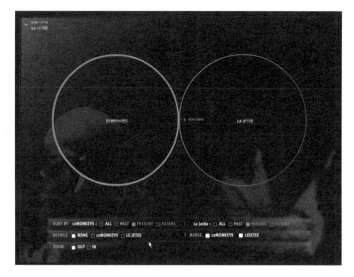
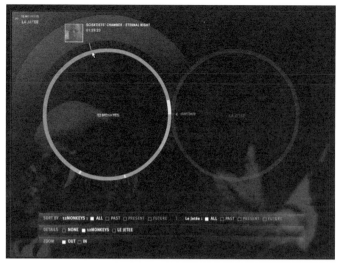
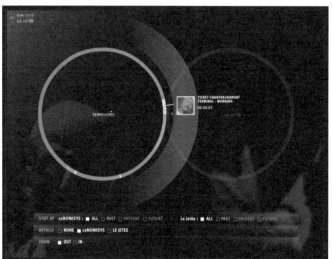

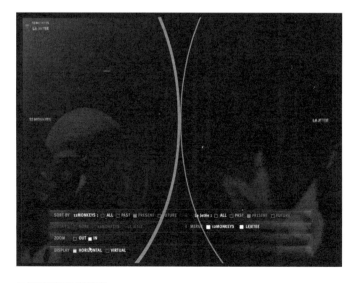

An interactive tool to help
a user explore meaningful
connections within the
complex visual content of
both films.

I then focused on the changes in time that occurred within these films. Since *Twelve Monkeys* and *La Jetée* are primarily time-travel films, I was curious to see how mapping time changes could be visualized. I developed a system to label each such transition in time as a horizontal line of a particular color — where the color would denote whether the moment belonged to the past, present, or future. I used yellow for the past, orange for the present, and blue for the future. I was curious to see what my analysis would reveal.

The two films were of different durations — *Twelve Monkeys* being about 130 minutes and *La Jetée* at about 28 minutes. In order to compare the two movies I mapped their results to the same length and juxtaposed them to view the differences. The result was interesting, in spite of *Twelve Monkeys* being inspired by *La Jetée*, the former was mainly composed of moments in the present (yellow) as compared to the latter. While this was just one observation that I had made, I began to realize the many possibilities that lay in creating a learning tool that would allow for a variety of explorations and discoveries. This would be of particular use to an audience interested in studying cinema.

INTERFACE EXPLORATIONS: SEARCH FOR A METAPHOR

Having made some progress on mapping, I looked for metaphors that would help with designing the interface to include the functionality and interactivity I needed for the project.

In order to design an appropriate interface that could compare the narrative aspects of the two films, it was essential for me to find an ideal visual metaphor. Not only is the interface the primary medium to understand the stories in these films, but to also appropriately depict my understanding of two films' depictions of time travel. The choice of the interface affects the nature of user interactions.

Initially I considered the use of two horizontal lines to represent each of the two movies. The user would traverse through each of these lines and get to know what happened in a given movie at a particular

point in time. Navigating the two movies in a linear manner was useful, but seemed like the most obvious solution to me. I was trying to find other ways in which I could push the user's ability to compare and contrast the narrative aspects of the two films. To do so meant the need for additional design elements that would engage the user's curiosity.

As mentioned previously, the action of main characters constantly going back and forth in their memories and in their place in time characterize the two films. In many ways, this aspect helps to build climactic outcome, but also reminded me of the circular nature of time.

After several more sketches, I decided to use a circular shape to embody my interpretation of the nature of time in these two movies. My process revealed that the circular shape was a more effective and meaningful visualization as opposed to using a horizontal line.

Firstly, the circular shapes placed next to one another allow for an easier comparison of the timelines of the two movies. Should I have chosen the horizontal lines over the circular shapes it would have presented a challenge in accommodating the entire duration of each movie within screen space. In this regard, the two circular shapes displayed next to one another was a more efficient use of screen space.

Secondly, a circular shape allows for users to traverse the movies in nonlinear ways, thus allowing for potentially interesting and unexpected discoveries in analyzing the movies. This flexibility also allows for the user to compare and contrast the narrative aspects of the movies in non-traditional ways.

FUNCTIONALITY AND INTERACTIVITY

After having decided on the circular shape, I put the two circles (one for each of the movie) side by side on the screen with a black background. I felt a black background would help users distinguish the various colored categories.

The opening screen shows the two circles meeting at a common point but they each rotate in opposite directions. The left circle denoting the *Twelve Monkeys* turns clockwise from this meeting point, and the circle on the right denoting *La Jetée* turns

counterclockwise. The idea for this kind of a behavior came to me while evaluating ideas on where to place the circles and how best to have them interact.

There are two reasons why I feel the turning of the two circles is of importance. Firstly, as the user turns these circles, the point at which the circles meet creates different and dynamic overlapping connections. The meeting point of the two circles serves as a place where the user can start to compare the similarities and differences between the two movies — particularly around the past, present, and future events given that *Twelve Monkeys* was inspired from *La Jetée*.

Secondly, the circles are my interpretation of the role of time in these two movies and the act of turning around the circles in either direction serve as a metaphoric representation of the back and forth that goes on in both movies.

Three additional features were envisioned in the interface to allow its users to sort, obtain further detail, and to zoom in and out of particular points in time within the two movies. These features were intentionally placed at the bottom of the interface, as they are secondary to the circular shape that serves as the primary means for interaction, navigation, and exploration of the content.

FURTHER DESCRIPTION OF FEATURES AND FUNCTIONALITY

The "Sort By" Functionality

This functionality allows users to sort (isolate) selective points in time within each of the films. The user can pick from the past, present and future points in time. When the user selects the present (orange) option, the past (yellow) and the future (blue) break apart and disappear from the circle leaving only the present selection on screen. Soon after, a new option called "Merge" appears beneath the "Sort By" function. If the user selects it, the present (orange) merges into the full circle. In this way, the user can compare the thickness of the two circles, which is a visual indicator of the amount of 'present' time in both the movies. The "Sort By" option is the principal functionality

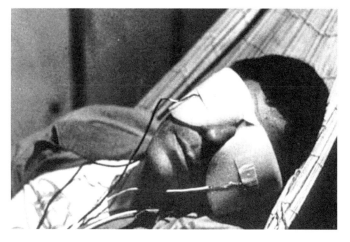

The 1995 *Twelve Monkeys* by Terry Gilliam (right), was inspired by the 1962 film *La Jetée* by Chris Marker (left).

of this project when comparing the films because it in turn affects how the other two functions — the detail view and zoom in/zoom out-behave.

THE "DETAIL VIEW" FUNCTIONALITY

This option allows users to individually view additional information about a particular clip within a movie. This function helps the user to understand and analyze a scene in greater detail. Users can rollover a scene from say the past (yellow), present (orange), or future (blue) on both circles; they can additionally view details consisting of a synopsis and can watch the movie clip on a screen that appears over the main screen.

THE "ZOOM-IN" AND "ZOOM-OUT" FUNCTIONALITY

The default setting of this feature is at 100 percent. If the user selects "Zoom-In," both circles are immediately magnified and they focus in on an area where the two movies meet at the center on the screen. At this level of maximum zoom, the user sees a pair of vertical lines that represent the timeline of the two movies. The reason for this feature is to make it easier to review and compare the two movies. It also provides a

display of content at that particular point in time as embedded clips. This ability to view in detail specific clips of the movie allows the user to make unique discoveries and thus develop new perspectives about the two stories.

CONCLUSION

Throughout my entire process in making this interactive learning tool, I realized three key aspects to dealing with a complex body of information, such as narrative:

1. Need for grouping and labeling parts of the information in order to find interesting areas worth exploring;
2. Need for visual metaphors to enable the creation of meaningful and informative connections;
3. And finally, design a final outcome that enables discovery.

By allowing the user to navigate through past, present, and future points in time of the movie, my project helps the user explore the narrative aspects of the two movies. Manipulating the circle-shaped interface results in discovery of interesting and potentially meaningful connections within the complex visual content that is part of these two movies.

However, I was unsure if my discovery would be meaningful to the user or not. When I posed this question to my professor, he indicated that I did not need to explain every single valuable aspect of the experience since some aspects of it need to remain for the user to discover and realize.

The final outcome of this project received the international Adobe Design Achievement Award in the non-browser based design category for 2008.

The Field

ERICH DOUBEK
Class of 2008

The Field is deeply inspired by the work of Camille Utterback and her *See/Saw* installation. I consider *See/Saw* a very successful example of object-based interactive narrative. I tried to focus on how Utterback used the seesaw's physical traits to engage the participants and bring the seesaw beyond the familiar through the experience. I realized that the seesaw had two basic interactive functions that built directly off its natural form and use.

The first was the seesaw's up and down motion as the interaction that drove the story forward. The second element was the seesaw as a metaphor. The person in the down state of the seesaw holds considerable power over the person in the up state. This shifting role beautifully mirrors the power shifts between the two characters in Utterback's narrative.

MY THOUGHT PROCESS

This insight enabled me to see the physical traits of my cube differently. If I wanted to give the viewer control over time, I needed to think about time in abstract ways that could be connected directly to my object.

My thoughts swirled around the ideas of modularity in clocks, calendars, and sundials. From the sundial my ideas expanded to that of the sun's rotation around the earth. Building off this astrological concept of day and night, I started to see the cube as two hemispheres. The top and bottom sides of the cube could function as two separate times zones. With one side designated as day and its opposite side as night. The user could now change time by changing the top (day) and bottom (night) orientation of the cube. With the cube's time controls established, I needed to turn my attention to building a sense of place.

As humans, our eyes are placed in an articulated turret: our head. The resulting visual experience is a roving view capable of 360 degrees of rotation. Our eyes are how we determine distance and position — our location in the world. When we communicate direction we simplify that experience down to variations of four basic paths, the four points of the compass.

When I started to think of a compass in relation to the cube it started to form a metaphor for the human head. The cube has six sides but when held, only five of the sides are visible as the sixth side is face down in your palm.

This gave me five sides of the cube to think about. When I thought of the cube as a head I imagined each side being a viewpoint. In my mind, the cube now was a head with five eyes. I saw four of those eyes on the four sides of the cube, each pointing down the arrows of the compass North, South, East, and West. In this mental image the fifth eye naturally pointed skyward. This fifth eye was the most powerful.

The orientation of the fifth eye pointing skyward was significant for a number of reasons. The first of which is our connection with the sky goes way beyond a simple viewpoint. From the origins of our species, our relationship with the sky has been integral to our survival. It was the original foreteller of our immediate future. Is the sun out or is a storm brewing from which we should take cover?

The skyward view's second significance is its function as our species' first chronograph. Our ancestors' knowledge of the sun and moon's passage across the sky is the oldest means to measure the passage of time. We instinctively know the difference between a cool-colored dawn and the warm hue of dusk and how they differ from the peak of a noonday sun or the black of night. In *The Field*, the users would unconsciously read the sky as an ambient marker of time.

THE USER-EXPERIENCE

For *The Field* installation, the cube sits on a table in front of a projected image of the daytime sky. I saw this as the natural state of the cube when it was not in use. The skyward view invites the user into the experience by defining, in relative time, the moment the user is witnessing.

Depending on the face of the cube pointing upward, the user gains access to the view of the playground to the West, the fields to the North and South, or the houses abutting the park to the East.

When the user inverts the cube, he does not find a view of the grass at his feet, but instead he experiences a time shift. What was day is now night, the daytime skyward view becomes a night sky. The time shift also carries over to the four sideviews of the field. While the location has stayed the same, by simply inverting the cube, the user's experience changes. The entire experience has altered. The daytime field takes on a different life at night. The children are no longer playing on the swing sets to the West. The well-lit green field is now a shadowy darkness with dew glittering under field lights with haloes of color, high in the distance. To return to the daytime, the user only needs to flip the cube and the field is again filled with sunlight.

Using an apple as a natural
interactive component to
an interface.

ASSESSMENT

In the case of *The Apple*, its size and natural interaction lent itself
well to the experience. The cube enabled the user to easily equate
what they were seeing in their hand and layer the alternate reality
of the projected visual experience on top of their physical actions.
In other words, the user's actions and the visual experience matched
up as parallel happenings that made sense being connected. The
interactive element successfully changed the user's relationship with
the cube, fulfilling a thesis goal of putting the cube (the object in this
case) in the role of interface as a way to articulate a virtual apple.

This was not the case with *The Field*. Although it was successful
at creating an interaction that addressed the concepts of time and
space, the user interaction with the cube was wholly unnatural and
not intuitive.

In the building stage of *The Field*, I realized that Camille
Utterback's interactive function with the seesaw built directly off its
natural form and use. By moving up and down on the seesaw your
kinetic input moved the story forward. This relationship of cause
and effect made sense.

Unfortunately, while the sides of the cube related to the directions of a compass, the user interaction did not. The interaction
of rotating the cube to change the view projected before you felt
disconnected. I had missed an important aspect of human-object
interaction; the physical interaction didn't make sense with the
resulting experience.

If I were to remake *The Field*, in addition to the object navigation, I would also like to address the visual experience and materiality of the object. I feel as if the wood cube was too generic and it
would have been nice if the material and tactile nature of the object
in the user's hand helped connect it to the field. When I think of a
field in a park, I think of dirt, grass, jungle gyms, and chalk on pavement. Materials like these would connect an object tacitly to a park
in ways that are impossible with the wooden cube.

I also would need to address the projected image. Still images
worked to prove the concept but video with sound would have
enhanced the user's experience by pushing the user's perception
to better alter the user's experience with the object. I would also
consider changing the space to accommodate multiple walls of projection. This way the user would be contained in a space where the
visuals could encompass them instead of just being shown on a single wall in front of the user. Mirroring an actual field by wrapping
the projection around the viewer might help in building a stronger
sense of place.

When the user inverts the cube,
he experiences a time shift. The
daytime field takes on a different
life at night.

Garden City

DAN JOHNSTON

Class of 2009

I was interested in developing a design strategy that would connect gardeners from around the world. The *Garden City* concept is a channel of communication for urban gardeners of all skill levels. It is a platform for gardeners to ask questions and provide answers, or simply share information about past experiences.

Why gardening? First, this concept of locally grown food has become increasingly popular in American society during the last few years. There are many examples of artists/designers/writers developing new content in this new environmental direction.

So what does gardening have to do with dynamic media? It's not the subject itself, but the systems associated with the process. Those who identify as gardeners have a strong sense of community, but only in their local area. I was interested in exploring different ways of interacting that would be of interest to gardeners. Could they find common ground based on the size of their plot? By the crops they are growing?

There were a few specific goals I had in mind when putting this project together. Most importantly, I wanted people to grow some of their own food. Since the scope of the project is focused on urban gardens, the amount of food grown would be small. That's fine! I wanted people to have the experience of growing something from a seed, so they could have a better appreciation of how food gets to their marketplace.

A secondary goal was strengthening the locality of a place. I was hoping *Garden City* would cause the ranks of existing gardening communities to swell. Other practical goals included allowing everyone to participate regardless of skill level and providing a clear path for beginning gardeners to follow.

Is there a difference between gardening and farming? Isn't it all just "growing stuff?" The following quote from Wikipedia is helpful: creative communities — designing to invite participation in the creative process

> *The key distinction between gardening and farming is essentially one of scale; gardening can be a hobby or an income supplement, but farming is generally understood as a full-time or commercial activity, usually involving more land and quite different practices.*

This is an important distinction to make. I am not interested in addressing farmers who have lots of arable land, and have an interest in maximizing their returns. The audience here is home gardeners, working at a small scale during their free time. They are of course interested in growing things, but may also want to meet other people, talk about gardening, or just get out of the house!

Since each user of *Garden City* will be different, is it beneficial to compare one garden or gardener against another? I believe it would be, as someone with a rooftop garden will encounter different problems than someone growing herbs on a windowsill. The size of the user's garden is the most useful piece of information to use when comparing two gardens.

How do you go about making those comparisons? I decided to create an open standard unit of measurement that can be applied to all gardens. An SGU (Standard Gardening Unit) would be the amount of soil contained in half a cubic foot. As more dirt means more work, I feel users with similar SGU counts would have other commonalities as well.

Will implementing an open standard for gardening be successful? I don't know. I do know that open standards have been wildly successful in other mediums. Train travel was vastly improved when a standard thickness of rail was laid down, liminating the burden of switching cars as the influence of one region gave way to the next.

Now that you have defined a target audience, a goal for them to accomplish, and a quick way of comparing one garden against another, how do you build an online community? What information can be found online that is relevant to physical actions taking place in this community? During my research, I uncovered three locations where data relevant to a particular community lives. A successfully designed system would draw on all of these types of data.

First, there are facts. This is a collection of information that is scientifically true. An example of this type of data as it relates to gardening could be two simple charts. One chart outlines daily sunrise and sunset times, another lists the amount of sunlight plants need to flourish. By combining these two charts, the power of these facts emerge, revealing the optimal times for plants to grow.

Facts alone can be overwhelming, there are so many! But they can be narrowed down by a second data type, personal data. This could be anything from a user's location, to their dislike of mushrooms. Since this is information of a personal nature, users may feel reserved in providing it. Getting users to trust the motives of the system is key in getting good data here.

For me, the information generated by the community social network is the most interesting. This is information largely based on

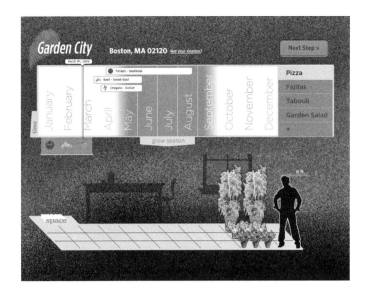

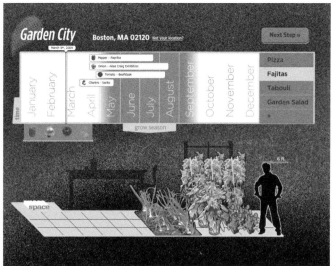

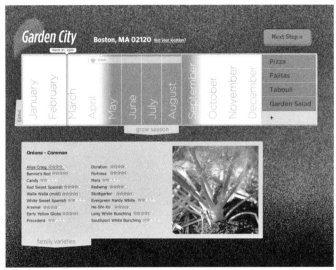

Garden City is a platform for gardeners to ask questions and provide answers, or simply share information about past experiences.

opinion. These opinions may be accepted as fact by the community at large, and could even be scientifically true. A gardening example of this could be, "Planting tomatoes and marigolds together reduces pest problems." This is interesting, as the decision whether or not to trust the information is left up to the user. This data is at the heart of any successful system.

My next step was to begin researching current business models that use these categories of information in their design systems. I'm looking for successful companies; gardening shouldn't be the focus yet. But each company's design system should contain all three of these informational categories to varying degrees.

Zipcar was the first company I took a closer look at. Providing a car-sharing service, Zipcar describes itself as "Wheels when you want them." Users go online to reserve a car. They use that rented car for a few hours to run errands or go to the beach.

When their rental period is up the car is returned to its parking space, and the availability status of the car is updated online. An individual benefits from this service by saving time and money. Lowering the price point of using a vehicle makes cars accessible to more people. The community benefits by seeing fewer cars on the road, a reduction in traffic, and reduced air pollution.

How do these different data types manifest themselves in the Zipcar model? Factual, external data here is related to the cars themselves such as make, model, MPG, and so on.

Zipcar captures lots of personal data as its users interact with the system. Your location, how often you drive, how far, and your renting patterns are all logged. This information is likely used to know when to increase the size of the Zipcar fleet.

There is a small amount of social network data here, consisting of users sharing past experiences: things like road trips taken, and memories made possible by Zipcar. This information is only presented on the website in a marketing context, however.

As you can see from the diagram, there is not much overlap between data types. The only real crossover is the availability of the vehicles with the users requested rental time.

There is virtually no social network here. Users cannot inform one another as to the state of the vehicle they are renting. Does it smell? Is it making a funny noise? The success of this system relies on the fact that driving is tacit knowledge. Everyone has taken driving classes at some point and is aware of the benefits of driving. The size of the external data reflects the many extra services available to drivers Zipcar doesn't have to provide, such as driving directions, traffic updates, and more.

A second successful business model that brings together community information is Nike+– is another melding of digital and online worlds. To achieve this Nike created a device that measures and records the distance and pace of a walk or run. Users can take the information generated by their workout session, and upload it to the Nike+ website for friends or training partners to see.

Experiencing something
from a seed to better
appreciate how food gets
to the marketplace.

Differing from Zipcar, the external data here is limited. The only real tie-ins are to more products! Users have the option to buy a pair of Nike sneakers, or an iPod in order to get the most from the system.

Personal data here is by far the most abundant. The accelerometer in the device detects your pace, distance, calories burned, time spent exercising. It also remembers all workouts and can compare one against the other.

Users must go online to access their social network data. There are options to schedule a time to go running with friends. Groups of runners who have never met can even join the same digital team, pledging to run a certain number of miles each week.

The real success of Nike+ is the overlap between the personal and social network data. By allowing runners to form teams online, they no longer have to exercise with others who happen to be nearby, or run the same speed, or have a similar schedule.

Solo runners using Nike+ reported staying motivated to run, and stuck with a regimen longer than individuals not using Nike+. Your digital teammates can see the amount of running you are doing online, and use that to stay motivated. Although not running in a group, runners on a team still felt camaraderie and would work harder to avoid letting the group down.

Now that I knew the types of data that were important to me, and had seen them working in other applications, I began researching garden-based information systems.

There were many websites dedicated to gardening out there, but few showed much in the way of active communities. Fewer still had any gizmos, like vehicles or shoe sensors.

The National Gardening Association has lots of content and is updated often. They offer ideas, information, and expert advice relevant to your location. Unfortunately, the NGA's site is based on a newspaper model with no space for users to get involved.

Some other sites, such as Guerilla Gardening had a great community. But their sites really just function as documentation for their activities, they do not invite you to participate.

Probably the most successful site I could find, is maintained by the American Community Gardening Association. This site has factual information, like what to grow and when to grow it. It also provides start-up guides for first time gardeners, as well as a community garden locator. Allowing visitors to find the nearest community garden to their home.

During my research phase I uncovered a few gardening-specific systems. Some approaches are high tech, while one, Square Foot Gardening, is a bit more straightforward. The author of this book, Mel Bartholomew, began preaching his style of square foot gardening in the early '80s. The concept of sectioning off your garden into tiny little plots fit nicely into what I was doing.

Botanicalls is another interesting system designed by several students at NYU's Interactive Telecommunications Program. They have developed a system that uses several open source technologies (asterisk, arduino, php) to detect a plant's moisture level and places a phone call when it needs watering. The Botanicalls team goes one step further by assigning personalities to species of plants, reflected by the accent the plant speaks with when placing calls. This is an interesting concept, and technically stunning, but I felt it was a little too lighthearted in the end. There is a community created, but it's an artificial one built from one person's plants and the pre-recorded voices assigned to them.

The last plant-based system I found had me reconsidering the direction of *Garden City*. A company called EasyBloom marketed its titular device, designed to help people learn what they could grow. In their words: "The EasyBloom Plant Sensor shows exactly what vegetables, fruits, herbs, flowers, trees, shrubs or houseplants will grow anywhere, inside or outside. For over 5,000 plants, EasyBloom has step-by-step plant care, pruning, fertilization and gardening tips."

You just place the sensor wherever, and based on your geographic area and the time of year, it will tell you which plants would be most successful in that location. My research had been pointing me towards developing a product like this. Once I learned it already exists, I knew I had to focus on the community aspects to have a successful project.

I decided to focus on potential gardeners who might be interested in beginning, but didn't know where to start. To do this, I put myself in the place of someone who doesn't know anything about a topic. What kinds of questions would these people have?

In gardening, like any other hobby, there are millions of questions that need answering at a range of skill levels. A beginner might want to know how much money they need to get started, how much time needs to be invested, and just how difficult is this anyway? Intermediate users have got their plants started and will need different answers. Maybe just some encouragement to keep going, or specifics on how to deal with bug problems. Experienced gardeners may be interested in talking to other gardeners on their level, or even taking the time to help a few beginners!

After deciding the type and location of the information breakdown, it was time to draw a site map. I attempted to bring together all the information I had learned during the research-and-requirements gathering phases.

I decided on giving the site three phases, roughly correlating with the potential user's diagram. The first few pages should be seen and digested very quickly. Here, users should be learning what they will be getting themselves into. Discovering who else is doing this is important here, as well as the larger societal reasons for starting.

At this point, users have two options. They can decide gardening is not for them, and go on to their next project, or they might be interested to know how they can get started.

If the "Get Started" button is clicked, this brings the user to the next area. Here they are presented with several common meals to grow. I chose to represent choices to beginners in terms they are already familiar with, such as pizza and fajitas. I hoped that providing these options would prevent people from feeling overwhelmed when faced with choosing from the thousands and thousands of different growable vegetable varieties.

These common meals would not be the last word, but function more as a customizable template. They're there to get you started. As the user is experimenting with the tool, they are seeing relevant growing information for each vegetable. When is the best time to start it? How much space does it need? How did others fare when growing this plant? These are the questions that are being answered for the user.

Once the user has selected and tweaked their virtual garden to their liking, they are ready to move on to the next step. By clicking the "Next Step" button, the user is taken to a screen listing the materials required to grow their specific creation.

Now, for a second time, the user is given the option to disengage from the system. They've planned their garden, they know how much time and space they need, and they've got a printed list telling them what they need now and in the future. They can walk away now with the tools they need to succeed, or they can choose to stay. If they decide to register as *Garden City* users, the next level of options would be made available.

One option available after registration, is location-specific updates for your garden. *Garden City*'s algorithms could cross-reference user-plant information with weather information based on that user's location. Updates could be texted telling users when to bring plants indoors, passing on severe weather alerts and so on.

Would users really be interested in entering all this detailed information about each plant? They already have! The planning tool serves a dual purpose. It remembers the final garden layout chosen, and fills in information related to those plants.

How do users communicate with one another? How are passions shared, photos exchanged, and questions resolved? For the online world, the answers are a simple message board. Although not glamorous, the message board has been around a long time, and it is quite simple to post and search user content.

An alternative way of broadcasting garden information, would be through the use of a social networking application. For example a Facebook plug-in. Users with shared interests in gardening would be able to follow and share experiences with one another, expanding pre-conceptions of a gardening-based community. People no longer have to be near each other to share their gardening experiences.

When I showed this concept to actual gardeners, the response I got back was muted. The gardeners in my audience were quite experienced, and have had years to perfect their techniques. They were nice about it, but expressed doubt that they would find much value in a tool like this. I could see their point, as the materials here are targeted at a more inexperienced audience.

I felt compelled to do this project based on some current trends in our society. The United States has seen a huge resurgence in green/sustainable initiatives across the board. Michael Pollan's book *The Ominvore's Dilemma* has become a best seller, crossing into the realm of pop culture. Even the president is getting in on the action, by planting his own victory garden on the south lawn of the White House.

In hindsight, my desire to work with this material may have led me to push it further than it needed to go. After my research uncovered the EasyBloom device and the American Community Gardening Association website, I could have stopped there and been happy with my progress. One is an amazing piece of diagnostic technology, while the other does an excellent job of performing the social/community function. Using the two of these products together would produce similar results to what I was hoping to achieve with *Garden City*.

I'm glad I kept on with it however, as I was able to explore the core concept of what a community really is. What components are necessary to cause a community to form? What are all these people bringing to the table, and how can I help them share their knowledge with other interested parties?

Sound Machine

DAN JOHNSTON

Class of 2009

The goal of the *Sound Machine* is to give people with limited or no musical background the experience of being a performer. The *Sound Machine* is designed to challenge users to communicate in modes, nonverbally for example, that they may be unfamiliar or uncomfortable with. Screens are omitted in an attempt to push the computer into the background, allowing participants to focus on their fellow performers.

The reason why I chose the *Sound Machine* is simple. I love music, but I am not a musician. I have always enjoyed watching the dynamics that occur between performing musicians. I wondered if such communication, informed by those professional individuals knowledge of music, would be possible to replicate using non-musicians. This project also presented itself as a great platform for moving away from screen-based media and into physical interfaces.

When constructing this instrument I felt it was important to take three things into consideration. First, audience participation would be a key feature. By allowing people to easily change their role from performer to observer, I hoped to make *Sound Machine* more approachable. Second, the distance and location of the performers would be key to the success of this project. Too far and there could be no communication. Too close, and people would feel their personal space was violated, and they would be unwilling to participate.

Finally, the performers had to be placed in a way that makes it easy for them to interact. If these people are going to work together to create a piece of music, they need to feel comfortable giving and receiving instructions to one another.

During the brainstorming phase, I tried out different concepts on paper to find the voice of the project. At the beginning you can already see the performative aspects taking shape. Would there be some kind of projected keyboard on a wall? Is there a stage performers are standing on? The projection idea was quickly dropped, but the touching of the object remained. Maybe there would be panels hung on the wall? This had the fatal flaw of not allowing performers to see what the other is doing.

The idea of touch stayed with me, however, as I moved into production. How could I alert users they were allowed to touch this device? Text instructions? An icon of a hand? I became interested in the mechanics of how users would activate a sound.

Ideally, there should be no barrier between the users hand, and the sound they triggered. Many long weeks were spent researching touch-sensitive capacitance switches in search of a perfect solution. The technical complexities of this route were ultimately beyond my grasp, however, and I settled on using a simple push button. In the end the little red buttons perform their job admirably. We have a cultural knowledge of what buttons are, and the red color makes it hard to resist pushing!

Constructing the physical frame of the instrument allowed me to use my dormant industrial-design human-factors skills. It had to be built at the right height, of course, but its shape was a core design element as well. Users of the Sound Machine needed to stand facing each other in order to facilitate nonverbal communication (such as eye contact, nodding) that is traditionally observed being used by live musicians. Restricting the amount of inputs on the *Sound Machine* to four was necessary in order to make the machine approachable. No one wants to use something that makes them look dumb! These input buttons were placed with enough distance between them so no single user can trigger them all. A group must be formed.

The actual sounds emitted by *Sound Machine* are probably its weakest aspect. The samples used during testing were too long and complicated. Some samples were matching halves of popular songs, included in the hope that users would attempt to recreate the original song. The first testing period was very brief, perhaps with more time to experiment, users could have made those connections for themselves.

The machine could be more effective by producing shorter, more percussive sounds. During user-testing, users had problems identifying which sounds they were generating. I believe this was due to sound samples going on for too long. Making it easier to identify which performer is responsible for which sound, would allow for better cooperation and communication between individuals. Shorter samples would also focus the reward for users on releasing the buttons so they could be pressed again. This would

Sound Machine gives people with limited or no musical background the experience of being a performer.

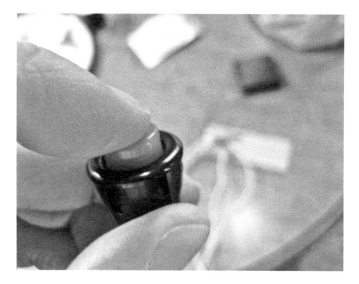

help overcome a technical problem, where the sounds start clipping if too many buttons are held down simultaneously. Hiding the wiring a bit more wouldn't hurt either.

Recently, I revisited this project. I placed the machine in a gallery setting, and allowed people to approach it at their own pace. It was quite interesting to see different personalities working together. Some users were totally uninhibited. At first they would try to activate all the buttons alone, and when they found this impossible, they went out and recruited friends. Others were shy, and wanted to see friends engage with the system before they felt comfortable jumping in. Still others were only interested in hearing what sounds the different buttons would make. Uninterested in participating with others, they only stayed long enough to press each button once. Unsurprisingly, I found that people who had an interest in music were more likely to interact with the machine for a longer period of time. When building the machine, I was aiming to attract people who were not necessarily musicians. I hadn't even considered the fact that non-musicians were much less likely to be interested in playing music!

Ultimately, I felt like the gallery showing was a success. *Sound Machine* was interesting enough to get people to interact with it. At the same time it was simple enough so as not scare away casual users. And it held just enough content to hold people's interest for a moment.

For me, that moment of interest was the litmus test result signifying success. It was great to see a group of friends get together and share a smile at the experience. It was even more rewarding to see strangers, or groups of strangers getting together, forming an impromptu community, and using the machine.

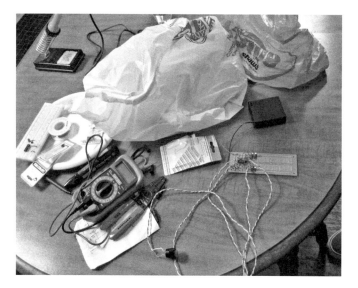

Johnston researches
touch-sensitive capacitance
switches in search of a
perfect solution.

Falling Up

MARY MURRAY

Class of 2008

By walking down a hallway, visitors control the video and audio playback of plates falling and crashing. The speed and direction of the plates falling is controlled by the speed and direction of the user's movement. For example, if the person moves slowly in one direction the plates fall down slowly. Conversely, if he or she moved quickly in the opposite direction, the shattered plates would quickly regroup and rise again.

Over the course of conceptualizing and creating *Falling Up,* I've developed three related interpretations.

Controlling Time: In our thoughts, we often go back in time and replay events, but in our everyday experience the flow of time is something over which we have no control. *Falling Up* gives people the experience of controlling the flow of time by manipulating digital media.

The Difference Between Reality and Representation: In our thoughts and through media we can imagine changing events or undoing events. But in reality time only flows in one direction. A plate that is broken stays broken. You can't hit "undo."

Expanded Perception/Different Perspective: Falling Up is recorded with high-speed video which, when played back, slowly allows a visitor to experience time in a way that is not possible through their normal perception. For example, the high-speed video allows the visitor to see that at the moment of impact the plate holds its round shape for a second before exploding outward.

By creating a playful digital interaction, which allows users to control the speed of the video and sound, I hoped to create an experience that would demonstrate that there is more information in the world than can easily be perceived with our senses.

Visitors control the video and audio playback of plates falling and crashing.

ShapeMix

COLIN OWENS

Class of 2009

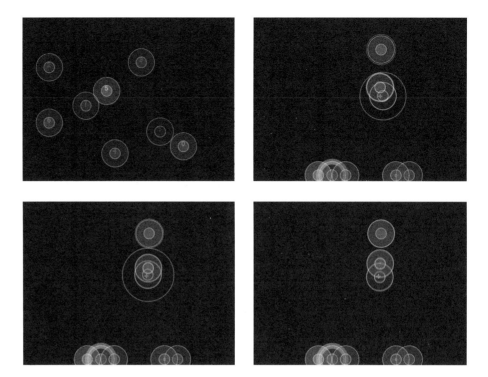

CASE STUDIES

ShapeMix is the project I created as a test bed for several theories of audiovisual exchange. I wanted to create a place where one or more audiovisual objects could live in one space and be manipulated.

At the heart of the project is the notion of a confined space that represents left-and-right pan and up-and-down volume. Each of the shapes (circles in this case) represents a sound. Inversely, each sound represents a shape. The two are synonymous. Each of the circles can be manipulated with sonic and visual effects that give audiovisual cues.

AUDIOVISUAL CUES

I wanted to create a flexible software interface with an eye toward portability and ease of use. For the gallery show, I created a small touch interface on a screen inside of a box with an accelerometer inside. Because of the small size, the user could pick the box up and shake the shapes around. This probably could be done with a larger table, but I doubt it would have been easy to pick up and move around!

Several early experiments led me to the creation of the fully working prototype.

BEAT DETECTION

I started working with a library based on Frédéric Patin's algorithms for detecting sound energy peaks. I took several recorded tracks from the same musical piece and assigned them to a circle. I then had the program enlarge each of the circles according to the beat detected.

The beat detection worked very well with percussive sounds (as you would expect). On the downside, it randomly assigned beats to sounds that didn't have as much definition. I dropped the idea of using beat detection in favor of volume data.

PAN AND SPACE

I had circles placed in space, but it bothered me that they appeared in different places — yet sounded like they were coming from the same place. I experimented with audio pan by mapping the horizontal space of the circles in relationship to the left and right ears. One of the sounds to the far left was more apparent to the left ear. The two sounds near the middle sounded more in the center, with the one on the left leaning toward the left and the right one leaning toward the right.

MOVEMENT AND SPACE

I had a single circle move by following the cursor. The movement of sound and shape from left to right worked well for panning, but nothing happened when I moved the circle up and down. I thought to use height as volume, making the circle bigger and the sound louder as it approached the bottom of the screen and smaller (becoming almost nothing) when it reached the top.

MULTIPLE SHAPES AND VOLUME

When I introduced multiple shapes, the size of the circles became a problem. Circles closest to the top would become difficult to find when I tried to click on them. Circles closest to the bottom would become difficult to locate and maneuver because they overlapped so much.

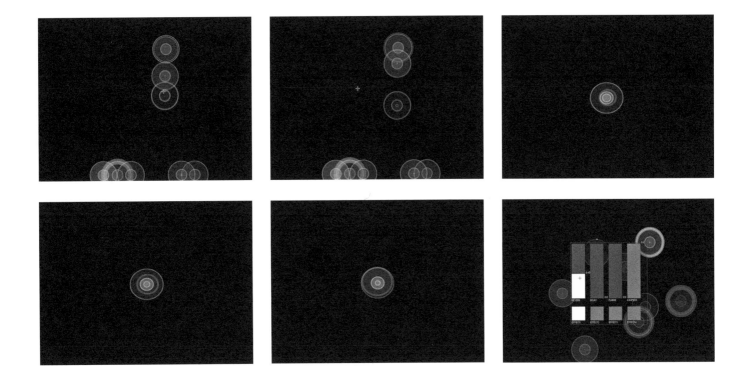

I settled on keeping the shapes the same size as one another so I could identify them as different objects of the same type. This would also make it easier later, when I would use a touchscreen to move the objects around. If objects of different sizes were difficult for the mouse to locate, a touchscreen with a much larger clicking area would drive someone crazy trying to locate and move individual circles.

Since I didn't want the base shape of the circle to change, I had to represent volume in another way. There were several possibilities: represent volume as a non-filled second circle emanating from the middle; use the edge of the circle as volume; or use the opacity of the circle. I didn't want to use opacity because if I had any more than a few circles of similar base color it might get confusing. Using the circle's circumference for volume was mathematically difficult for the computer; the presentation method too limiting and having to read around the circumference would be odd.

I chose to represent the volume as a non-filled circle emanating from the center. It was far less distracting than the other two proposed methods and it made the interface easier to use.

PHYSICS

I wanted to find a way to keep objects from overlapping too much on the screen. It didn't make sense to have two objects in the same place at the same time, since our version of physics doesn't support two things being in the same place at the same time. In audio mixing theory it's also prudent not to place two things in the same exact space (there are exceptions to this rule).

Each of the shapes represent a sound and can be manipulated in space to give sonic and visual effects.

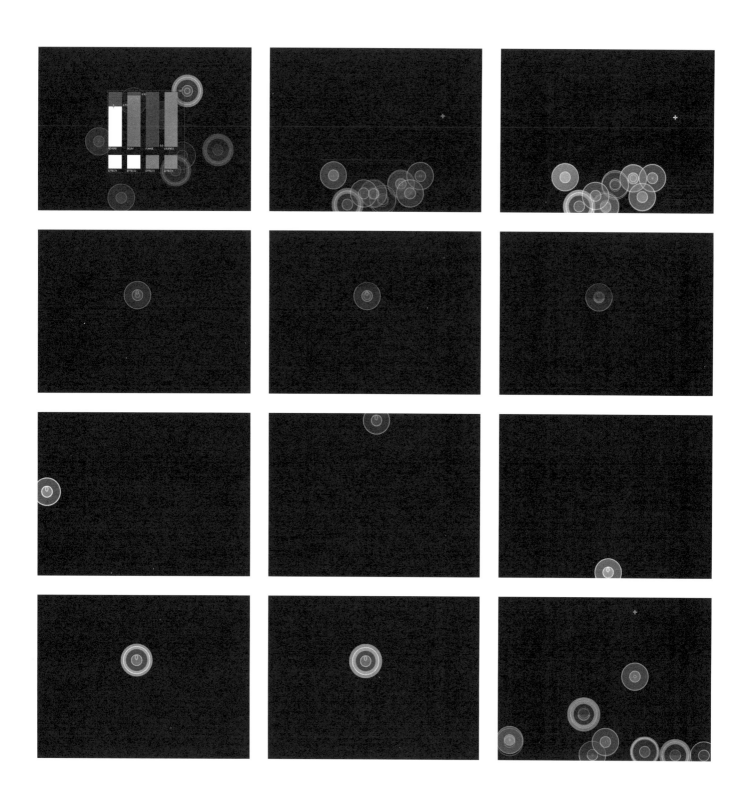

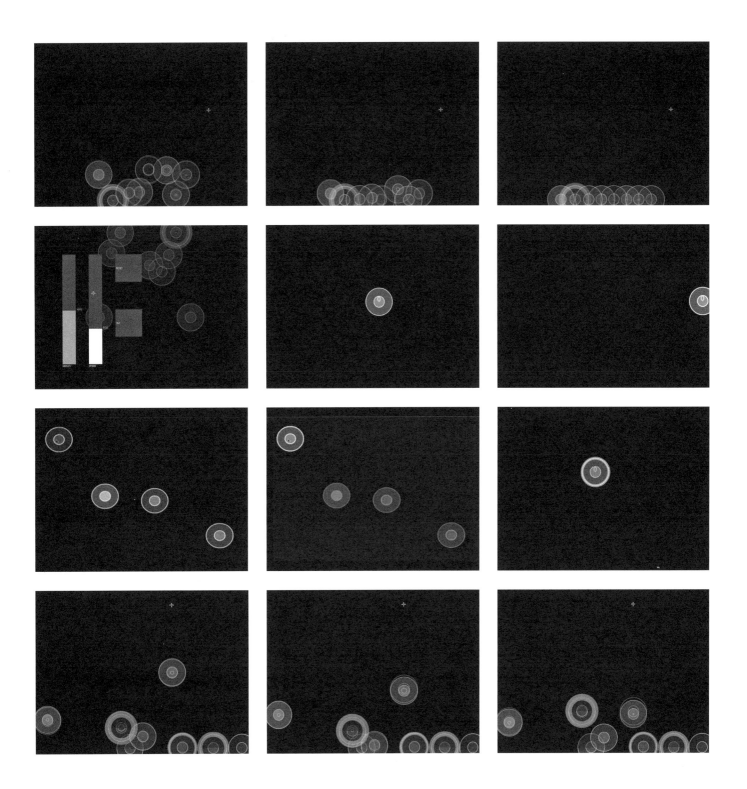

I adopted some simple physics principles of collision detection and separation. In addition to keeping the circles apart, I opted for them to "spring" or repel away from one another, like magnets with the same polarity. I turned the whole space into a "box metaphor" so that the circles wouldn't pop out of the side and end up on the other side abruptly. I applied a simple gravity that, when turned on, would make all of the circles fall to the bottom and bounce like superballs.

The direction of volume had to change at this point. Up means volume-up and down means volume-down in audio mixing. In physics, rest means silence. When the volume was changed so that the bottom meant silence and the top meant full volume, it made sense because objects resting at the bottom didn't have any movement whatsoever attached to them.

Later, I added an accelerometer that, when place on the bottom of an LCD screen laid flat on the table, would bend gravity in different directions depending on which way it was turned. It reminded me of lifting a pool table and watching the balls fall to the bumper. This effect helped in instances where every sound needed to be nudged up or to the left a bit.

Adding gravity, spring, and collisions to the mix had some fun, unintended consequences. The act of randomly bouncing balls changed the volume and pan and created its own set of effects. Using a single ball to move the one next to it helped to widen the distance between two mixed objects, creating better audio separation. This reinforced the idea that natural metaphors can extend the language of motion using sound and image in physical space.

EFFECTS

Effects seemed to have correlations between image and sound on a wavelength level. Every time I came across an audio effect, I found a corresponding visual effect whether it was experienced by the naked eye or on a smaller, molecular-atomic level. Panning is a psychoacoustic audio effect and the visual artifact of seeing an object in its relation to our heads.

Delay was a little more difficult to comprehend, since the corresponding audio effect was based in astronomical physics. However, looking at the theory of audio delay, it too can be measured in wavelengths. This formed the basis of the edge effect, or effect based in levels much smaller than we can see translated to our naked eye as audiovisual correspondence.

CONCLUSIONS

If I want to extend this language, I will have to spend some considerable time analyzing and testing each effect type of image and light analogy. I realize that both the research and the software environment are just in their infancies. I could create a set of motion studies to look at the results of a Doppler effect on the pitch or arc motion of a shape. I could look at the elasticity or rigidity of shape as a way of giving cues about sound. There are many others.

There are other metaphors beyond 2D space. Video could be used in place or along with shape to give a sense of space to both the sound and video. The ReacTable Environment could help give tactile feedback using physical markers on the screen that act as distinct objects. This could be useful in low light situations or for people with vision impairment. A true 3D space could give way to a totally immersive environment. However, until we invent a true 3D projection system, this is not possible.

This work was made possible with the computer, but its usefulness as a tool is limited. The mind is a much more powerful tool. The computer is merely a vehicle to enable the theory that there are connections between light and sound waves and that we behave in particular ways in space.

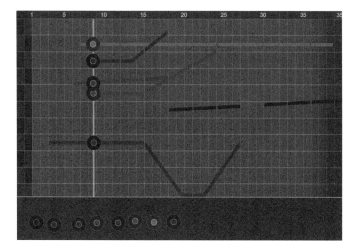

Camp Ta-Kum-Ta

BRIAN MOORE
Class of 2009

PROJECT GOAL

Taking what I had learned from previous project and documentary film classes, I would create a comprehensive interactive narrative that covers an event and tells a personal story.

PROJECT OVERVIEW AND PROCESS

By the end of my fall semester in 2008 I already knew I was going to focus on *Camp Ta-Kum-Ta* for my final thesis project. For more that two decades, *Camp Ta-Kum-Ta* has provided, free of charge, a resident summer camping experience for children from Vermont and upstate New York who are battling or have had cancer. For one week each summer, a group of more than 90 volunteers come together from all over the country to create summer camp adventures for nearly 60 kids affected by cancer. The mission of the camp is to help heal the mind, body, and spirit of children 7-17 who either are fighting cancer or have had cancer in the past. By bringing together children who have experienced the physical and emotional pain and isolation of cancer and its difficult treatment, the camp creates an environment of mutual understanding. Kids aren't individual patients, kids are just kids.

Being a part of the camp as a volunteer for over six years, I feel a strong connection to the campers and staff as well a great understanding of what exactly the T-K-T experience means. My time at camp has had a profound effect on my own perspective. The individual stories of triumph, loss, joy, and pain are inspiring, heartbreaking, and all very real. In my short time volunteering with camp, I have watched campers grow up, some get better, some get worse, and some return as different kids the following summer while some don't return at all. As part of the media staff, I have listened to and captured their stories. I have tried to understand and report the challenges of living with and dying from cancer as well as the empowerment and hope of overcoming disease.

When I received my application for the 2009 camp staff in January, I wrote a lengthy project proposal to the camp board explaining my intent. I proposed filming the week to produce a short documentary film the camp could use for parent education and fund-raising. I also wanted to use the footage and photography to create an interactive narrative. My goal was to tell the camp's story through the experience of individual campers.

From my previous experience developing interactive narrative, specifically *"Recounting Iraq,"* I knew that I had to establish a story. I envisioned the overall piece including many from the T-K-T community, but I needed to focus part of the content on one individual's experience to tell the story of all the campers' experience.

During the previous summer, I became friends with a 16-year-old camper named Scott. He is a sweet kid with a great attitude and extremely dry sense of humor. Scott lost most of his hearing and eyesight temporarily due to an inoperable brain tumor when he was 6. With time and treatment, his tumor stopped growing. He spent his seventh birthday at *Camp Ta-Kum-Ta* and hasn't missed a summer since. The summer of 2009 he turned 17 and looked forward with excitement and sadness to his last week as a camper. I reached out to Scott and his parents to ask them if he would be interested in being featured in a documentary for camp. Camp had given so much back to Scott and his family that they didn't hesitate to say yes.

With Scott I had the veteran perspective. Working with the camp medical director, also the head oncology nurse at Fletcher Allen Hospital in Burlington, Vermont, I was introduced to the Ardren family and their 9-year-old daughter Meghan. She was just finishing treatment for leukemia and responding well. Several emails and phone calls with Meghan and her parents explaining my intentions convinced them to participate. Meghan had never been a part of camp before. She was nervous and excited about attending camp.

While obtaining approval from the camp and getting access to the campers, I was taking a summer class in documentary filmmaking with David Tamés. This class and its companion, Documentary Film Boot Camp, which I had taken previously, helped prepare me for the first part of this ambitious project. David's classes covered everything from the basics of lighting and camera operation to editing to production planning and legal advice. I would not have been able to take on such a big project without David's classes and support.

My plan was to follow one camper as she is introduced to the camp experience for the first time and another camper as he graduates from camp after attending 7 consecutive summers. In addition to these two featured campers, I include material from the week highlighting the various events, campers and staff that make up the camp experience.

Prior to the camp week, I created a shot list and key events I could predict based on previous camp experience and the 2009 camp schedule. I was sure to include traditional moments such as saying goodbye to parents, meeting cabin counselors, high-ropes course, squirt-gun fights, campfires, formal dance, and reunions with parents. I scheduled preliminary interviews with both campers' parents the first day of camp before they said goodbye for the week. I followed those up with interviews as they took their tired children home.

I left for camp-week July 31, 2009, with two HD video cameras, 3 microphones, two tripods, a digital camera, 40 hours of digital cassette tapes, and a box full of cords and other accessories. Richard Swenson, another volunteer and former camper, was going to be my assistant for the week to help me capture as much as we could. The day before the campers were set to arrive, we made sure we were familiar with our equipment and divided the camp schedule. I was to primarily follow Meghan throughout the week and Rich was to follow Scott. I went to sleep late that night very anxious to start filming and feeling the pressure to do a good job capturing the personal stories for a community that I considered myself a part of for many years.

The first day of filming, we arrived at the hospital in Burlington, Vermont, where most of the campers had been treated for their cancer and where, now, their parents would drop them off for the week. It took some time for campers and staff to get used to having cameras at every event. I also had to get used to my role as cameraman/observer at every single event, no longer an active participant as I had been in previous years. Eventually, I over-came my shyness and went about the business of observing and recording.

Rich and I spent nearly every waking moment at camp with a camera in our hands. Together we shot over 29 hours of footage in seven days. After the first night of shooting I tried to review each day's footage and catalog it for editing. That lasted one night. I was exhausted and spent what energy I had preparing the next day's shot list. When I was shooting the last parents' car leaving the camp road with their tired camper in the backseat, I remember the cramp I felt in my hand from holding the camera all week. I turned the camera off as I walked back to our makeshift office, which doubled as the camper's game room, exhausted and relieved but mostly excited as I remembered some of the amazing footage I captured throughout the week.

Following Meghan's experience throughout the week, I was hoping to capture a slight transformation of a timid kid, unsure of her new environment into a camper who found a new community and support for her

I have tried to understand the challenges of living with and dying from cancer as well as the empowerment and hope of overcoming the disease.

personal challenge. But Meghan is shy and barely spoke to anyone all week let alone me with a camera. I did however witness some memorable moments and captured them including Meghan playing piano in front of the whole camp before dinner, her being fitted for a dress for the formal, and simply connecting and laughing with her cabinmates and counselors.

Scott's last week as a camper was like a farewell tour. He was clearly a favorite of the veteran staff members. He addressed the whole camp the final night retelling his earliest memories of camp and, through tears, what the 10-year experience had meant to him. Other staff members told me numerous stories of Scott as a young camper and how he had matured into an adult heading off to college a month after this year's camp. Months later when I sit at my computer, slowly reviewing, noting, and cataloguing each scene across 32 tapes, I can't help but smile and enjoy reliving the experience.

INFORMATION ARCHITECTURE
AND INTERFACE

As I developed the interactive project, I was motivated by the connection I felt to camp and the kids. Between capturing and reviewing all 29 hours of video, I started to sketch out the information architecture for the interface. I researched interactive projects that incorporated timelines to better understand common conventions and successful user interactions. I compiled rough, flat prototypes based on my findings. Thinking

about past projects such as "*A Garden of Questions*" and "*Recounting Iraq,*" I realized I didn't have to over-design the interface. A simple and easy-to-use interface that let the content be the focus would be a more successful approach.

In addition to the hours of footage, I had over 600 still images from the week. Thinking about my *Facebook Filter* project, I decided early on the goal of the interface was to give quick access to the videos and photos I had collected while guiding users through the stories I wanted to convey. I knew I was going to use the idea of filters to turn the content on and off. Information architect Richard Saul Wurman's thoughts on the five ways of organizing information were a helpful first step — Location, Alphabet, Time, Category, and Hierarch (LATCH). I decided that time would be the primary way to organize or filter the information. I selected a total of 14 videos or photos for each day and displayed them horizontally with a little more than half a day's worth of content visible on the screen at any time. Clicking on a media piece in the main timeline will bring up a larger version and play a video clip if it is a movie.

A smaller version of this media timeline appears above the main timeline with a controller indicating the visible space. By grabbing and moving this viewer/controller, the user is able to scroll through the full week and see all the media. Clicking on a thumbnail within the smaller timeline moves the larger timeline to that area.

The option to filter the content drops from the top-level menu. Each media piece has been tagged with meta-information allowing it to be filtered by story, media type, activity, and emotion. The activities filters were based on the events of the week. This was similar for the emotion filters, but more subjective. Filtering by story, clicking on one of the preset stories, highlights all the media pieces along the timeline that are part of that particular story. After clicking and viewing the first media piece in the story, you can read the headline, description, and scroll though the rest of the story. Filtering by media type, activity, and emotion has a similar effect on the time, highlighting relevant content and receding content that doesn't match the filter chosen. While viewing a specific media type, a user can see and explore the threads of other filter tags that contain the same media piece. For example, if you were watching the fourth video in "Meghan's Story" you would see that it is also tagged with "Laughing." If you were to click on the "Laughing" link, you would leave "Meghan's Story" but continue to view the same media piece. You would now be in the "Laughing" thread.

I developed a feature where members of the camp community could create their own story using the media pieces in the timeline. By selecting a number of videos and photos, a camper or staff member can collect a thread together and save it for others to watch, enjoy, and respond in kind. More than just scrolling through the images

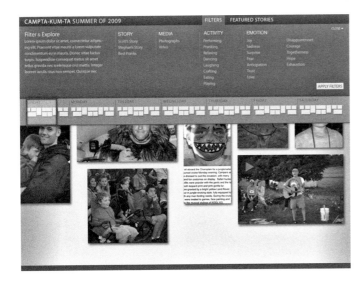

and videos, users could now manipulate the content and create their own story of images to share.

I originally hoped to include a map of the camp alongside the smaller timeline. Using pinpoints on the map to represent each of the media pieces, a user could rollover the points, see a thumbnail of the media, and then click for a larger view to continue with the piece described above. Ultimately, I decided to drop the map component of the project. I felt it didn't really add too much more to the interface since most of the action happened primarily in three locations. Additionally, most people exploring the system wouldn't be familiar with the camp's geography.

The Flash ActionScript 3 programming involved in producing this piece pushed my coding skills further than any other project. I cobbled together the interface and functionality from tutorials and things I learned while auditing Brian Lucid's Elements of Media class. In the end I needed to bring in someone with professional development experience in ActionScript 3 to make it work exactly as I envisioned. He helped me by writing a function that searches the XML file and filters the media content based on a users interaction. I had reached a point just after the middle of the semester where the object-oriented programming was beyond my skills. Whenever I was frustrated with the coding, I would take a break and scan through the images or video footage to re-mind myself of why I chose this project.

WHAT I LEARNED FROM THIS PROJECT

If I could go back and redo the filming, I would have set aside more time for personal interviews rather than the amount of quiet observation that I capture. Just as important as showing the experience is hearing the participants describe it in their own words.

Normally, a project like this would include a team of people with a variety of skills. Ideally I would have had 2 videographers, 2 sound technicians following the campers throughout the week. After shooting, a transcriber and Final Cut Pro editor could have handled the post-production. Along with the ActionScript developer, an in-depth look at information design would have been helpful. I had to wear many hats during the nearly year-long process, some fit better than others. I struggled with the filming, editing, and coding and there are clearly other people that are more talented in those areas. I love telling stories and for this project, program, and degree, I wasn't going to let that hold me up.

CONCLUSION

My overall research and studio investigations guided me in the development of *Camp Ta-Kum-Ta*. Decisions about interface, story, interaction, and user-control were based on previous successes and failures. I plan on continuing my work on this specific project. I hope to present it to the camp community in early 2010 for their use and feedback. I feel I can further refine the

experience and perhaps develop it into a platform for other interactive narratives.

More and more people are getting their news from online sources. Most news content is similar to its counterpart in news-papers and television providing text and images. Interactive journalism not only tells stories and provides information, but can entertain, excite, and engage users in a story. The power of the medium is to deliver a unique experience that includes elements of discovery, control and participation. Creating an element of discovery for the audience can draw their interest into the piece exploring how the interface design can reveal part of the story. The interactive timelines are a good example of a simple interface that allows for exploration, discovery, and at the same time provides context for each component. Users are given control, to explore their path through the content. Providing options about direction or opportunities to localize the content, create personalized experiences that build connection and promote retention.

Interactive narratives, like my *Camp Ta-Kum-Ta* project, are broken up into various story parts. The designer needs to balance the user-control and the story. Too much user-control and the story might get lost and conversely, too little control and you may lose the interest of the audience. It is impossible to make a blanket statement about how much control or user participation is needed for a successful interactive

narrative. You must look at each project individually and determine the right balance that effectively conveys the overall story and creates an active audience.

The variety of specific skills that are involved in developing interactive news presents challenges. It is unique for a person to be skilled at the writing, information architecture, interface design, and programming that go into comprehensive news packages. This list expands if you include capturing video, audio, and photography — all disciplines by themselves. While working as a one-person show, I had to balance these various roles based on the story I was trying to tell. After defining the goal and purpose of the project, I developed a plan to best deliver the content. Will the maximum experience be found through a written story that gives more control to me as the author or by a series of audio or video clips of the main characters themselves? Depending on the content I am reporting on, I had to make decisions about which skills needed more focus. A character-driven piece would have more story development and less information design.

One thing that interactive journalism does well is visualizing large amounts of information, raw data, or user-submitted content through story, context, reinterpretation. Elements of personalization and control allow users to see all, dig deeper, or follow their own narrow interest creating a unique experience. It is the role of the new-media journalist to look at databases of information as news sources and develop interactive systems to make them accessible.

An interactive narrative needs a story — a concept so basic and obvious. The best interactive narrative journalism projects on the web today are grounded in a good story. I think it is easy to get excited and a bit lost in the fascination of creating a new narrative form in the digital world. The design, organization, and delivery of the material are crucial to support the story and extend the experience. Interaction made possible through a user-controlled interface and new-media elements such as non-linearity, variability, personalization, participation, and computation present an opportunity to enhance reporting and the art of storytelling.

The means by which the best digital stories are presented today will continue to evolve. While writers and reporters continually perfect their craft, technology creates innovative ways to communicate and media becomes more accessible.

Interactive narratives, like *Camp Ta-Kum-Ta*, are broken into various story parts. The designer needs to balance the user-control and the story.

Motionary

AGATA STADNIK

Class of 2009

MOTIONARY

Motionary is an online, user-generated database of improvised words and expressions given meaning through silent improvisation. *Motionary* helps people learn and understand new words and at the same time, it supports both physical and online social interaction. *Motionary* members can create an entry for each new word; record performances individually or in a group, submit and meta-tag their improvisations online. *Motionary* is a confluence of concepts from other case studies I created during my first year in the Dynamic Media Institute program. *Motionary* offers three different modes: Learn, Play, and Create that support different learning styles.

LEARN

The Learn mode is the most important and essential part of *Motionary*. Through improvisations, it offers vocabulary and expressions, definitions, and pronunciations. The Learn mode helps people understand the meaning of words, see them being used in the context of a situation and also helps them remember these words. Users will be able to create their own accounts with vocabulary preferences, galleries of favorite performances, and sign up to receive an improvised word every day. Users will be able to select the clearest or the most popular performance or add their own improvisation.

PLAY

This mode offers games that are based on nonverbal communication, i.e., a kind of online charades. It allows people to play with improvisations, meanings, and words. Users have the option to select the level of difficulty, play with their friends. and keep score online. Play mode offers a challenge for people who know vocabulary very well, but who want to experiment with their ability to comprehend body language. Playing with words and improvisations allows playful interactions for people who enjoy games, riddles, and challenges.

CREATE

This mode lets people remix existing performances to create new sentences, poems, and stories. In "writing" sentences using recorded improvisations, users are able to choose from a wide range of improvisations and give a very specific meaning to what they wish to convey. They can share their stories with their close friends or with the entire *Motionary* community. The white background used in the improvisations allows the clips to be linked seamlessly into one visually uniform story. In the future, I would like to see the Create mode used for creative online collaboration and filmmaking.

ORIGINS

The idea for *Motionary* was born during the Spring 2007 semester, when in my Design Symposium class I was asked to create a dynamic interpretation of a poem. I chose *The Great Figure* by William Carlos Williams, because its simple and seemingly random words created an intriguing story. Poetry is a combination of words, which, when juxtaposed with one other express unexpected and unique meaning. I contemplated the various ways each of us read, improvise, or interpret a poem and how this results in unique and very personal interpretations. I remembered poetry readings that were longer as the reader used gesture. I wondered if I could push the envelope even further in my project, and ask people to act out and perform the poem. While I was working on the interactive poem project, I was also looking at English words which are difficult for

Motionary is a user-generated database of improvised words and expressions to help people learn new words through silent improvisation.

me to understand or to remember. English is my second language, so I decided two years ago to expand my vocabulary. I signed up to receive a new word every day from the online site Dictionary.com.

Since then, I have received hundreds of words but it is difficult to remember them all. This new vocabulary often seemed as abstract as the words in the Williams poem and it could be used and imagined differently by various people. I wanted those unusual words from the online dictionary to be presented in a more appealing, unique and memorable way. I am a visual learner and so images help me build and maintain a growing fund of English words and concepts. Consequently, I imagined how helpful it would be if a person performed each new word for me each day. That is exactly how the idea for *Motionary* was born!

THE GREAT FIGURE
by William Carlos Williams

Among the rain
and lights
I saw the figure 5
in gold
on a red
fire truck
moving
tense
unheeded
to gong clangs
siren howls
and wheels rumbling
through the dark city.

POEM IMPROVISATION
Originally, I asked a group of strangers on the street to perform parts of Williams' poem together using only body language without any spoken words. I lined up five volunteers along the sidewalk and gave each one a card with their particular words from the poem. The performers had to anticipate their turns in order to act out each word or phrase sequentially and to maintain the flow of the poetry. It was fascinating to see how the participants used their bodies, the space around them or even the other actors to express the words. Two

things struck me, first was the moment when one of the actors clung to another — a perfect stranger to her, to express the word "gold." Another happened as an actor stepped apart from the alignment and used the entire surrounding sidewalk. Clearly this one loved to perform. It was revealing to watch the group interpret the poem, improvise, and let go of societal norms — in this case to touch a stranger. Though the performance was very engaging, without knowing the words of the poem it was abstract and hard for the audience to decipher. To solve the problem, I introduced a reading of the Williams poem as an option. I thought about adding "buttons" to each performer so that by rolling over the viewer would be able to replay, see the text, or hear the poem read aloud. To improve the project it was clear I needed to involve better or even professional actors.

RECORDING CYCLES
For the subsequent take of poem improvisations, I asked my classmates to perform separately in the blue room. I wanted to have a clean background and the flexibility to replace one person with another. The second group of performers was more skilled in improvisation than the first group. Their first task was to express the whole poem using only body movement. Since I had them in the blue room I took advantage and required the actors to define additional groups of words. It was not about spontaneous improvisation anymore. With terms such as "instructions" or "beautiful," the actors now had to explain and define meaning as clearly as possible. Those first

Motionary performances were excellent. They looked wonderful on a white background and demonstrated the advantage of being able to seamlessly combine all the clips. It was observing the reaction of the audience to those clips that I realized another aspect of language and meaning acquisition. The audience was using a combination of wild guesses and reacting to one anothers interpretation in order to seek meaning. That inspired me to build another component of the *Motionary*, online charades. Viewing many performances gives the learner the option to choose the best performance or their favorite actor. The next step in the development of *Motionary* was to build a larger database of words and improvisations. I was determined to record more individual improvisations on a white background. However, it was challenging again to get more volunteers. I became more confident in what I was doing and started asking more people to improvise for my project.

RESEARCH

During the process I had to lower my expectations and for research purposes I asked many people to improvise in random locations, without the advantage of the blue room. I conducted a series of photo shoots at the MIT Media Lab, where I was able to get my class-mates to perform for me. Whenever I explained that *Motionary* is about helping people learn, understand, and remember words, most people were eager to participate. They also did not mind sharing their performances online, which I found surprising in a positive

way. Another insight occurred while I was shooting a performance, with two actors obviously in a hurry and anxious about time. To accommodate them I suggested they improvise together. This acciden-tal situation resulted in a terrific performance. Without any direc-tions and left to negotiate on their own, the two actors collaborated and turned in an amazing performance. I realized that having a pair of actors adds another level of stimulation to the performance. In time I decided to ask three or more people to participate in the next performances. I was a bit skeptical about having a group of people agree on something and perform without a director. Here again my assumptions were wrong. The largest groups I was able to get to perform for *Motionary* were five children and on another occasion four adults.

GESTURE PATTERNS

All group improvisations were full of lively atmosphere and heated discussions, because people had to negotiate and agree on elements of each scene first. What also amazed me was the ease participants displayed while performing even with some unfamiliar people. Strangers touched, unconsciously mimicked each other, and as-sumed postural-echo body positions. I watched enthralled as people who had never talked to each other before, embraced, touched and had fun together. I also tried to see if *Motionary* could help people learn a new language. I recorded native speakers improvising and pronouncing the word aloud, so that the learner could both see and

MOTIONARY WORDS

– jollification: merrymaking; revelry.
– *deus ex machina:* an agent who appears unexpectedly to solve an apparently insoluble difficulty.
– bellwether: a leader or leading indicator.
– ostentation: excessive or pretentious display.
– camarilla: a group of secret and often scheming advisers.
– importunate: troublesomely urgent.
– woebegone: woeful; also, run-down.
– voluble: characterized by a ready flow of speech.
– afflatus: a divine inspiration.
– pugnacious: combative; quarrelsome.
– caesura: a break or pause in a line of verse; also, any break or pause.
– salubrious: healthful.
– abulia: loss or impairment of the ability to act or to make decisions.
– pin money: money for incidental expenses; also, a trivial sum.
– miasma: a thick vaporous atmosphere, often noxious.
– objurgate: to scold or rebuke sharply.
– roister: to revel; to carouse.
– inveigle: to persuade or obtain by ingenuity or flattery.
– portent: a sign or omen.
– lambaste: to scold sharply; also, to beat.
– chimera: a mental fabrication.
– lionize: to treat or regard as an object of great interest or importance.
– ubiquitous: being everywhere.
– winsome: light-hearted.
– epigone: an inferior imitator.
– confluence: a flowing or coming together.
– posit: to postulate; also, to suggest.

Source: Dictionary.com

I asked many people to improvise in random locations with terms such as "instructions" or "beautiful."

hear the new word. I decided to zoom in to frame only the person's upper body. That way, I thought, the viewer could see the facial expressions in detail. I assumed that we mostly use our upper bodies to gesture while talking. Thus by watching the speaker's lips, we can see the positions needed to make certain sounds. Another fascinating aspect of *Motionary* performances is the fact that although I recorded all performances in separate shoots, some performers used exactly the same gestures and moves to express certain words. It is more understandable to see performers using the same gesture for very specific words, such as in performances of the word "camarilla," however seeing actors using the same sets of moves for the word "epigone" fascinated me. Three different groups of people, from different cultural backgrounds and different schools, used the same context of a person marching and an "imitator" following him. I was surprised because I would think of a dozen other ways to represent the "imitator" before I would think about walking, but maybe it is just me. I think it could be revealing to research this matter further and see why people use identical gestures to interpret the same word.

NO DIRECTOR

One of the most remarkable aspects of *Motionary* performances is the fact that performers took only a few minutes to think about their words and how to act it out. The actors had to be creative and improvise in an instant. It was amusing to see that at first participants would say, "It is impossible to show this word," and then a couple minutes later they would turn out an amazing performance that clearly expressed that particular word. Soon, I realized that the participants also needed some time to "warm up" and with each new word they would become more free and relaxed. They needed time to get used to the space, to the camera, and the challenge. I recorded and interviewed professional actor and director Joshua Dolby. Because he has extensive experience in front of and behind the camera, his feedback was invaluable. Dolby acknowledged that he also needed time to warm up, get used to the space and surroundings, the camera range and to my expectations. Usually, directors have a specific vision of the performance and they want actors to play according to that plan. In *Motionary*, I simply gave people words and encouraged them to express it using only body language and no words. I had no rules, no directions, and no time limits. Some participants told me that in the beginning, they were confused because they did not know what exactly was expected of them. *Motionary* participants were surprised that I was happy with the first take. I did not judge or criticize the performances. I only re-shoot a performance if the actors were stuck in their scene and needed more time to work it out. I wanted all *Motionary* performances to be "raw," spontaneous and very real. I think that this is one of the reasons why those improvisations were so successful. Often I was able to observe the joy the actors felt during and after improvisation sessions. I often heard "I did not think this would be so much fun," which gave me enormous satisfaction.

EXPRESSED WORDS

For *Motionary*, I asked people to perform uncommon and very specific English words taken from the online site Dictionary.com's — Word of the Day. I also imagined that people would be able to create sentences about their feelings and emotions. That is why I asked people to show me "I love you" or "I hate you." Most American participants expressed hate with very animated body language and facial expressions. Then, when I asked people from Asian cultures to do the same, they told me they do not know how to communicate "hate" because in their culture they do not express this emotion. International students from Korea, China, and India had to think very long to improvise a "feeling that is close to hate." Even when they expressed it, it was not as powerful as expressions by American students. Asian cultures are known for not demonstrating emotions ostentatiously, or in public, which is likely the reason for their reticence. The participants were also given some basic verbs that are usually learned when a person is first acquiring a new language. I asked students from Germany, Korea, and India to show and say the verbs: cook, sleep, forget, measure, and other basic expressions. That experiment made me realize that motion could really work as a tool for learning a language. However, for a better learning purpose it would be useful to zoom in even closer to capture facial expressions and upper body gestures. Some languages and sounds are very hard to hear and even harder to repeat. Improvisation enhances seeing, seeing enhances learning. That batch of recordings turned out to be fascinating on another level. I discovered that students from different countries used the same gesture to express certain verbs. For example, each student leaned her head on her folded hands to express the word sleep. It would be revealing to research even more gestures in order to discover universal patterns of body language.

CHILDREN

Filming children participating in *Motionary* demonstrated another fascinating aspect of my motion and interaction studies. I filmed five children: three, six, nine, ten, and twelve years old. I noticed right away that children utilized a great variety of movements. Kids crawled, pretended to fly, jumped, made stars. I gave them simple or simply defined words from *Motionary* to perform. It was amusing to see that their performance of "zoo" was almost the same as "ubiquitous." When standing alone in front of a camera a child looked nervous and self-conscious. The same child in a group with other children would forget about everything and concentrate on interacting with others. When moving and interacting with each other, children looked more carefree, cheerful, and more relaxed than the adults. The nine-year-old actor used the same gesture and facial expressions to express anger or concern as the adult actors did. Was this genetics or can children mimic adults and even by the age of nine recognize and replay certain meanings with their own body language? Mimicking was obvious in interaction between kids, especially when younger children tried to copy the older ones.

PROFESSIONAL MIME

My last photo shoot happened at the end of April 2009, when I recorded and interviewed a professional mime, Ian Thal. He performed words for the *Motionary* contest and other unusual words from the *Motionary* collection. Thal's improvisations were captivating and dynamic. He presented and explained to me his "gesture alphabet" that he uses as a foundation for his improvisations. Thal trained in classical mime but he tries to discover new venues of improvisation through his own acting, writings, and direction. Thal looks at the body through a philosophical, spiritual, and mystical prism. He does not agree with famous philosophers, for example, Descartes, that "the Body is just a machine." Thal believes that acting, improvising and using body motion integrates people's body and mind into "real" unison. Thal thinks that being in tune with their bodies helps people feel better and be happier. In his opinion, verbal and nonverbal communication operate in different realms. These areas overlap, but while verbal communication is very precise corporal language leaves more room for interpretation. Thal believes that *Motionary* is a confluence of explicit vocabulary, the highest form of verbal communication, and mime, the highest form of nonverbal communication.

MOTIONARY CONTEST

In April 2009, Brian Moore helped me organize the First Annual *Motionary* Improvisation Contest. He helped me create a system of rules for contest submissions and judging. The contestants had to perform one of four words: gesture, narrative, sensors, and visualization, and upload their performance on YouTube. I received five submissions this year but I am hoping next year it will get bigger. The winner, Tristan Pine, was chosen based on ratings from YouTube users and the opinion of four judges chosen from the DMI community. The *Motionary* judges surprised me with their extreme ratings, and it was tough to choose the winner. Negotiating across different opinions and preferences is essential to the concept of *Motionary*.

INTERACTION ONLINE

The main concept for online interaction is based on new media tools that already exist and are widely used by millions of people. For example, on Wikipedia or YouTube users often generate their own content. I intend that the *Motionary* database be authentic and original. Before any performance will be introduced to a new learner, it has to be revised and approved by a group of community members. So far, I've recorded over five hundred performances, edited, and posted some of them online. I also designed the *Motionary* website, blog, and a working prototype to provide an example of how each performance represents a specific word. *Motionary* constantly expands.

INTERACTION IN PHYSICAL SPACE

By creating the *Motionary* community I want to foster social learning and interaction, enhance people's communication skills, and encourage the exchange of creative ideas. I want to motivate people to have fun learning and playing with words and improvisations. For the physical *Motionary* interaction, I want to design spaces that could be located in large public places, for example in shopping malls, schools, or on playgrounds. I want people to have the opportunity to stop by and perform with their friends or invite passers-by to improvise with them. Those *Motionary* spaces will be set up with filming equipment, a white background, good lighting and Internet connection. Having such a setup ready against a consistent background will enable users with little effort to share their performances online.

STATISTICS AND META-TAGGING

During my process of recording for *Motionary*, I filmed over 50 different performers and over 500 word interpretations. Performers' ages varied from a three-year old boy through teenagers, students in their twenties, to adult actors in their fifties. I recorded many individual and group performances. The performers came from different countries and some spoke in their native language. Most people improvised for the first time in their lives, others were professional actors. I recorded performances in different locations and with a different background. Most *Motionary* performances lasted at least 4 seconds but others were longer than 30 seconds. Actors utilized a variety of moves, gestures, and facial expressions. My *Motionary* database grew enormously and I hope it will get even bigger. That is why I decided to prepare a system for users to meta-tag their video clips, gestures, and interactions.

FUTURE DIRECTIONS

Motionary is based on a simple but at the same time complex idea. I think the *Motionary* concept can be researched further in countless different directions. Some of the most important directions might be language acquisition, social interaction, and body language. During my thesis research, I concentrated mostly on experimenting, observing, and interviewing participants. I realize that my research would benefit from a more controlled and methodical approach. I think it would in the future be helpful to conduct more specific studies. I think that games, motion, and creativity can put people in a "flow" state. I strive to engage people deeply in my projects and I create situations where they can immerse themselves in what they are doing. Most of the people who performed for *Motionary* told me: "I did not know this would be so much fun!" I also noticed that although I asked them to do three words, once people started performing and "warmed up" they always wanted to do more. I believe that some participants experienced a "flow" while interacting with my projects. In the process of creating improvisations, recording for the *Motionary*, my perceptions came full circle; from the initial group of people performing at the same time, to experimenting with a single performer, and finally understanding the value of the groups of people collaborating to express meaning.

The participants were given basic verbs that are usually learned when acquiring a new language. The experiment revealed that motion could be used as a language-learning tool.

Bathroom Writing

DENNIS LUDVINO

Class of 2010

An interactive anthology
of bathroom writing.

The writing found on bathroom walls amuses me. It is often crude and is almost always bad, but there is something universal here — across time and space people have always written on walls, and bathroom walls are reserved for the juiciest of content. The writing can be funny, puzzling, dirty, and even sad. *Bathroom Writing* is an interactive anthology comprised of this writing. In this collection, no writing is too bad — bad is better.

The goal was to create a database of 100 objects and a series of filters to hide and reveal information based on certain properties. While there are infinite potential properties to choose from, I narrowed it to seven: genre, color, tool, location, time, typography, and illustration. This database relies on the physical properties of text to define the user-experience. How specific information is revealed and when it is revealed creates a dramatic story. More importantly, the design must reflect and protect this story.

In order to do this I created a virtual bathroom wall that displays information dynamically. Within the design, the user is presented with certain choices that control the initial experience. For example the homepage reveals the first filter — the user needs to choose to go number one or number two. The path chosen determines what information will be accessible. The user can always go back, but the choice will always alter the experience. In the culture of interactive media, choice matters.

TECHNOLOGY

ActionScript became my friend (or at least a friend of a friend). It was the architecture I used to build all of the interactive elements.

At the end of a couple of week's worth of coding and debugging, I had a semi-workable prototype — a huge success in my book.

There isn't anything revolutionary in the code, but the challenge of having a functioning prototype allowed me the opportunity to work with programming long enough to get comfortable with it. This foundation was enough to help me build more complex projects like the *Dada Machine* and *Sound Writing* where I begin working with arrays, multi-dimensional arrays, conditionals, and loops.

While my uphill battle with programming continues, I made some serious progress in the development of this project.

PROCESS

The design process was broken into three phases: research, wire frames, and visualization. Breaking down the process this way helped to better understand the content and how to visualize it in a way that represents and further enlightens the experience.

Most of the research phase was spent collecting content, which meant spending numerous hours in public restrooms. During this time I discovered the shared qualities of bathroom wall-writing — the tools, writing styles, and content commonly found in the bathroom space. With this in mind I questioned the various characteristics of each specimen collected. First, where were the images written, in the stall or by the urinal? What tools were used to create the messages? What was the content of the message? What type of building was the message written in? By categorizing each post based on visual, thematic, and spatial characteristics, I developed the structure necessary to begin thinking about the overview of the database.

The wire frame sketches provided the skeleton of database, how information would flow, and areas of interaction. In the beginning of this project I thought of the database as nothing more than a simple collection of images that visitors could look through. But from the wire frames I developed a level of participation and communication based on three modes: viewing, sharing, and commenting.

When visualizing this information, I created three different concepts. My first reaction was a more conventional interface that wasn't specific to the content. The second concept used the content to drive the design. For this visualization I created a virtual bathroom wall that sorted and displayed writing based on a variety of filters. Finally, the third concept was an abstract system of circles that allowed for a variety of different information to be displayed, but again wasn't content-specific.

I decided the virtual bathroom wall was the most appropriate visualization for the content and used a variety of bathroom specific interactions as the basis of the design. The user first decides to visit the stall or the urinal, which initially filters the content based on where it was written in the bathroom. The paper towel dispenser contains the filters and to view more content another toilet is visited. When the user wants to return to the home page, the toilet must be flushed.

The main goal for the visual side of this project was to bring the user into a dingy typographic space. The authenticity of this space centered around the creation of hand-drawn text and images. I discarded all the basic rules of craftsmanship. No line was too crooked and messy, no image too childlike, and certainly no animation too crude. I channeled all of the time I spent in the bathroom photographing different specimen.

The bathroom wall database was most successful in bringing meaning to the design from the content and bringing meaning to the content from the design. In this sense every aspect of the design was meaningful to the user and created a rich experience in the process. While the project doesn't answer any questions about bathroom wall writing (which was not my goal), it does create an interesting virtual space to explore

Collaborative Drawing

JASON BAILEY / DENNIS LUDVINO

Class of 2010

Collaborative Drawing is an online collaborative space that allows multiple users to draw together in real-time. It explores the use of networks as creative environments to encourage interaction through a shared mark-making experience. The goal was to create a network where users had complete control over their environment. In the collaborative drawing space people can write, draw, or create shared marks — the web page is a blank slate, it's up to the group to decide what to do with it.

Many of the communication tools we use on a daily basis provide little room for a person to exert their influence. For example, Instant Messaging is a quick and effective way to communicate but, aside from creating a smiley face with a colon and a parentheses :), there are simply no creative options for users. The space restricts us to typing and displaying messages.

Collaborative Drawing sits at the opposite end of the spectrum. It is not yet an effective tool for written communication, but it is a completely nonrestrictive environment. I say not yet because I do see potential in this application for many real-world uses. It could evolve into a handwriting chat similar to IM and text messaging (it's not far off from this already). I see potential for editors to have the ability to write directly on documents sent to them electronically. The strength in this project is its emphasis on collaboration.

The ability to share in the mark-making process with others is unique to the digital experience. While the bathroom wall is a collaborative space where authors share their work with one another, it is an asynchronous collaboration. Networks, on the other hand, provide the means to communicate in both synchronous and asynchronous time.

By throwing numerous people into the same time and space, we noted many interesting experiences. Occasionally a leader emerged whom all other users followed. The leader, for example, might draw a robot and others would draw robots or add on to existing robots. On other occasions, users would try to dominate the space and a struggle for power emerged. There were also times when no collaborations occurred at all. Users simply stayed in their corner of the screen and showed no interest in the drawings of others. These findings highlight the potential for new methods of communication to emerge from more collaborative spaces.

TECHNOLOGY

This project got off the ground with the help of a couple of open source Processing projects written by Daniel Shiffman and Alexander Galloway. It turns out creating a networking connection between two computers in Processing is surprisingly simple. One computer acts as the server and the other machines connect to it via its IP address. The nature and stability of the network, on the other hand, is a much more complicated animal.

Jason and I received a crash course on networks and their strange and scary protocols. One of the problems early in the project was related to static and dynamic IP addresses. A network's IP address changes frequently and each time it changed, the Processing code had to be altered. Jason came up with a solution when he found DynDNS, a company that offered free dynamicDNS service. This allowed us to create a subdomain to connect to a computer even though its IP address was constantly changing. This fix helped stabilize the network and kept it from continuously crashing, but

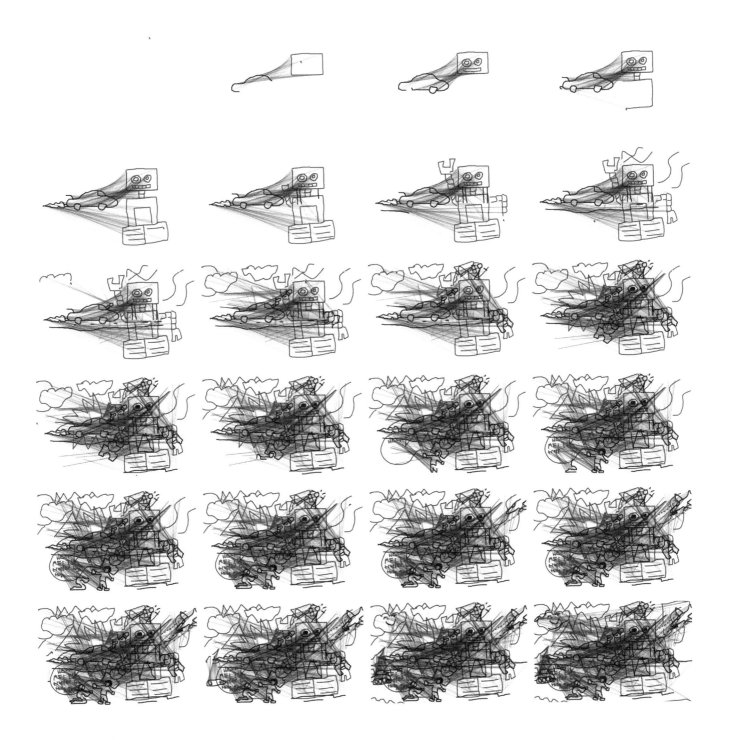

In the collaborative drawing space people can write, draw, or create shared marks — the web page is a blank slate, it's up to the group to decide what to do with it.

we continued to struggle with the speed with which the network handled all the data coming in.

In order for each user's drawings to be fed and displayed by other users, the network is bombarded with information. The program kicks out four numbers (previous x/y and current x/y) 30 times per second for each client and then passes those numbers to all other users. The more people signed-on to the server the slower the network. Because this delay inhibits collaboration — the main goal of the project — it was a huge bug. The problem seemed to be in how much information was being passed from the users to the server and then from the server back to the users.

We initially thought that if we set a slight delay to give the network some time to buffer, it would be able to keep up with the flow of information. This solution helped stabilize the network a bit, but the lag time still existed. Jason came up with the final solution. We bribed a kind MIT student to look at the code and tell us what we did wrong (Jason gave him a television). It turns out that the solution was simple: Change one of the conditional statements from "if" to "while." This optimized how the server looked for the information to send out and sped the entire project up significantly (Thanks Pol! I hope you are enjoying Jason's television).

While using a network to create an interactive environment is somewhat difficult, it turned out to be a rewarding process. There were many problems to solve (most of which we didn't), but in the end we had a workable prototype to share with our peers. Success!

PROCESS

At the end of the third semester I presented a project proposal to create a virtual bathroom wall where users could communicate with one another via writing or drawing. After my presentation, Jason said that we should collaborate on creating a networked drawing application that we could get up and running relatively quickly. As his thesis was about the potential of drawing in the digital world and mine was about writing, it seemed like a perfect fit. We met before class one evening and were able to successfully connect to each other's machines and draw together. Admittedly, this sounds much grander than the reality. The code for a basic shared canvas application already existed, but this was simply a first step.

This project progressed organically. We would draw together, decide what refinements we needed, and separately make changes. We first dealt with adding some functionality and refined the default brush used to draw. Additionally, we had to deal with the network problems like server crashes and unrecognized users. The initial design (or lack of design) was intended to solve these issues. Somewhere along the way we made some changes to the code and crazy geometric lines started shooting all over the screen. After looking closer at what was happening, we noticed that we were sending the server additional line coordinates that connected our mouse positions. This became a mapped view of the relationship between our drawings. After tinkering with it some more we made the primary drawing lines much larger and the network lines smaller to recede into the background. After receiving some good feedback from other

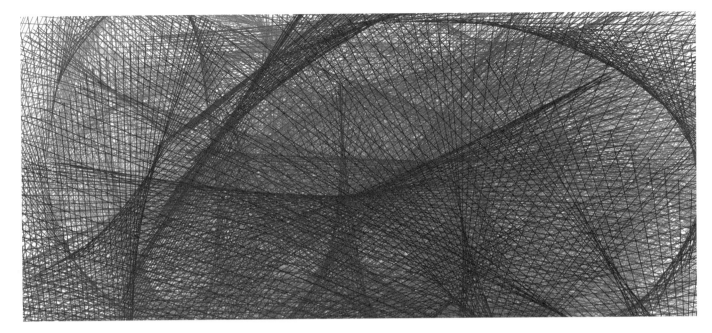

Bailey and Ludvino created an online collaborative space that allows multiple users to draw together in real-time

students and faculty who joined in on our drawing sessions, we began to focus on three aspects of the project — stabilizing the network, visual output, and line behavior.

The network lines and the general drawing lines became too chaotic after a few minutes of drawing. We decided that we should be focusing on the experience of the collaboration and the network lines got in the way, so removing them seemed like the best option. This created a more pleasant drawing experience, but with multiple people drawing (more than 2), the screen still filled up quickly and it became difficult to draw anything visually coherent. To solve this we decided to have the drawings slowly fade over time creating an infinite canvas.

The visual output was pretty basic. Users had a single colored line with a fixed width. There were no special tools — only lines. Changing the simple line to shapes gave us some interesting visual results. The new brushes ranged from the practical — like thick and thinner weights — to the impractical — such as crazy colored triangles shooting out randomly and uncontrollable 3D lines. The more experimental brushes radically changed the nature of the drawing application. The farther away the brushes moved from the simple line, collaboration seemed to diminish. For example the 3D brush, our most radical visual output, made beautiful compositions but the collaboration suffered because users were no longer working together. The more practical brushes refined the drawing capabilities and seemed to encourage further participation.

Our final modification to the behavior of the lines was an attempt at further encouraging participation. By averaging the distance between the users, we were able to use physical proximity to drive the brush size. Users farther away from one another would have a smaller brush size, but as their mouse positions came closer together, the size would increase. Again we got some unexpected results that changed the drawing experience. When the users got very close together, the brush size magnified into a visual explosion and filled the entire screen. After this discovery, we let proximity drive the size, color, and transparency of the brushes. The visual results were beautiful and it added a game-like aspect to the program as users chased one another around the screen.

Working collaboratively on this project was by far the most gratifying experience in graduate school. More often than not, collaboration in the educational realm fails. People have different schedules, methods of working, and feel more comfortable with their own ideas. Jason and I, it turns out, work very well together and neither of us tried to steer the project one way or another. The process of working together constantly generated ideas and helped the project to evolve into its final form. From the beginning Jason and I wanted this project to be open-sourced. Our end goal was to get the program to a stable condition (which it has not quite reached) and then release to a broader community of users to help refine it. A project about collaboration should be created in a collaborative spirit.

Drawing With Data

JASON BAILEY

Class of 2010

As my thesis work with programmatic drawing developed, physical gesture became irrelevant. The way I pressed the keys on the keyboard did not affect the resulting drawing. I started thinking about the mouse gesture, and how I had thought of it more as a limitation for drawing than anything else. I eventually asked myself why I was writing-off the mouse gesture as irrelevant? After all, I spend more time gesturing with my mouse than I do making just about any other type of gesture; it's the nature of working with computers. What if I captured the data from the everyday gestures of my mouse and turned them into a drawing? What would it look like?

Normally, I would spend a lot of time trying to write a program to capture my mouse position over time, but I knew I wanted this to be a short, experimental project. So instead, I found some free software that would track the X and Y coordinates of my mouse and save them to a text file. I turned on the mouse tracker and generated thousands of lines of data as I went about my regular computer-related tasks. I tried not to change my behavior as I was interested in capturing the unmodified gestures of my daily mouse-driven activities. I realized pretty quickly that I would have more data than I knew what to do with, so I grabbed a five-minute chunk of the data and put it into a format I could use to import it into Processing. Once I was able to get the mouse data into Processing, I started playing around with drawing different colored shapes and lines to represent the data.

At first, I thought of this exercise as a data visualization project. I tried to make it clear where the mouse started and stopped by adding circles at these departure points. I lost interest in that approach and started to tweak variables and add new code to add randomization to the color and location of the lines, testing the drawing each time I made a change. The drawing transformed very quickly from a visualization of my mouse gestures to a more abstract and appealing image.

The dense network of colorful lines spanning the screen created a complex dimensional space. Often my goal in creating drawings is not to recreate what I see, but rather to create an entirely new visual space comparable in intricacy to the world around me, less familiar yet still inviting.

Initially, it seemed ironic that breaking from the data acquired from actual gestures had made the composition more gestural in its visual qualities. Unlike drawing with a pencil or brush, my programmed drawings relied more on conceptual decisions than physical gestures. That process was different yet strangely similar to drawing with programming.

My analog drawing process, particularly when creating more abstract work, involves making a few marks, stepping back, and evaluating. Often I spend more time evaluating than making marks. After that period of contemplation, I usually feel like I know where that next mark belongs.

Frequently when drawing, something outside of my control will happen, an accidental drip of paint, a smudge of charcoal, etc. These elements have become a welcome part of the creative process for me and frequently take the composition in new and interesting directions. When programming drawings, I have a very similar process. I start playing with code, checking in periodically to see what the resulting image looks like. More often than not, I am surprised by what comes on the screen when I run the program. Sometimes I like what I see, sometimes I don't. One of the great advantages of programming drawings is that my accidents are repeatable. If I tweak the code and like what I see, I can reuse that code in new combinations and turn what was initially an accident into a tool.

After completing the mouse drawing series, I realized I had a tool that could make drawings out of any data with a similar two-column format by mapping the data to the X and Y coordinates and creating lines. Thinking back to my ideas on driving one media with another, I started thinking about using this same code to make drawings out of songs.

BREAK POINT ONE
I knew that the music I played on my computer was really just a sequence of numbers at a base level, regardless of whether it was an .mp3 file, a .wav file or any other audio format. I experimented with different formats trying to find one that would produce data that I could use with my mouse-position drawing program. It turned out that exporting music to the ASCII format produced exactly the type of data that I needed. I was convinced that the patterns in music would translate to numeric patterns when digitized, which would become visible when processed trough my drawing application.

I have always enjoyed John Coltrane's music and decided to use his composition "Giant Steps" for my experiment with drawing music. I tried to export the entire song into ASCII format and crashed my computer. Realizing that it was just too much data, I cut it in half, and crashed my computer again. I proceeded to cut the song into smaller and smaller chunks until I found a manageable chunk: the first five seconds. I dropped the data into my drawing program and a beautiful composition came out.

I knew that five seconds was likely not enough time to establish much of a pattern in the song, but it didn't matter to me as I had proved to myself that I could write a song-drawing tool by taking advantage of the common language across digital media of ones and zeroes.

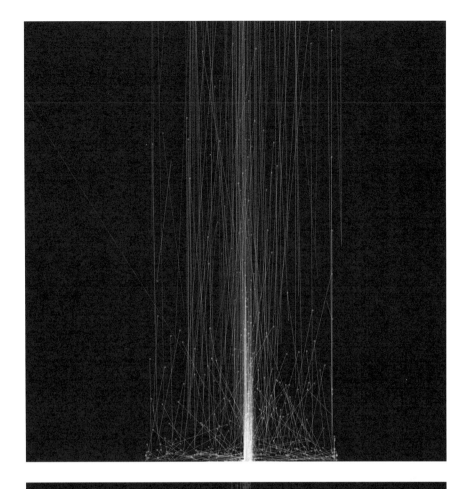

While I was happy to have visualized the data from the John Coltrane song, I wanted something that I had more control over: less of a visualization project and more of a drawing project. What if I produced the music live and created the drawing with real-time audio data?

BREAK POINT TWO

I play several instruments equally poorly. At different times in my life I have tried to learn the clarinet, drums, and harmonica with varying degrees of success. For my live-music-drawing program, I settled on the harmonica as it was the most portable. I had a little experience messing around with krister.ees, an audio library for Processing, so I decided to utilize it for this project. I hooked up my microphone, started writing code, and eventually worked through a tutorial that created real-time waveforms responding to the data captured from my harmonica. While I was pleased to have completed the loop of real-time audio input to visual output, the visualization itself was still just a boring, run-of-the-mill waveform. So I started to adjust the code to try and make the visuals feel like the audio sounded. I made adjustments to color, motion, line thickness, and every other variable I could find until the visualization organically evolved into a visual equivalent of my sounds. No longer just a series of waveforms, I was now drawing with my harmonica.

Drawing with a harmonica

Sparks

KENT MILLARD

Class of 2011

*Wanting connections, we found connections —
always, everywhere, and between everything. The
world exploded in a whirling network of kinships,
where everything pointed to everything else, everything explained everything else...*

– **Umberto Eco,** Foucault's Pendulum

I went to a lecture once by Seymour Chwast in the early '90s. I remember being absolutely awestruck by the variety and depth of his
work. I mean, here was someone who had creativity oozing from
the very fiber of his being. Having a career that had spanned four
decades at that point, Chwast's work continued to exude the same
vibrancy and relevance that it always had. I just had to know how
he did it!

I reverently approached the lectern after his talk. I looked up,
starry-eyed, and asked, "Mr. Chwast, how do you continue to keep
your work so innovative and fresh after all these years?" The moment of discovery was at hand, the veils of secrecy would soon be
swept aside, and all would be revealed! I waited with bated breath.
His response was the verbal equivalent of a shrug. The creative process has always been something of a mystery to me (and, I imagine,
many others). Oh sure, we can talk about what we create. For many
of us, describing something that already exists is usually not a challenge — and on good days, we can probably even string together a
few insightful comments about our work.

But how we create a particular piece — the myriad inspirations
and influences that shape our thinking and ultimately what we create — is among the most essential and elusive parts of the creative

process. What are the influences that shape our work? How do others
perceive our work? How can we be exposed to other influences and
move our work in new directions?

I find this decision-making process embedded within the creative process particularly interesting. The designer must evaluate
and revise work based on external and internal factors. These external factors come together during the "critique," broadly defined
here as interactions between the designer and clients, instructors,
colleagues, etc. The internal factors include the designer's education
and experience, among other things, which inform and shape
their work.

During critique, in addition to providing specific comments
on what is and isn't working, people often reference other creative
works that are relevant, or connected to the work being discussed
and can serve as a model. These connections or "sparks" are invaluable in three ways: 1) they expose us to new work that can act as a
catalyst for our own; 2) we understand how our work is perceived;
and 3) gain insights into the creative process of others based on the
references that they make.

Face-to-face, or synchronous critiques are a vital part of the
creative process but the quality and scope of these exchanges are
limited to the people present. This raises the question of how these
limitations can be overcome in order to gain the insights and interpretations of a broader group of people. While not replacing synchronous critique, asynchronous exchanges conducted online can
open up the process to many more participants.

Internally, we draw from our own personal databases of experiences during the creative process. This highly individualized process

Sparks is an online community to provide references for uploaded creative work and to make connections through associative thinking.

synthesizes a number of personal variables and external factors to produce a creative response that is then refined through a series of iterations. This response is typically sprinkled with bits and pieces of existing creative work that served as inspirations, or influences to us. The question here is, how can we effectively harness and organize our personal databases and those of others into a coherent system?

Sparks is a visualization tool that would allow online communities to provide references for uploaded creative work. The tool is based on the premises that there are no wholly original creative works and we make connections through associative thinking.

The users interact with the system as Authors and/or Audience. Authors upload their work, citing the creative works that shaped it; these "sparks" take the form of five types of media: sound, written, video, image, and interactive. Author sparks are also tagged by how they are used in the work (Inspiration, Influence, Parody, Homage, etc.). In addition, Authors can include brief comments about the spark as well as quantitative attributes such as date, author, title, etc.

The Audience provides feedback on the uploaded work by answering the question, "What does this remind you of?" and then citing their own sparks. The Audience also reviews and votes for sparks that they consider relevant, which helps the Author see how their work is being perceived.

The *Sparks* interface includes a Timeline and Explode view. In the default Timeline mode, the Audience can see the work and sparks arranged along a timeline. Sparks can be added at precise points for time-based media and be filtered.

In Explode, several projects are viewable at once. This permits users to see how certain sparks are connected to other projects. The macro scale of Explode allows patterns of connectivity to emerge and provide new areas of discovery.

Sparks could be used to extend the functionality of a site such as Vimeo. Authors upload their time-based work to Vimeo and then use the *Sparks* plug-in to document their creative influences. By documenting these influences, authors are compelled to reflect on their own creative process, helping them become more thoughtful and purposeful. *Sparks* allows the Audience to understand the context of the work through the influences or sparks that shaped it. This provides them with new insights into the work as well as the Author's creative process.

Sparks allows participants to share their creative catalysts and gain an understanding of how others engage in the creative process. It opens up another channel of communication and allows people to interact and potentially collaborate. By extending the critique experience, and helping to organize and access our personal databases, *Sparks* can provide an important tool in the creative process.

Practice

SCOTT MURRAY

Class of 2010

Practice is the culmination of my explorations at Dynamic Media Institute. But to call it a culmination implies that it is something of a terminus, when it really is just the beginning of a new course of study. Let me explain how the project originated before I delve into that new direction.

I knew that I wanted to complete the year with one substantial project that integrated much of my learning from the program. Yet after two years of immersing myself in interaction design, data visualization, systems design, and narrative studies, I was at a loss when formulating a thesis project. I couldn't imagine what the content would be, but I had a list of elements that it should incorporate:

data-as-narrative

interface and visualization

dynamic, streaming, or live data sources

visualizing the invisible

These were my favorite bits and pieces from past projects, but this list needed simplification. What was the one, single quality I wanted in my project? Immediate engagement. I wanted my thesis project to be engaging. And for that reason, I selected mirrored, interactive video as the primary input/output medium. Processing, of course, would be used as the development and execution medium.

EARLY EXPERIMENTS

Using video as an interface input allowed me to explore some fun technologies, like computer vision and live video processing. One of the computer vision libraries available for Processing offers face detection, which lets the system look at each frame of incoming video and analyze whether or not any faces are present in the image.

Although face detection is more popularly associated with the security industry and, more recently, point-and-shoot digital cameras (which can identify faces, and adjust exposure settings accordingly), this technology is ripe for exploration in the context of interactive art. Faces are emotionally loaded entities; they are our primary means of both identifying others and recognizing ourselves. The emotional responses we have to faces cannot be overstated, and this power makes them prime targets for artistic exploration.

More pragmatically, face detection can be used to isolate a person's position against a background of visual noise. Many interactive video projects track "motion" by looking only at which pixels changed from one frame to the next. (*Gesture Project* used this simple definition of motion.) By using computer-vision algorithms to look for faces, our systems can disregard all other visual input, such as objects moving in the background. Different face detection "profiles" can be used to identify faces from different angles (head-on, ¾ profile, or full profile, for example), so we can even differentiate between people facing directly toward the camera, and those turned away from it.

Of course, computer vision is nowhere near perfect, so good lighting is critical. The algorithm needs to be able to see two eyes and a mouth in order to identify a face. If only half the face is well-lit, it will not be detected. In my experience, false positive identifications are actually more common — such as when the system "sees" a face that isn't really there, in the folds of a shirt or among shadows cast far in the background. The computer has no sense of physical depth, so a small circle near the camera will be perceived the same as a much larger circle very far away. Both could be interpreted as "eyes" of the same face, even though they are hundreds of feet away in physical space. The camera knows only pixels.

Despite these technical considerations, I was committed to exploring face detection's possibilities. My first experiment was ostensibly very simple. It captured the video image, analyzed it for faces, and then blurred a portion of the video around the user's face. The blur gradually intensified, then diminished, cycling through varying levels of clarity. I incorporated easing, so the blurry box would move smoothly, gliding, not jumping, into place. Technically, it supported identifying only one face at a time, so introducing a second or third user confused the system. (The blurry box would jump quickly from face to face.) But for a quick sketch, it worked well.

Users hated it. I showed the project to a number of friends, and the universal reaction was to move around, trying to dodge the blurry rectangle. Some tried to physically push the blurred box away from their faces using their hands. I quickly realized that this blurring effect was operating

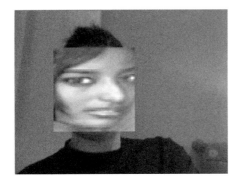

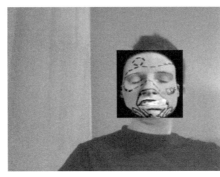

Using the Flickr API, a face was selected at random and mapped over that of the user.

contrary to the engagement effect of mirroring. Users were seeing themselves, and the system's motion (of the blurry box) was coupled to their motion, but because the mirroring effect was interrupted visually, users were immediately annoyed and put off. People wanted desperately to see their own faces, not just torsos and necks topped by fuzzy squares. I had designed a frustration machine.

I interpreted this user frustration to mean the project was not successful, but Gunta Kaza encouraged me to explore it further. She pointed out that the experience triggered a strong emotional response from users (if not a positive one), and for that reason, at least, was worth exploring further.

For the next iteration, I wanted to know how people would react if the blurry box was gone and they were shown a face — just not their own.

I tapped into the Flickr API to retrieve the most recent photographs tagged with "face" or "person." Then, the system would run face detection on those photos. If no obvious face was found, the image was discarded. If a face was found, the image was cropped and stored in memory. Then, when someone stepped in front of the camera, one of the Flickr faces was selected at random and mapped over that of the user. Every 10 seconds or so, a new face was selected and displayed.

Users found this version much less frustrating, but extremely creepy. They wanted to know where the other faces came from, and why they were being placed over their own. Some juxtapositions were more entertaining than others, such as a baby's face, or a face with a shape and hairline that visually matched the user's. In the event of the latter, users would reposition their bodies to best fit the image being shown, like the inverse of a carnival cut-out: a clown's face on top of your body.

  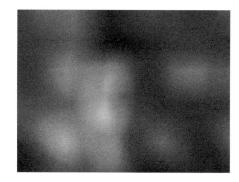

CLARIFIED DIRECTION

Neither of these quick projects were the engaging, rewarding experiences I wanted to create, but the discomfort they induced provided me with some valuable insights. Gunta encouraged me to consider framing the system-user interactions in terms of challenge and reward. My *Gesture Project*, for example, was 100 percent reward — there was no challenge. But maybe a reward would be sweeter if users had to work for it by tolerating some amount of intentional, designed discomfort.

Yet, how can we challenge someone while keeping them engaged? When users have essentially no commitment to the project (e.g., they have not paid money to see it or worked to create it), how can we incite them to overcome the discomfort of the challenge? As described earlier, establishing a sense of anticipation is essential. By hinting at the rewards to come, without revealing them too soon, we hold out a proverbial carrot for our users to pursue. But such a challenge/reward structure may be too simple. We must remember that we are trying to create a positive, aesthetically unified experience on the whole, not just sequential alternations of bad and good elements.

In *Rules of Play*, game theorists Katie Salen and Eric Zimmerman review the research of psychologist Mihaly Csikszentmihalyi, who has written extensively on cultivating the peaceful mental state of "flow." Csikszentmihalyi's state of flow corresponds roughly to my definition of satori: a quiet, concentrated mental state, in which the subject's focus is entirely on the task at hand in the present moment. (1990) Salen and Zimmerman apply this research to game-design theory, arguing that any challenges must fairly match the user's skill level. (2004) A challenge that is too difficult leads to anxiety and failure. One that is too easy leaves users bored and disengaged. To elicit an engaged state of flow, the challenge must be of appropriate difficulty. As the user gains experience with the system, the challenges must escalate at a corresponding rate in order to sustain the same level of engagement.

Game designers, of course, strive to create games with "replay value" and even addictive qualities. Gamers should be engaged not only "in the moment," but sustainably as they return for subsequent sessions. Salen and Zimmerman consider games as systems of rules and actions. They write, "If you create a space of possibility that rewards players for exploration, then you are likely to have players that want to see more permutations of how the rules play out." (2004) All the while, the ideal design would elicit what Csikszentmihalyi calls an "autotelic" experience, meaning "a self-contained activity, one that is done not with the expectation of some future benefit, but simply because the doing itself is the reward." (1990) Use of the system, then, becomes a reward in and of itself, inclusive of all the challenges presented within that interaction.

So the primary design challenges for my thesis projects became: to engage participants, construct a sense of anticipation, and then reward them for tolerating the discomfort elicited from sustained engagement. My

approach had shifted from an attempt to create a universally engaging and memorable experience to a study of human behavior. By designing increasing levels of challenge and reward, I could gather data on the intensity of participants' engagement, tolerance for discomfort, and patience for reward.

So, then, what reward to offer, and what challenges to precede it? To my mind, the ultimate reward is enlightenment: all-knowingness, clear perception, right seeing, oneness with the universe, and the thoughtless awareness of the present moment that comes with satori. Enlightenment cannot be literally bestowed upon users, of course, but I could allude to it figuratively, and at least try to trigger enough physical discomfort and emotional ambiguity to elicit a state of satori.

With enlightenment as the reward, stillness would be the challenge. Stillness can be interpreted both metaphorically, as in stillness of mind, as well as physically, as in a lack of motion. The latter is easily measured by computer, so users could progress toward enlightenment by being physically still. Movement would trigger regression away from the goal.

Nearly all video-based installations reward motion — jumping up and down, waving one's arms, ducking and jumping. *Practice* rewards stillness, which should not be confused with inactivity or a lack of interaction. My early user tests showed that maintaining stillness is, indeed, quite a challenge, and the level of interaction, as reported by users, can be intense. Once participants understand that the key to success is not moving, they grow very quiet, still, and focused, watching and listening closely to whatever the system does next.

SOCIAL CONTEXT

As described earlier, video-based projects are always fundamentally social projects, since they can be used by multiple people at once. In many installations, participants may either interact independently of each other or work together. In my project, I built functionality that allows me to test either giving one user control of the piece (tracking the motion of only one individual) or giving all users some input (all user's motions are

considered). My hope was that, by considering the motion of all participants, the system would encourage social negotiation between its users. This would make the challenge of stillness even more difficult to attain, since interacting with others requires some amount of motion (at least a gentle nudge or mumbled instruction).

Also, we are used to staring silently at screens, but ignoring a fellow human being is impolite. So there is not only tension between the users and the system, but among the users themselves, as they struggle to maintain focus on the project while negotiating each other. Thus, the participants inadvertently become performers, and the system expands to include not just the screen and sound, but also the people in front of that screen, and the observers who are watching those people. As with a flash mob, anyone present becomes an active participant at some level, whether willingly or unwittingly so. Even pure "observers" are engaged in the dynamic, because their very presence serves to distract participants from the task at hand.

STRUCTURING THE SYSTEM

With a primary metaphor of stillness as a means of progressing toward enlightenment, *Practice's* initial display had to be grayscale, blurry, and dark. The experience begins with my interpretation of the hazy state of everyday life. We move quickly, going through the motions, without reflection or clarity around why we make the decisions that we do.

But with stillness comes clarity, so when the user stands still, facing the screen, the system gradually removes the blur, and the image comes into focus. Beyond that, color is slowly restored, until the participant finally sees him or herself reflected clearly, as though looking into a mirror.

Of course, any participant motion disrupts the stillness, in which case the system regresses — color fades away, and the sharp image grows blurry. We return to our default, unclear state.

I knew that the system would do at least this much, but I also envisioned the addition of several more advanced stages during which the mirroring would be augmented with increasingly complex imagery. This sequence of stages would culminate in a final interpretation of enlightenment.

Soon after beginning work on the project, I had to consider the structure of my code. How could I organize these different programmatic elements in such a way that would support the experience I wanted to create, while also ensuring a straightforward process for developing and inserting additional stages that I hadn't yet designed or considered?

I settled on using a single number — a progress value — to track the participants' "position" within the sequence of stages, while each stage was assigned a whole number. For example, imagine each stage as a point along a line, starting with 0, then 1, 2, 3, and so on. In the beginning, the progress value is 0.0. At 0.5, we are halfway through the initial stage (stage zero). The scene is grayscale, but some blurriness has been removed. At 1.0, the scene is clear, and at 2.0, we see in full color.

This structure was useful because, for each frame of video, the system had only to reference one number to know where it was in the sequence. So during each frame, two steps occur: First, the face tracking algorithms are applied, and an averaged "stillness value" is calculated. If the stillness value is above a certain threshold (meaning, there was little or no motion), then the progress value is increased by a small amount. If the stillness value is low (meaning, there was a lot of motion), then the progress value is decreased by a substantial amount. The increment/decrement values are unequal, so progress is lost more easily than it is achieved — another way in which the operating metaphor was expressed in code.

Once the stillness and progress values are calculated, the system simply renders the appropriate stage. So, if the progress value is 4.7, the system executes the code for stage four. In addition, a normalized value is used to determine the position within each stage. That is, 4.7 tells the system both that we are in stage four, and that we are 70 percent of the way through the stage. That normalized value is then used to drive different events within the stage, such as how much blur to apply or color to restore.

Events that happen between stages, such as triggering sounds or resetting elements'

positions, are controlled by comparing the previous frame's progress value to the new one. So, if progress moves from 5.99 to 6.02, the system knows that we've just entered the sixth stage, and it executes the appropriate actions. Similarly, moving from 3.1 to 2.84 means we're regressing, so any audio played during stage three should fade out.

Structuring the project around multiple, self-contained stages tied to one numerical progress value gave me a great deal of control over each stage, and simplified the process of adding new stages.

USER TESTING

Since my professional background is in user-focused web design, usability research is always an essential part of my design process. I had tested the "blurry box" and "replaced face" experiments only informally. But with *Practice*, I applied more structure to my user testing and conducted tests at least weekly, enlisting around 20-30 different people over the course of a few months.

The earlier user testing can occur in the design process, the better. Ideally, the designer can test early and often, making refinements to the design along the way.

The most difficult design challenge with *Practice* was figuring out how to instruct stillness. In my first tests, users were content to see themselves reflected in blurry grayscale. But they never progressed through the system, because nothing was telling them to be still. My testers would invariably wave their arms and jump around in front of the camera for about half a minute, and then try to act impressed, despite their obvious disappointment that there wasn't more to my big art project.

I thought it might help to communicate that the system was seeing participants' faces, so I tried drawing a primitive, rotating spiral shape around each detected face. That only made testers move more, since they enjoyed watching the spiral spin and change size as they moved closer and farther away from the screen.

Thinking the problem was in the rotating motion, I tested a simpler treatment: every time a new face was detected, a brief tone played and a soft, blue circle appeared, covering the face. The circle quickly faded away, so I thought there would be no

incentive for additional motion. But I was proven wrong, and my testers only moved farther and faster this time, confusing the face-tracking system, triggering many more blue dots and xylophone-like tones.

It was time to reevaluate my approach. This initial instruction was absolutely critical to the project's success. I was certain that, once participants understood the interaction model (stillness leads to progress and reward), they would smoothly advance through each stage. But stillness is such a foreign concept in our culture, especially within the sphere of dynamic media, which always incites us to go, go, go and never stop moving. So a completely new treatment was needed.

Since all testers found the mirroring element invariably rewarding (even when blurry), why not "punish" their motion by taking the mirror away? I removed the circles and sounds, and coded the system to quickly fade to black upon detecting too much motion. This worked perfectly — finally, people stopped moving! By removing the visual stimulation altogether, I could provide immediate, negative feedback. With a blank screen in front of them, users have no incentive to keep moving. That, combined with confusion around why the video suddenly "went away," causes them to hold still. They lean in close, squinting and perplexed, asking "What happened?" Then, once they become still, the black fades out and the video returns. It usually takes no more than two or three of these disappearances for participants to understand the interaction model.

At this point, I observe an "aha" moment in participants, when they understand that the system is looking for stillness. This initial stage zero is completely silent; the first audio plays only upon reaching stage one, when a bell chimes. Entering each subsequent stage triggers another discrete bell-like chime (a different chime for each), and begins looping other ambient audio. (In testing, users correctly understood these chimes as indicators that something is "about to happen.")

The visual transitions, however, are deliberately very gradual and subtle, which contributes to the sense of anticipation. For example, it is only about halfway through

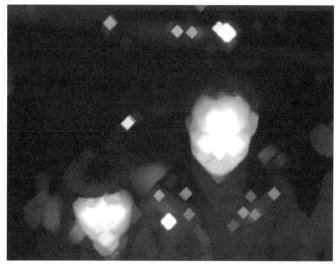

The system uses a primary metaphor of stillness as a means of progressing toward enlightenment.

stage two that users realize that the video is being colorized. The subtlety of these early stages primes them for focused observation and keeps participants watching and listening closely as they progress.

THE STAGES OF PRACTICE

There's no substitute for experiencing *Practice* in person, but for the purposes of documenting the project here, I will describe each of the eight stages and articulate the intent behind the design of each stage.

Stage 0 — Clarity

Video is initially grayscale and blurry. The blur is gradually removed, and by the end of this stage, it is in full focus.

Stage 1 — Color

A chime sounds, and video gradually transitions from grayscale to full color. Too much motion in this stage triggers a blackout of the screen. After this point, motion causes only regression (a decrease in the progress value), but not a fade to black.

Stage 2 — White Snow

A chime sounds, and ambient drumming sounds fade in. Assorted, semi-transparent white circles begin falling down from above.

They seem to be responding to gravity, yet they cascade around participants' heads. This is the first indication to users that the system "sees" them. They discover that the shapes are indifferent to waving hands and arms. Moving their faces (or whole bodies) affects the circles' trajectories, but that motion also triggers regression within the sequence. In testing, some participants look up to see where the circles are falling from. The circles' relative sizes are proportional to how close users are to the screen, so standing up close magnifies the circles' diameters.

Stage 3 — Colorful Snow

Another chime sounds, and the drumming loop continues. The physics of the cascading circles remains the same, but they

Each physical space offers its own technical challenges and opportunities.

gradually transition from white to assorted colors. This transition mirrors the earlier shift from colorlessness to full color.

Stage 4 — Orbiting

A chime sounds, the drum loop stops, and spacey, ambient audio fades in. The circles no longer avoid participants' faces, but are attracted to them. The circles then orbit and obscure the users' view of their own faces. This deliberate obstruction is intended to heighten the tension and discomfort of stillness. Just as my early experiments obstructed users' faces, so do the circles here. With the mirroring interrupted, there is greater incentive to move. But moving to the side to reestablish the view of oneself, of course, triggers regression. In testing, participants find this stage somewhat disorienting, and many tried to eat the circles as though they were floating pieces of candy.

Stage 5 — Emotions

A chime sounds, the space-like audio stops, and a friendlier, yet contemplative audio track begins looping. The circles have

disappeared, and now strings of text cascade down from above, pulled down by gravity. Those that pass near a face latch on and slowly orbit the face. The words are feeling statements, taken from the *We Feel Fine* API. The intent is to enhance the contemplative mood of the piece by forcing reflection on the statements presented, which are recent "I feel…" statements from blogs on the Internet. By visually attaching emotional statements to users, participants must consider whether or not they want to be associated with those statements. "I feel sad because of what I did today." "I feel happy that we were able to spend so much time together." Does the participant relate to these feelings? Do they cause him discomfort, possibly by exposing his own feelings that he would not have otherwise exposed in this public setting? In testing, since the source of these statements is not fully explained, a few users felt the system was somehow reading their minds.

Stage 6 — Personal History

A chime sounds, and the emotion statements

continue to drift and orbit. But a new visual element appears — a sort of flaming, colorful line that zigzags about the screen, ultimately coming to rest on each participants' third eye, at the center of the forehead. The line moves differently for everyone, because it is a visualization of individual participants' movements, as recorded by the system throughout their session. This element serves to bring each participants' focus back to his or her own self. As it cycles through a range of colors, it appears to pulsate and flicker, much like the flame of a candle, as observed in meditation.

Stage 7 — Enlightenment

Warm, electronic tones gradually build and reach a crescendo as the video blurs using a method that produces diamond-shaped patterns, like a photographic lens filter. As the diamond blur increases, the whole image grows brighter, until it is solid white. Just after the audio peaks, it becomes suddenly silent, the screen fades to black, and then video is restored once more, blurry and gray. We achieved the clarity of enlightenment, but only for a few fleeting moments, and now we are back where we began.

STREET TEST

After months of experimentation and refinement, it was time to test the project with people whom I'd never met and who didn't know anything about the project.

I contacted my friend Huy Le, who owns Revamp Salon here in San Francisco. I had installed the *Gesture Project* at the salon a few months earlier, and he has been a great supporter of my artistic process. Revamp is near 16th St. and Guerrero St., a busy corner in the Mission District with lots of foot traffic, especially on weekend nights. The salon has a window facing Guerrero, and an entryway protected by a lockable gate. It was a great opportunity. I could set up the video camera and projection screen in the window, and place speakers just behind the gate. Random passersby could experience the project, and no equipment could be stolen. I proposed this plan to Huy, and he agreed to let me take over the front window for an evening. I chose Friday, February 12, the start of the Valentine's Day weekend, hoping to reach the crowds of people headed out for dinners and drinks.

I sketched out possible layouts, and then went over to the salon to take measurements. I would need cables long enough to connect the computer to the camera, projector, and speakers without interfering with the projection. And I would need light — lots of strong, even lighting directed out onto the sidewalk — to ensure that the face detection would work at all. Finally, I would need to find a material onto which I could project video from inside, and have it be seen clearly outside, on the street.

Another friend, interactive artist Mary Franck, offered me the use of her projector for the weekend. On Tuesday the 9th, I picked up the projector, and made a trip to the hardware store to purchase clamp lights, an extendable curtain rod, and wire. Back at the salon, I maneuvered the camera, curtain rod, computer, and projector in place, and a plain white curtain I brought served well as a projection screen. The physical setup was ready, but I still had some changes to make to the software before Friday.

The final features I built into the *Practice* application enabled the system to save much of the data it was already capturing during operation. This included:

— A record of every face detected by the system, including when it first appeared, how long it was present, and how much progress it made through the various stages.

— For each face, a complete history of its size and x/y position for every frame in which it was seen.

Once each minute, a still image capture of whatever was on-screen at that moment. (I tried saving these screen captures more frequently, or even recording full motion video, but doing so slowed the system to an unacceptable degree.)

I made anecdotal observations during the installation, but all of this data helped generate quantifiable answers to my core questions: How long would it take people to first understand that stillness was the key to success? What was their tolerance for remaining still? And how many people would make it all the way to the final stage?

ANECDOTAL OBSERVATIONS

That Friday, *Practice* ran from 9:00 p.m. until 11:00. A number of friends that I'd invited stopped by, and a handful of other people stopped to observe or engage, most only briefly, but some for sustained periods. During those two hours, I made the following observations and conclusions.

1 — The physical context is critically influential to the overall experience, as it informs participants' expectations and what behaviors they will consider socially acceptable. A busy street is not necessarily the best place for an interactive installation. I had hoped for a lot of foot traffic, and got some, but most of those pedestrians were destination-oriented, not casually strolling. Guerrero is not very pedestrian-friendly, and the volume of car traffic encourages people to walk quickly, until they can turn off on a more welcoming street with wider sidewalks and fewer cars. That said, for my purposes, this element didn't make the installation a failure, but only amplified the discomfort and challenge of both remaining still and simply stopping in the first place. As the importance of context became clear, I understood that just one installation would

not be enough to definitively answer any questions about people's tolerance for stillness. If *Practice* were in an art gallery, or even a less hectic public space, I would see very different results.

2 — Each physical space offers its own technical challenges and opportunities. Although the salon window was a perfect size for my purposes, the street was noisy, and the outdoor setting dictated that I could only show the project at night, so the lighting conditions and aural environment were not ideal.

3 — Over the course of the evening, not one person stopped to observe or interact with the project unless there were others already engaged with it. It was critical that I had invited friends, because it's possible no one would have stopped otherwise. With only two or three people present, passersby tended to glance at the projection, but they wouldn't stop walking. But once there was a crowd of 10-15 people, every pedestrian stopped, partly out of interest, but also due to the physical necessity of navigating between so many people along the narrow sidewalk. This range of 10-15 functioned as a sort of critical mass, which would draw in new people as others left, and, for a time, was self-sustaining.

4 — To my great satisfaction, the social interactions that I had anticipated and designed for were fully present. While active participants interacted with the system, observers interacted with each other, and coached the participants. A fascinating dynamic evolved between the initiated and the uninitiated. In an ironic twist, the initiated — those who had already progressed to higher stages and understood that stillness was the key to success — quickly grew impatient with newcomers, becoming frustrated when the uninitiated would move too soon. Initiated observers were torn between withholding the "secret" and encouraging others. They seemed to be content watching for a while, but when a newcomer would "give up" or turn away from the screen, the initiated would be quick to offer urgent instruction — "No, no, don't look over here!" or "Stand still!" I anticipated this dynamic, to a degree, but not its intensity. I hope it reflects that the interactive experience itself is so emotionally engaging that, having

completed it, participants are motivated to coach newcomers so that they, too, may share in that experience.

DATA ANALYSIS

By the end of the evening, the *Practice* application had generated about five megabytes of face tracking data and 168 screen captures. I then dove back into Processing to write a new program that would read the data files and generate some visualizations. But first, some numbers.

The system detected and tracked 1,198 faces over the course of the evening, but about half of them "existed" for fewer than five seconds. I excluded these faces from my analysis, assuming that they were mostly false positives. Of course, many of the 605 faces that lasted for five or more seconds were also incorrectly "seen" by the face detection algorithms, as we'll see in just a moment. In any case, I proceed with the understanding that the data set is not quantitatively accurate, yet can still be used to derive some valuable insights.

My primary questions of the data were: How long were people engaged, and how many stages did they complete? Of those 605 faces, the average "lifespan" was 13.8 seconds — not very long. But an average isn't meaningful in this case because only a few participants were engaged for significant periods of time. The longest-lasting face existed for 5 minutes and 4 seconds, a considerable amount of time to stand up straight, look straight ahead, and resist urges to turn your head and acknowledge the people around you. The 50th percentile for time spent was only 7.6 seconds, and the 70th was 10.6 seconds. The top 10 percent of faces lasted longer than 24 seconds, and only 7 of those lasted more than a minute.

Time spent aside, how far did people progress toward the final stage? The chart below shows all the numbers. Of the 605 total faces, just 69, or 11 percent, made it to the first stage (as indicated by the first bell sound, and removal of blur), and only 6 experienced the enlightened ending, stage eight.

We would expect the numbers to decrease for each subsequent stage, and for the most part, that's the case. But notice that for stages four and eight, they actually increase.

This indicates either face detection inaccuracies (whether false positives or faces "lost," then "found," between stages), or instances of people stepping into the frame, joining others who have already progressed to a higher stage.

This technical limitation is also expressed in this analysis of the time needed to reach each stage (see chart below).

Since the stages are always shown in the same order (five is after four, e.g.), we would expect later stages to always require more time than earlier ones. But, instead of an upward trend, we see some downward dips, representing imperfections in the computer vision capabilities.

Although these numbers are not wholly accurate, they are still valuable. Participants may have been engaged for several minutes, then turned away for a few seconds, and returned to face the screen — which would have counted as two separate "face sessions," not one. Until computer vision systems can recognize and track people from all angles (and outside of the video frame), it won't be possible to automate this level of data collection around engagement.

Engagement is not limited to visible presence in any case. In my observations, several people, especially those who came with friends, spent anywhere from 15 minutes to an hour at the installation, engaged either directly with the system or as observers, socializing and communicating with others. This social engagement, that occurred outside the realm of the digital system, could not be tracked by the system, but was an equally important part of the overall experience. The social interactions, along with the physical environment, formed the context in which the interactive system was experienced, and thereby informed participants' tolerance for different forms of interaction. Having to balance internal curiosity (or lack thereof) with external, social stimulation ("Stand still!") and anxieties ("Everyone is watching me up here, and I look stupid!") supplemented the emotional range of an experience that, absent the social dynamic, would be quite different.

FUTURE

I am satisfied with these findings, and believe that they illustrate how, for the most part, the design successfully engaged participants on many different levels. In a world where video advertisements and motion graphics compete for eyeballs and measure success in duration of participation, I think it's valuable to take a broader view of engagement that accounts for the entire experience, including its physical and social contexts.

The data can only tell us so much, especially in an uncontrolled environment, such as this busy street in the Mission District. User testing and ongoing refinements to the design are still essential, but future research could focus on expanding the role of automated data collection — perhaps using a second overhead camera to monitor the meta-space around the installation, counting both direct participants and third-party observers, their physical proximity to each other, and correlating noise levels to events in the system. (For example, do cheers erupt upon successful achievements?) An ongoing challenge will be improving the quality of the data collected without dampening the challenge and joy of the overall experience. A highly controlled environment (such as a gallery space) may increase accuracy, but that physical context will trigger very different responses than that of a more chaotic, public space (such as a city street). Both are valuable for study, and each presents its own challenges and opportunities.

CREDITS

Practice uses data from We Feel Fine *(wefeelfine.org), by Jonathan Harris and Sep Kamvar, and incorporates recordings from* Freesound *(freesound.org) by the following authors: acclivity, chipfork, fauxpress, Freed, Jovica, kerri, suburban grilla, suonho, and zuben.*

Visualizing Network Relationships

SCOTT MURRAY

Class of 2010

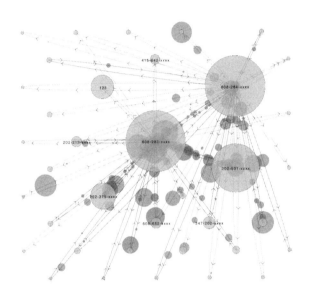

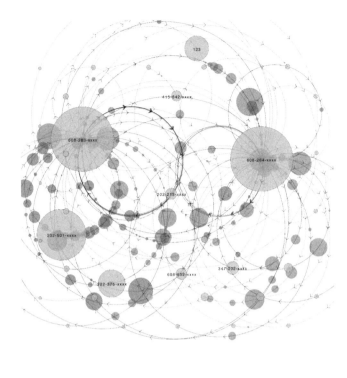

ABSTRACT

The vast majority of network visualizations are based on simple graphs and are rendered with connecting lines that communicate only one binary value: network nodes are either connected to each other or not. Information about the nature of the connections is either not available or not represented in these kinds of visualizations. *Relationship Visualizer* is an application that takes directed graphs with multiple edges as input and renders those edges visually meaningful. By incorporating directionality as well as assigning each edge a quantitative value, a new method of visualizing multiple-edge graphs is introduced.

The application accepts input in a simple data format and employs basic user interaction tools to enable custom renderings of data sets. This approach has potential for visualizing any directed graph data with multiple edges and quantitative values, such as phone records, emails, social networks, economic trade data, website links, and network traffic.

INDEX TERMS

Graph drawing, directed graphs, multiple edges, interactive graph visualization, network visualization.

INTRODUCTION

The vast majority of network visualizations use connecting lines that communicate only one binary value: network nodes are either connected to each other or not. Information about the nature of the connection — its strength, frequency, or direction — is either not available or not represented in these kinds of visualizations. Extensive research has contributed incremental improvements to methods for drawing simple graphs, resulting in more efficient renderings and intelligently clustered nodes and edges that reduce visual clutter. Little work, however, has addressed visualizing directed graphs with multiple edges, specifically those in which each edge has associated quantitative values — the focus of this paper.

Working with more robust edge data provides the opportunity for each edge to convey not just a connection, but the nature of that connection. Since directed graphs incorporate the directionality of each connection, there are opportunities to visualize the (im)balances between nodes — the two-way nature of the relationships, in other words. Also, when working with multiple edges, each edge can be assigned a quantitative value, which could be a measure of time, a priority ranking, or any other relative value. Potential data sets for directed graphs with multiple edges include: phone records, emails, social networks, economic trade data, website links, and network traffic. Data in simple graph form (single edges only) could not be used with this new method. The majority of recent research on graph drawing tends to focus on improving the visual readability of representations of simple graphs. Useful approaches include clustering related nodes and clustering related edges to reduce visual clutter, and even duplicating nodes in specific applications in order to make trends and patterns more identifiable by human eyes.

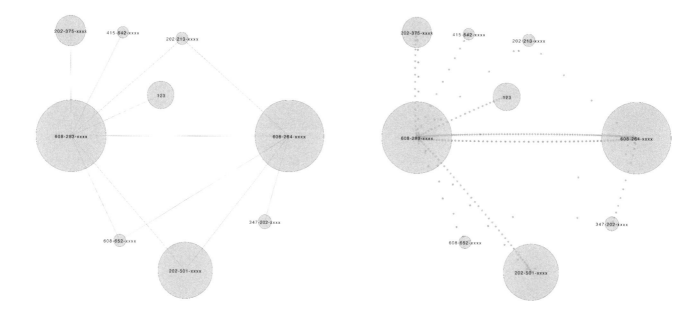

An exhaustive search of recent literature in the field failed to discover any visualization research using directed graphs with multiple edges that encoded the edges as anything other than lines. A significant paper introducing a new algorithm for generating flow maps was found, but even that uses lines for edges, with edge values encoded as thickness. The only visualization research that uses bidirectional encoding also employs lines.

APPROACH

The goal of this research was to develop a software tool that could:
- usefully visualize directed graphs with multiple edges,
- usefully visualize additional quantitative values associated with each edge,
- employ motion as a means of encoding data and making the end visualization more clear,
- employ interactivity and configurability to enable users to adjust the visualization to best suit their purposes, and
- take a very simple data format as input, to ease adoption of the tool for a wide range of purposes.

Useful Edge Representations

In the world of graph drawing, simple lines with uniform weight are common but reveal only that two members are connected — only one bit of information. Yet lines may carry more visual weight and even occupy a greater area (whether in pixels or ink) than the nodes to which they connect, resulting in a low Tuftean "data-ink ratio." New visualization methods with more dense (and useful) information resolutions are needed.

By visualizing not just binary connections, but properties of the relationships between members, we could perceive visually which relationships are balanced, lopsided, one-way, or reciprocal, and identify similarities and differences across relationships.

A relationship-centric network visualization would de-emphasize a network's members in favor of the relationships between them. The first key contribution of this research is to segregate individual edges into discrete visual forms. This approach runs contrary to the conventional rendering of edges as lines, but by representing each edge as its own visual object, we both drastically increase the dataink ratio as well as open up new possibilities for encoding even more data.

Encoding Quantitative Values for Each Edge

Taking Tufte's advice, if the visual representation is boring, we should start searching for more interesting data. Fortunately, there is an enormous amount of data in the world that can be structured in directed graph form and used with this tool. And now, with each edge as a discrete visual form, we can attach a quantitative value to each edge and represent that value in the visualization.

For example, it may be useful to visualize patterns of email traffic within a company network. Each user's email address could be treated as a node, and each email as a directional edge, from node A to node B. But a network administrator may also be interested in the raw data volume of the exchanges, so a quantitative value of the length of each email is appended to the edge. Then, in the final visualization, the visual forms representing long messages could appear larger than those representing short ones. Patterns may emerge around users' email usage, and high-traffic exchanges would be visible at a glance.

Employing Motion

Existing interactive graph visualizations use motion only to animate node placement and

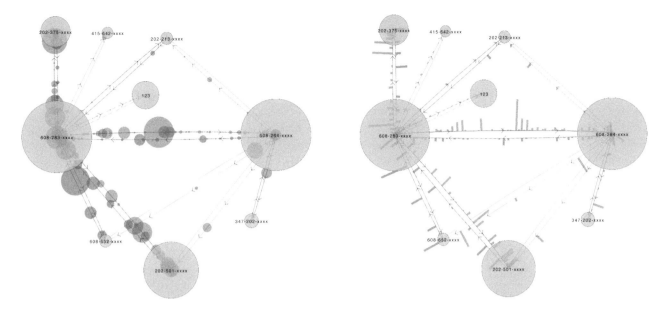

A new method of visualizing multiple-edge graphs.

adjust edge lines accordingly. *Relationship Visualizer*, however, employs motion (instead of arrows, for example) to indicate edge direction, so related edges travel along a path from node A to B, while opposing edges travel from B to A.

While inappropriate use of motion has the potential to distract and visually overwhelm the user (especially when viewing many nodes and edges), this development is nonetheless a new approach and may be considered a more intuitive representation for many users.

Interactivity and Configurability

This approach asserts that there is no single ideal visualization for any given data set. A visualization's success is best judged by its users, and each user will have differing needs and interests in the final output. Therefore, *Relationship Visualizer* employs basic interactivity (such as selection and dragging of nodes) and user-configurable parameters (such as rate of motion, and arc width) in an effort to enable each user to actively explore his or her data set and render the tool's visual output in the form that will be most meaningful to that user.

Simplified Data Format

To encourage easy use with the widest possible range of data sets, the tool has been designed to accept input data in a very simple, accessible format (see section 4.1 below).

Processing, a free, open-source programming environment, was chosen as the development platform, in part due to its strengths in easily capturing and parsing data sets, but also to ensure accessibility of the tool to others after its release. Version 1.0 or newer is required to use *Relationship Visualizer*. (Processing can be downloaded from processing.org/download.)

Also, it should be acknowledged that the final application incorporates and builds on simple graph drawing code developed by Ben Fry. All development work toward directional edges with quantitative values was done by the author.

RESULTS

This section provides a walk-through of the *Relationship Visualizer* application, illustrating some of its potential uses. Mobile phone-usage records have been used as the sample data set, with phone numbers obfuscated to protect privacy.

Data Input

To run successfully, a plain text file named "data.csv" must be placed in the sketch's data folder. The data file must contain edges in the form: from_node_name, to_node_name, edge_value.

Node names can be alpha or numeric characters, and should not be surrounded by quotation marks. Edge values must be numeric. All values must be comma-separated.

Default Visualization

When the application is first run, the default, *simple graph-like* visualization is shown. Nodes are represented by gray circles, and node names are shown when the circle diameter is wide enough to accommodate the text label. The radius of each circle reflects the number of connecting edges, so nodes with more connections are shown as larger circles.

Edges are aggregated and represented as simple gray lines between nodes. At this point, neither the multiplicity of edges nor their directions or associated values are shown.

Although nodes are initially placed using a basic force-directed layout method, they can be dragged with the mouse and positioned as desired by the user. Pressing the "L" key will switch to a clustered layout method in which large-value nodes are weighted more toward the center, and low-value nodes are pushed toward the outside.

When using the clustered layout, spacing between nodes can be adjusted using the "J" and "K" keys.

Initially, all nodes are shown. Low-value (small) nodes can be filtered out and later revealed by using the bracket keys.

A basic help screen describing all of this appears (not shown here), and may be toggled off and on using the question mark key.

Edges Encoded

Pressing "3" reveals the first visualization with edges encoded as discrete visual forms — small blue and red circles, in this case. Motion reveals the edges' directionality, which is also reinforced by the colors. The color choices are arbitrary, and a greater prevalence of blue or red in the visualization should not be considered indicative of any trend; they are simply used here to help distinguish edge direction.

Motion can be accelerated, slowed, or stopped altogether by pressing "S" and "F." Notice how, without lines present, connections with very few edges may be difficult to discern.

Increasing the rate of motion makes those low-value connections more easily perceptible, while slowing the rate of motion helps with high-value connections.

With all motion stopped, it may be useful to reveal path guidelines that indicate edge direction by pressing zero. The light gray lines and arrows are particularly useful for generating static visualizations, where motion cannot be used to indicate direction. Pressing "P" exports a copy of the on-screen view as a high-resolution, vector PDF file.

Quantitative Edge Values Encoded

Pressing "4" reveals an equivalent visualization, but with edge values (in this case, telephone call duration) encoded as the diameter of each edge-circle. Longer phone calls are larger circles, and shorter ones smaller. Immediately, a wealth of new information is present, and the user can identify imbalances and trends within the network

of relationships. Telephone number A may call B more often, but when B calls A they tend to talk for longer periods. Or A places few outgoing calls, but receives incoming ones from many different numbers.

Quantitative Edge Values Encoded (Alternate)

Pressing "5" reveals a similar view, but with edges represented as rectangles, and with edge values encoded as the height of each rectangle. This view is similar to a traditional bar chart representation, and may be more appropriate given the data set.

Also note that the paths traveled by edges between nodes are slight arcs, enhancing visibility of the edges, which would otherwise overlap. The plus and minus keys can be used to increase and decrease the width of the arcs, which may improve readability, depending on the desired node placement.

CONTRIBUTIONS

This project offers a number of contributions toward the future of visualization of directed graphs with multiple edges:

1) The presentation of edges as discrete visual elements;
2) The use of motion to indicate edge directionality;
3) The encoding of an additional quantitative value for each edge.

Nearly all prior visualizations of graphs with multiple edges maintain the convention of representing the edges as lines. The multiplicity of edges is typically encoded as a visual property of the line, either thickness, brightness, or hue.

The primary contribution of this project is to break with the tradition of representing edges solely as lines. As we can see now, when multiple edges are present, each edge can be visualized discretely whether as a circle, rectangle, or some other form. Not only is there no need to aggregate multiple edges into singular visual form, but visualizing each edge as its own entity provides opportunities for encoding additional quantitative values specific to each edge. More data can be communicated using discrete edges instead of traditional lines. While lines may be superimposed on this sort of visualization, they are necessary only when few edges are present. Otherwise, the arrangement and motion of edges communicates the

binary information originally represented by the simple line: whether or not two nodes are connected. Connections are still obvious, yet much more detail about each relationship is made visible.

CONCLUSION

This research opens the door to a number of other visualization possibilities, such as experimenting with alternate visual forms for edges (beyond just circles and rectangles), incorporating ordering of edges in date/time sequence, encoding additional values onto edges to render additional dimensions of data, and designing legible labeling systems to reveal exact values where appropriate.

It is the author's hope that others will expand upon the visualization and interaction techniques revealed here to present more valuable and data-rich presentations of all kinds of network relationships.

Cheeky

SCOTT MURRAY

Class of 2010

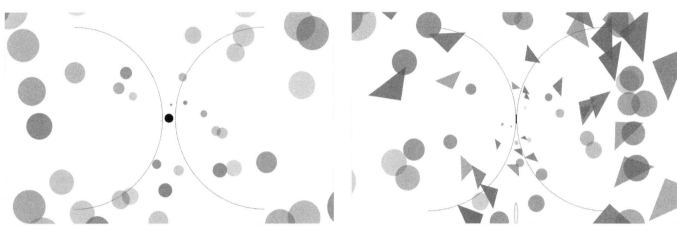

In early January 2010, fellow Dynamic Media Institute student Lou Susi announced that he was organizing a gallery show entitled "American Cheese" for the 28th of the month. This was a rare opportunity to apply the conceptual framework and technical skills behind *Practice* toward something less aspirational.

Over the course of two evenings, I came up with a concept, downloaded and edited the necessary audio samples, designed the visual system (which was rudimentary, due to the time constraints), and adapted the face-tracking code from *Practice* for use in *Cheeky*. When viewing *Cheeky* from afar, the participant sees a white display with a small curved-X shape at center, sort of like a rounded X. As the participant moves in for a closer look, the X shape slowly expands, growing roughly in proportion to the user's distance from the display. Face-tracking monitors the size of the participant's face

estimate how near or far a person is are from the video camera and display. A small amount of easing is incorporated, so even if the user jumps up close, the X shape will not jump in size, but smoothly scale up over a few seconds.

Upon reaching a target size of about 80 percent of the display height, the curved X separates in two, vibrating rapidly while an offensive, yet instantly recognizable sound is played, and brown, semi-transparent "gas bubbles" are ejected out from center screen and fly away in all directions.

User testing reveals that moment to be a very emotional one, triggering a range of reactions, often all at once, including embarrassment, shame, joy, disgust, love, and giddy excitement upon the realization that a computer has just released a digital fart in the participant's face. The abstract X can no longer be seen as anything but two cheeks resting against each other until the next evacuation.

The slow expansion of the X builds tension around anticipation of what will happen next. The tension is released in a very visual, highly audible form — a representation of a bodily release that is both commonplace and socially off-limits (except for eight-year-old boys). So the social context is important, of course, and informs the range of feelings and decisions to be made by the participant in that one airy moment. At a performance-art show called "American Cheese," it is probably okay to laugh at a fart joke, and not take yourself too seriously. But what if the work were presented in a more serious context, as though it were high art? Or, what if you are the artist, and your friends who have seen *Cheeky* can't stop recommending it to people you've only just met? How does that recommendation influence the first impression you're in the process of making, and do you position yourself closer to or further away from the project?

Even when *Cheeky* is not on display, it has ways of making me uncomfortable while making me laugh.

Although *Cheeky* is designed for only one active user at a time (which is appropriate, given the intimate nature of the bodily function on display), it employs many of the same design principles as *Practice* to engage third-party observers and become a social experience. In *Cheeky*, the visuals are important, but the audio is critical, since it expands to fill the space around it. At the "American Cheese" show, the display was positioned so that it couldn't be seen right away, but required some navigation within the gallery space to get a good look. So, as I had hoped, the uncomfortable audio caught the attention of uninitiated observers who looked over and witnessed the active participant, face close to the screen, either shocked and appalled (and, soon thereafter, even further shocked to observe that everyone else was watching), or laughing uncontrollably, or all of the above. The uninitiated knew, then, that this was some kind of fart machine, but without a clear view of the screen, its interaction model remained a mystery. This curiosity motivated them

to experience it for themselves, but in the meantime the sights and sounds of someone else experiencing the piece were almost funny enough. This is comedy, in dynamic digital form. And while our social self-consciousness may not be intense enough to induce a satori-like state, it elicits enough discomfort that we just have to laugh. It may not be enlightenment, but it's not bad.

It gets funnier when people come back for repeat performances. In my testing, new users tended to jump back in surprise, or at least look away, trying to connect with the other people in the room. ("Oh my god, can you believe what it just did?" "This is in such poor taste!" "Make eye contact with me so I can communicate to you that I do not approve of this filthy, so-called art!") But those who came back for more were rewarded with any one of ten pre-selected fart recordings, all acquired from Freesound, the online sound sample archive. In these subsequent interactions, participants may have noticed some of the subtleties of the design, such as how the cheeks' vibrations are synchronized with the audio (so louder noises produce greater cheek separation), as are the speeds of the outgoing bubbles (which move faster for loud ones, and slowly for softer ones). The small, black circle at center is glimpsed only briefly, but its identity and function are unmistakable and cannot be forgotten. The ten sound samples are selected and played in random order. While that randomness helps explain part of

what keeps the experience varied, it doesn't tell us why people are willing to (and even excited about) voluntarily approaching a machine that will fart loudly in their faces, even once they know that it will do so! I guess fart jokes never stop being funny.

Once *Cheeky* was working, the randomized sounds and vibrating cheeks weren't quite enough; I felt it needed one more thing to keep users coming back for more. So I created the "lighter" stage. About 10 percent of the time, when a release is triggered, the audio will play, gas bubbles escape, and cheeks vibrate — everything as normal — but with an additional twist: A small "flame" rises from the bottom of the screen, which lights the emerging gases on fire. Corresponding audio is played (click, click, WHOOOOOOOSHHH!), and red triangles crudely represent the gas that has been set aflame. (Unfortunately, due to a version control issue, the *Cheeky* shown at "*American Cheese*" triggered the lighter nearly every time, instead of just 10 percent of the time.)

The lighter sequence adds another layer of depth and possibility to the interaction, and provides an incentive for participants to knowingly put themselves in an uncomfortable position, deliberately sustaining repeated blows, until they achieve the reward of the flaming fart. Because the lighter sequence is played at random, users may have to suffer through the humiliation of anywhere from one to twenty or more evacuations. When the reward does come, it is very big and very

loud, a release befitting the discomfort and effort required to attain it.

Despite the low-brow content, I hope to have made clear how a number of techniques were consciously used to make *Cheeky* emotionally engaging — especially that of exploiting the tension of anticipation, pairing physical and social discomfort with satisfying rewards, and employing random elements to ensure variety in the experience. In the end, *Cheeky* may actually be more engaging and successful (if less philosophically pure) than *Practice*. It is certainly a shorter experience, since it requires the user to stand still not for minutes, but only moments. *Practice* is slow-moving, deliberate, peaceful, and contemplative, while *Cheeky* is explosive, shocking, humiliating, and downright offensive. Yet people love it.

CREDITS

Cheeky incorporates recordings from Freesound (freesound.org) by the following authors: elmomo, IFartInUrGeneralDirection, monterey2000, NoiseCollector, scarbelly25, and Walter Odington.

Comedy in dynamic, digital form — user interaction reveals the moment to be a very emotional one.

Perceiving Interaction: Heartbeat

AUDREY FU

Class of 2010

OBJECTIVES

The objective in this project was to explore the possibility of bringing a projected, lighted space into the language of performance. I invited a dancer, Ching-I Chang who performs professionally for multiple dance groups in both New York and Washington D.C., to work with me.

From the design of the stage and selecting the music, we thought, created, and performed together. We brought her performance into my system of three projectors to explore how the human body might act as a physical filter in our perception of space.

Ching-I performed the concept: the heartbeat. The projection projected the metaphor of the *heartbeat* as the blood pumping. Not only did I want to create a new generation of stage design for a dancer but also to have the performer's body move and pull audiences into this experience.

PREPARATION

My first project in the Dynamic Media Institute program for every incoming student was *I Am Now here*. It was a two-weeks warm-up project. I took the meaning of *I Am Now Here* as the concept of my culminating

Heartbeat project. I approached the concept from two points: I am now here; I exist. I am aware of myself mentally through my thoughts, and I am now here; I am alive. I feel life flowing through my blood and the stroke of the pulse. I am aware of myself physically through my sensations. Both of the two points conveyed a sense of "I am now here."

This project focused on testing the language of performance by using my three-layer projection system with three projectors into a real stage space.

Two directions were planned for the audiences to observe this performance. First, the audience only observed — they could merely watch the artist perform with light and space. Later on, I directed the artists to invite the audience to get involved by acting and interacting with the light and the other audience members.

Based on the experimentation with three projectors in a three-layer projection system, the artists' motion was both the physical filter and the spatial surface. Then I made two areas, which were the center where the multiple projections overlapped and the periphery, without light. In addition, I added

lots of balloons as the medium; some were hanging and some were floating on the floor.

For the three light sources, I continued working with Processing for interactive sound detection. There were visual sound patterns as solid circular forms with different colors. Each circular form represented a heartbeat — each sound created the meaning of "alive." When the sound was detected, the solid circular forms grew and interacted with each other.

Ching-I and I considered large white paper, a simple shaped chair and objects with dissimilar forms when we selected a medium to place between the projections. We finally adopted the balloons to be the main medium to create a dialogue with the projection of the solid circular forms as the visual language. The balloons were everywhere.

We selected a classroom, which was about 20 by 20 feet with curtains as a background. Before this decision was made, we tried an empty dark room that was about 10 by 10 feet and a public staircase at MassArt.

PROCESS

The first time Ching-I experienced the light projections, I turned on the projectors and

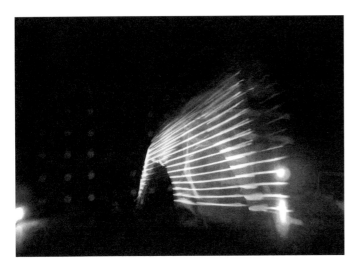

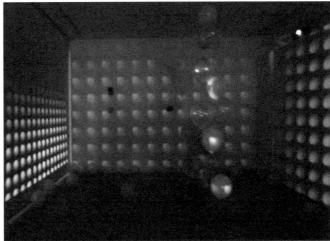

she tried to feel the whole light and space with her body and without too much thinking. She stayed still and moved slightly. Although I told her how it would look on the phone several times, she thought that it was too difficult to imagine by my description and the photos I sent her. She was shocked and surprised.

Extending her body naturally in the empty dark room to sense and catch the light was the first practice she made. She asked me to take pictures and shoot video for our discussion because she could not really see how the light changed and moved on her body. She moved every part of her body. She stood upside down, jumped, laid down on the floor and walked on tiptoe.

For another practice, we chose a transitional site in a public stairway at school. It was a busy area where people often walked around. The place was massive and light projections were projected onto the far and near walls, glass windows, and ceiling. The perception had been made boundless and limitless. She gradually gained more understanding of my experimentation and the effects of the light.

Exploring the possibilities of light and space in the language of performance.

Using the performer
to pull audiences into
the experience.

On the second day, we moved the equipment to the classroom. I built the stage with curtains as a background for the performance. She first asked for more objects with different forms such as a white box, and a cylinder bar among others on the stage to catch the projections. In my opinion, there were too many interruptions. So I suggested using one simple chair in the scene. She created a scene and slid it onto the stage slowly with music and light. Then, we both thought about the paper we tested before. We practiced all the different possibilities.

Between our conversations, we negotiated and tried our ideas until we focused on the heartbeat and determined that the balloons were our main medium to interact with the circular sound forms. The influence of the balloons and light was dramatic to see as she danced between the light projection in the illusory perception of space.

Ching-I and I collaborated again at the DMI *inter-akt* exhibition on April 15th, 2010. I set up the installation with her performance and my lighting space. She first danced for a short segment and then invited the audience to walk onto the stage and interact with her, the light, and space.

PROJECT REFLECTION

The most important thing I gained in this project was the support of a performing artist. Ching-I contributed a lot of her thoughts and dance. We had a tacit understanding and unspoken agreement during the process. She helped me in brainstorming and to generate new ideas. It was a new start for testing the language of performance. The discussion about the possibilities on the stage inspired me. She and I would like to push this idea more in the future.

On the other hand, the action for the performance was changing. Instead of a show, which was only for watching, the artist invited the audience to walk onto the stage successfully. The balloons were a nice and playful medium I used to function in the installation and the light and illusory space were attractive. The motion of the performance was the main part that introduced the concept of the light projections and space for people to interact with.

Because of the interaction and the invitation from the dancer, the audience easily crossed the edge of the "stage." They became part of the installation and re-created the performance.

Some people stayed in the periphery and kept observing. They saw the effects between the human motion, and lighting space. It was a joyful observation. Then, they maintained the spirit of performance by continuing to watch the show. Some people generously moved their bodies, gathered on the stage, and blew the balloons I gave them and played. I have investigated and explored this topic for two years; the scenes pleasantly surprised me. This result was marvelous. I had never used this huge scale of light, space, and human motion to gather this kind of interaction.

The next step for this project would be to create a group performance. I wonder if it will give performers an impulse and inspire their work. Moreover, how will they interact with my light projection and illusory space?

Drawing by Emotion

MINGXI LI

Class of 2009

I. INTRODUCTION

Drawing by Emotion is a system that recognizes human emotions generated by vocal cues and then uses that data as input to operate and activate a drawing machine.

Drawing by Emotion aims to express human emotion from the whole set which includes object metaphor, motion, and visualization statement. Five machines are based on five selected basic emotions: anger, happiness, neutrality, sadness, and boredom. The object metaphors chosen are a hammer, a spinning top, a weaving loom, an IV set, and a pendulum. Each machine transforms a vocal emotional statement into a visual expression of that emotion.

The project has two basic parts: one is to develop a system that can accurately detect a person's psychological state by analyzing the output of vocal cues. The other is to process this information in real-time (as it happens) and convert it into visual evidence.

According to Hiroshi Ishii, head of the Tangible Media Lab, Interaction requires two key components. One is control, through which people can manipulate access to digital information and computation. In this project, "control" is the human voice (speaking naturally) which may or may not encode emotion. Also, it's very important to have external representations that people can perceive to understand the result of the computation. And in my project, the drawing result is the decoding of the emotion.

The research begins with several questions: whether or not human speech encodes emotional cues? What is emotion? What is the standard determining emotion? What is the function of emotional expression? The following sections review the research that has been used to address these questions.

II. THEORETICAL CONTEXT

a. Theories of Emotion

What is emotion? "Everyone knows what an emotion is, until asked to give a definition. Then, it seems, no one knows" (Fehr & Russel, 1984). Emotion is a notoriously hard concept to define and there are no generally agreed upon criteria for what should count as an emotion and what should not.

b. Emotion Classification

There are many different emotion classifications. Andrew Ortony and Terence J.Turner (1997) collated a wide range of research on identification of basic emotions such as acceptance, anger, anticipation, disgust, joy, fear, sadness, surprise, courage, dejection, desire, love, sorrow, etc. Secondary emotions include feelings such as affection, admiration, pride, conceit, nostalgia, remorse, and rancor.

c. Functions of Emotional Expression

The communication of emotion is often viewed as crucial to social relationship and survival, and many of the most important adaptive problems faced by our ancestors are assumed to have been social by nature. Emotional expressions can shape social behavior through two interrelated mechanisms. First, by expressing emotions we can communicate important information to others, thereby influencing their behaviors, and by recognizing others' expressions we can make quick inferences about their probable behaviors (Darwin, 1872). Secondly, expressions can regulate social behavior by evoking emotional responses in the decoder.

There are many cues to enable accurate recognition of emotions including vocal intonation, facial expression, posture, behavior, skin color, and temperature. Facial expression is thought to be one of the most important elements in the expression of emotion. Ekman and Oster claim, "In humans the face seems to be a richer and more dependable source of information about emotion than any other expressive modality." In fact, many of the studies involving the perception of emotion from vocal cues present high levels of recognition, in some cases higher than those obtained from (at least static) visual stimuli (Julie Robson and Janet Mackenzie Beck).

d. Prosodic Emotion Recognition

Hypothesis: Different emotions have varying effects on the properties of the different speech sounds. Most studies have considered vocal expression as a means to communication. Hence, fundamental issues include:

A. The content (what is communicated?)
B. The accuracy (how accurately is it communicated?)
C. Code (how is it communicated?)

METHODS OF COLLECTING VOCAL EXPRESSIONS

Most studies of vocal expression to date have used some variant of the "standard content paradigm." That is, someone (an actor) is instructed to read some verbal material aloud, while simultaneously portraying particular emotions chosen by the investigator. The emotion portrayals are first recorded, and then evaluated in listening

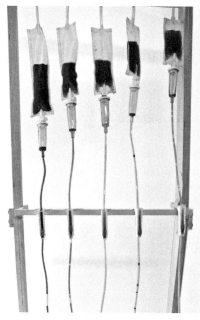

experiments to see whether listeners are able to decode the intended emotions. The same verbal material is used in portrayals of different emotions and most typically has consisted of single words or short phrases (Laukka 2004).

Other common methods include the use of emotional speech from real conversations, induction of emotions in the speaker using various methods, and the use of speech synthesis to create emotional speech stimuli.

VOCAL CUE IN EMOTION RECOGNITION

A fundamental question is: what aspects of the voice signal should be measured? The most obvious answer to this question is: "As many as possible." The current research on emotion recognition based on vocal cue tests are: Prosodic features (the patterns of stress and intonation in speech) including pitch, voice intensity, duration, frequency, pauses (Fairbanks & Hoaglin, 1941); Quality features: phonation type, precision of articulation manner, voice timber, micro-structural regularity (Davitz, 1964); Spectral features: bandwidth energy.

K. R. SCHERER'S THEORY OF VOCAL EXPRESSION

The general principle of Scherer's theory is that physiological variables, to a large extent, determine the nature of phonation and resonance in vocal expression. Scherer offers predictions for acoustic cues associated with anger, disgust, fear, happiness, and sadness; these are the "five major types of emotional states that can be expected to occur frequently in the daily life of many organisms, both animal and human."

My data and method of research, based on the work "Emotional Space Improves Emotion Recognition" by Raquel Tato, Rocio Santos, Ralf Kompe, J.M. Pardo, has helped to answer the two key questions: whether speaking (vocal cues) encodes emotions and which emotion statements currently can be decoded, and what methods are used to decode?

In the aforementioned paper, the authors aimed to recognize five emotional states: anger, happiness, sadness, boredom, and neutrality. They used two classifiers looking at prosodic features and giving as output three levels in the activation dimension (high = anger-happy, medium = neutral. Low = sad-bored), and a second classifier, looking at quality features, and making the final decision concerning an emotional state. In their first study, a speaker-dependent experiment: an experiment was carried out taking the whole set of 37 prosodic features as input to the neural network classifier (NN), with no hidden layer, to assess the confusability among the five emotional states.

Although the recognition rate is not particularly high, the output values clearly differentiate the position of the emotional state on the arousal axis. Another thing to be read clearly from the table is that emotion is a relative quantity.

Based on these facts, the five machines for *Drawing by Emotion* were coordinated simultaneously to draw together.

III. PROJECT ANALYSIS

Drawing by Emotion uses the whole set, including the machine itself, the motion of the machine, and the visual result as a process to transform vocal emotion cues to visual emotion expression.

The entire process combines human senses and a system installation to create a visual expression of emotion. Overall, in *Drawing by Emotion,* the interaction between human and machine can be treated as part of Human-Robot Interaction or Human-Computer Interaction. Usually, the function of robots is to extend the range of the physical capacity of humans, especially in dangerous or extreme conditions. The basic goal of Human-Robot Interaction is to develop principles and algorithms to allow more natural and effective communication and interaction between humans and robots. *Drawing by Emotion* seeks to elevate the process of interactivity. It envisions a way of manipulating a robotic machine that is capable of reacting to human voice that carries emotional cues — a human way — rather than a command-line interface. Its function would expand and integrate human senses.

OBJECT METAPHOR

When I designed each component of the project, the central questions were: How could the machine express emotion, and how could the expression be accepted by people as an emotion?

A past experience with a meaningful object can easily wake up memory and then connect a person to a new meaning. Metaphor describes an expression of speech "in which a word or a group of words is transferred out of its actual context of meaning into another, without there being a direct simile between the descriptive term and that which it describes" (Duden).

Metaphor is connected with memory. It connects the past experiences and new experiences to become a brand new unit and convert the unfamiliar and the unaccustomed to become familiar. The use of metaphor is a process of transferring and connecting from the past to the present toward the future.

Drawing by Emotion selects five object metaphors to represent five basic emotions: anger — a hammer; happiness — a spinning top;

A system that recognizes
human emotions generated
by vocal cues to operate
a drawing machine.

sadness — an IV set; neutrality — a weaving loom; boredom — a pendulum.

The reason for selecting those metaphors is based on my own experience. The image of a hammer crushing things reminds me of the emotional statement of anger. The pleasant memories of spending hours playing with a spinning top as a child influenced my choosing a spinning top for a happiness machine metaphor. When I was in the hospital with a fever, I experienced how infusion is a long, painful process. That is the reason an IV set was chosen as the sadness machine metaphor. The motion of a clock pendulum always remains at the same speed and rhythm, which leaves a person feeling very bored. The mode and pattern of a moving loom leaves a neutral impression.

When I wake up my own memories for selecting metaphors, there are design questions: when we design, what is the balance between "new" and "old"? How do we keep people feeling that ideas are fresh but not overwhelm them? In his book, *On Intelligence*, Jeff Hawkin observes:

"Brains like familiarity, but they get bored. They are genetically programmed to want to discover new patterns; you don't want it too new because that seems dangerous. You want it somewhat familiar and somewhat new. Somehow new and old at the same time gives the best design. If a design is so new that people can't relate to it, then they reject it….you want it to be just slightly different, enough that people say, Oh, that's cool."

DRAWING PROCESS

How does drawing specifically express emotion? Which drawing, which visual element, could represent which emotion? Not only does what I draw matter, but how I draw it matters too. So two parts need to be taken into consideration: the drawing process and the visual result. What matters in the process of drawing are both motion and the tool used in making the mark. The speed, the force, the rhythm, the fluency, and the loudness; each aspect of the movement matters in communicating the meaning and expression of an emotion.

The *Drawing by Emotion* system sets up the variables of motion in each of the five machines. The expression 'anger' is based on other related words, for example: choler, conniption, infuriation, quick short temper, all of which help me to visualize the image. The basic movement of the anger machine is hitting. The variables are the height from which hitting begins, the speed of hitting, the rhythm of hitting and the force (intensity) of hitting.

The expression 'happiness' is based on other related words, like delight and cheer. The basic movement of the happiness machine is circling. The variables are the size of the circling, the speed of circling, the rhythm of circling, and its fluency plus the width of the brush and the number of brushes.

The expression 'neutrality' is based on other related words, such as disengaged and inactive. The basic movement of the neutrality machine is making straight lines. The variables are the number of strokes.

The expression 'sadness' is based on other related words, such as dejection, dismal and blue. The basic movement of the sadness machine is dripping. The variables are the starting height of the dripping and the frequency of the dripping.

The expression 'boredom' is based on other related words, such as lethargy and monotony. The basic movement of the boredom machine is short repetitive stroking. The variables are the speed of stroking.

THE VISUAL RESULT

Color

Perception of color is the strongest emotional part of the visual process. Color has a strong affinity to emotion. Color also carries symbolic meaning and associative meaning.

There are many color theories. Donis A. Dondis states that color has three dimensions which can be defined and measured: hue, saturation, and brightness. In *Drawing by Emotion,* I chose colors based on the general knowledge that bright colors often express excitement, while duller or darker ones can express relaxation, depression, sleepiness, or other low-key emotions. In the system, red, yellow, black, blue grey, and grey represent anger, happiness, neutrality, sadness, and boredom. Each of the colors, except grey, which expresses boredom, has five different levels of hue, saturation, and brightness to express different degrees of each emotion.

Shape

Each shape has its own unique character and characteristics and meaning. A great deal of meaning is attached to each one. We get meaning in several ways, some through association, some though arbitrary attached meaning and some through our own psychological and physiological perceptions.

A splash shape, has qualities in irregularity, scalability, and can express an intense emotion. Therefore this shape is used for representing anger in the system.

Curved lines are lively and suggest energy, they can express a pleasant emotion; so curved lines easily represent happiness in the system.

Straight lines convey neutral feelings, which are useful for representing neutrality in the system.

Dots are delicate and tiny like rain drops. They can express a "down" feeling and represent sadness in the system.

Strokes are monotonous and represent boredom in the system.

Pattern

Pattern conveys multiple levels of information. One level combines the tools and the force of drawing. For example, in works with sharp, percussive strokes, like a Vincent Van Gogh painting, the brush strokes always give the painting an anxious tone.

The neutrality machine in *Drawing by Emotion* uses sharp pencils and consistent force.

The anger machine uses a block of wood, a hammer and powerful pounding.

The happiness machine uses soft brushes and rapid light circular motions.

The sadness machine uses gentle dripping water.

Another level of pattern is connected with movement. Pattern is a representation of motion on the timeline. The layer of patterns reveals the movement and its attached meaning.

Movement

Movement in a visual representation is described as the compositional tensions and rhythms in visual data, even when what is being seen is actually fixed and unmoving. The layers of meaning in the drawing (pattern) are indicated by the intensity, the size, the speed, and the length of time expended by the person making the drawing. From that, a great deal of emotional information is conveyed by the visual itself; the self-recorded visualization. The degree of emotion is conveyed in patterns related to movement.

REFERENCES

Darwin, Charles. *The Expression of Emotion in Man and Animals.* New York, London: Appleton. 1872.

Ekman, Paul. "HYPERLINK "http://www.paulekman.com/wp-content/uploads/2009/02/Facial-Expressions-Of-Emotion.pdf "Facial Expressions of Emotion." American Psychologist, 48:384-392. 1993.

Hawkin, Jeff / Blakeslee, Sandra. *On Intelligence.* Times Books, Henry Holt and Co., 2005

Laukka, P. "Vocal Expression of Emotion: Discrete-Emotion and Dimensional Accounts," PHD Dissertation, Uppsala University, December, 2004.

Ortony, Andrew / Turner, Terence J. "What's Basic About Basic Emotions?" *Psychological Review,* v97 n3 p315-31 Jul 1990.

Robson, Julie / MackenzieBeck, Janet. *Hearing Smiles—Perceptual, Acoustic and Production Aspects of Labial Spreading.* ICPhS-99, San Francisco, 219-222.

Scherer, K. R.. "Vocal Affect Expression: A Review and a Model for Future Research." *Psychological Bulletin,* 99, 143-165, 1986.

Tato, Raquel / Santos, Rocîo / Kompe, Ralf / Pardo, J. M. (2002): "Emotional Space Improves Emotion Recognition," in ICSLP-2002, 2029-2032.

collaborations

"A Dynamic Partnership"

The Dynamic Media Institute
and Isabella Stewart Gardner Museum

HEATHER SHAW / BRIAN LUCID

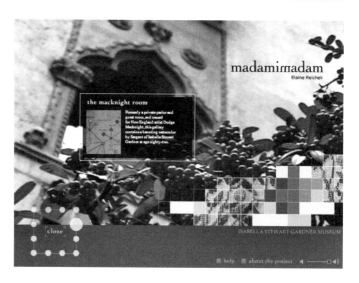

The interface uses several behavioral and visual metaphors to depict the transformation that takes place within the galleries.

My first visit to the Isabella Stewart Gardner Museum transpired during my interview process for the Dynamic Media Institute MFA program in the Spring of 2001. Being the first DMI candidate interview for the day, with a late lunch scheduled in the afternoon, I had some time to kill between appointments. I wandered over to the Isabella Stewart Gardner Museum to fill the gap.

There was a slight hesitation in my step as I embarked on my first excursion to the Museum. As a Massachusetts native, I tried to ignore the pangs of guilt from not having frequented it prior. Once inside, my shame quickly transformed to enchantment. From the open airiness of the courtyard; to the meta-detail of Isabella's installations in each room, I can only describe my experience as a complete immersion in Gardner's hypnotic.

I spent the majority of my visit in the Gothic Room. Originally closed to the public, it was a studio for John Singer Sargent. Currently, the Gothic room is a dimly lit ecclesiastic space containing stained glass windows, altarpieces, paintings, and furniture. However, it wasn't the history or spirituality that implanted me in this room — in the far corner was Sargent's 1888 portrait of Isabella. I simply could not take my eyes off this piece.

Aside from Sargent's mastery with the medium, I was captivated with the subject — Isabella. Although the portrait appears "posed," further study reveals discreet acts of motion suspended in time. Isabella's lips are just parted, as if to speak, with her gaze directly at the viewer. This portrait makes eye contact with you. Sargent's finesse captures the essence of Isabella in a way that only a close friend can initiate — her poise is fixed, yet fluid — evidence of grace under pressure as she mercilessly pursued her dynamic vision in support of the arts.

Bewitched by this apparition, I mused before Isabella for more than 20 minutes. What was she about to say? What projects was she executing during the time of the portrait? Simultaneously, how does the Museum continue to implement her work? My silent dialogue implored more information about Isabella, the Museum, and its vision. Little did I know this brief interaction, coupled with my acceptance to the DMI program, foreshadowed many future successful collaborations with the Gardner.

It was time for my next appointment. I turned back to look at the portrait one last time before leaving the museum. Out of the corner of my eye, I thought I saw Isabella wink at me.

INTRODUCTION

For nearly a decade the Dynamic Media Institute has served as a creative partner to the Isabella Stewart Gardner Museum. DMI students, faculty, and alumni have designed and developed a wide array of projects as the museum increasingly leverages dynamic media within its programming. The work spans the Contemporary and Special Exhibitions, the Collection and Archives, the New Building Project, and the institution's overall brand.

The involvement of the DMI program brings a fresh and creative perspective to the Gardner. The Museum is a demanding and educated client, interested in communicating through dynamic media and exploring it as an art form in itself. Working with the museum extends the pedagogy of the DMI program. The projects follow a working model akin to the thesis methodology, merging deeply theoretical and metaphorical constructs with a creative approach to technology, approaching both design and development as creative processes.

Below is a chronological listing of projects The DMI has produced for the Gardner Museum:
- 2002: Heather Ackroyd and Dan Harvey: *Presence: The Ephemeral in Focus*
- 2003: Elaine Reichek: *madamimadam*
- 2004: Danijel Zezelj: *Stray Dogs*
- 2008: *Luxury for Export: Artistic Exchange Between India and Portugal Around 1600*
- 2009: *Isabella Stewart Gardner's Travel Albums*
- 2009: *Isabella Stewart Gardner Museum Site Audit*
- 2010: *Building on a Legacy*

CONTEMPORARY EXHIBITIONS: CREATING THE VIRTUAL EXPERIENCE

The Gardner Museum's Artist-in-Residence (AIR) program gives an artist complete access to the collection for a period of time, resulting in the development and exhibition of a new body of work. DMI has designed and developed several interactive pieces in tandem with AIR exhibitions, working in partnership with the artist(s) and the Gardner's contemporary curator, Pieranna Cavalchini.

PRESENCE: THE EPHEMERAL IN FOCUS (2002 / CD-ROM)
Artists-in-Residence: Heather Ackroyd and Dan Harvey
Museum Curator: Pieranna Cavalchini, Contemporary Exhibitions
Dynamic Media Institute Project Coordinator: Jan Kubasiewicz
Design & Production: Isabel Meirelles, MFA '02 / Fenya Su, MFA '02
Video: Mark Lipman, MFA Film '02

Presence: The Ephemeral in Focus initiated the partnership between the Isabella Stewart Gardner Museum and the DMI. Artists-in Residence Heather Ackroyd and Dan Harvey transformed the Special Exhibition gallery into their studio, germinating and growing seven organic photographs intended to be presented as works of nature — time-based and ephemeral.

The interactive CD contains 35 works, in addition to video documenting the artists' process and interviews during their residency at the Gardner Museum. The project parallels Ackroyd's and Harvey's artistic negotiation of germination, growth, and decay. The interface reduces the sensory and psychological distance — created by the mediated presentation of images — to activate the viewer's own memories. This intent creates associations as connectors to personal narratives, changing an objective presentation of the data into a subjective exploration of the artwork.

In 2004, *Presence* won an Honorable Mention by the American Association of Art Museums: Museum Publications Design Competition.

MADAMIMADAM (2003 / ONLINE EXHIBITION AND CD-ROM)
Artist-in-Residence: Elaine Reichek
Museum Curator: Pieranna Cavalchini, Contemporary Exhibitions
Dynamic Media Institute Project Coordinator: Jan Kubasiewicz
Development & Video: Heather Shaw, MFA '03 / Michael Wiggins, MFA '03
Photography: Yoav Horesh, MFA Photography '03
Voice: James Engel
Sound: Adam Brown

> *...embroidery is in any case closer to the pixel method of constructing images than to traditional painting; yet it is at the same time a method of the hand, and inherits a tradition that can compete with painting for longevity.*
>
> **— Elaine Reichek**

Isabella Stewart Gardner's will stipulated that nothing in the museum's galleries could be changed or altered in the face of the public. To overcome these restrictions, Artist-in-Residence Elaine Reichek temporarily installed her samplers among the Gardner's permanent collection while the galleries were closed. Reichek's embroidered samplers — containing themes of creationism contrasted with science fiction — were placed in an artful context both visually and thematically within each room. These temporary installations were captured with digital video, producing 16 one-minute videos threading these connections through motion and time. The Gardner's first "virtual exhibition"— *madamimadam* documents this transformation of space within the permanent collection behind public eye.

The interface, designed to reinforce the virtual domain of the exhibit, uses several behavioral and visual metaphors to depict the transformation that takes place within the galleries. Large background stills of the rooms randomly change after several seconds. The navigation configuration is reminiscent of the courtyard, however the links around it have no bearing on the actual location of the rooms in the museum.[1] These metaphors maintain the ambiguity in the placement of Reichek's work within the virtual domain, reinforcing the transformation within the permanent collection.[2]

In 2005 *madamimadam* won first place in the American Association of Art Museums: Museum Publications Design Competition. It was exhibited in Reichek's 2004 exhibition: *After Babel, Alpha Beta* at the Nicole Klagsbrun Gallery, New York NY.

1. Homepage exhibits visual and metaphorical connections between Elaine's work and the Gardner. Navigation is reminiscent of the courtyard.

2. Background stills randomly change, maintaining the ambiguity in the placement of Elaine's work within the museum.

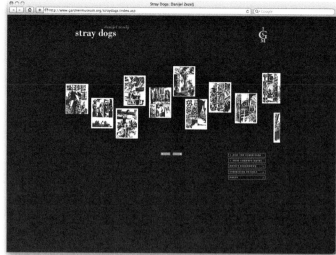

A virtual line-art simulation of the actual exhibit space, introducing walls that shifted and changed to reveal information.

STRAY DOGS (2004: ONLINE EXHIBITION)
Artist-in-Residence: Danijel Zezelj
Museum Curator: Pieranna Cavalchini, Contemporary Exhibitions
Dynamic Media Institute Project Coordinator: Heather Shaw, Alumna
Design: Brian Lucid / Heather Shaw
Development: Brian Lucid

> *…I do not see myself as a very good writer. So I'm trying to reduce the number of words as much as possible. It's similar to my approach toward images; often things are reduced to black and white, to the necessary. I think somehow through that, also, the words and pictures connect.*

— **Danijel Zezelj**

Artist-in-Residence Danijel Zezelj created an exhibition of paintings for his graphic novel, *Stray Dogs*. Set in a post-apocalyptic world, his narrative explores themes of exile and solitude. DMI produced an interactive website that embodied the spirit of the exhibition to promote Zezelj's paintings and novel.

Stray Dogs was modeled as a virtual line-art simulation of the actual exhibit space, introducing walls that shifted and changed to reveal information, paintings that pan and zoom, and book pages that turn and magnify. In the true spirit of Zezelj's reductionism philosophy, the site is designed to contain only the "necessary."

THE COLLECTION AND ARCHIVES: EXPOSING HIDDEN ARTIFACTS
The Gardner contains a wealth of archives and artifacts, many that are not on permanent display within the museum. Working in partnership with the Gardner's curator of the collection, Alan Chong, and the Musuem's former archivist Kristin Parker, the DMI has designed and developed two dynamic websites that provide public access to the archives through a digital means.

LUXURY FOR EXPORT: ARTISTIC EXCHANGE BETWEEN INDIA AND PORTUGAL AROUND 1600 (2008: ONLINE EXHIBITION)
Curator: Pedro Moura Carvalho
Museum Project Coordinator: Alan Chong, Curator of the Collection
Dynamic Media Institute Project Coordinator: Jan Kubasiewicz
Design: Brian Lucid / Heather Shaw, MFA '03 / Erich Doubek, MFA '05
Development: Brian Lucid / Erich Doubek
Video Editing: Erich Doubek

The *Luxury for Export* exhibition brought together a recently restored, large, embroidered Bengali wall hanging (part of the Gardner's permanent collection) with 16 artifacts crafted in India commissioned by Portuguese royalty. The exhibition explored the unusual cultural and visual "mash-ups" that occurred as Indian craftsmen re-interpreted traditional Portuguese embellishments.

The DMI team conceptualized two "modes" for accessing and viewing the exhibition: Guided Tour and Explore. Guided Tour features a collection of videos and media from the exhibition, allowing a viewer to be led through the collection by the curators.[1] Explore mode provides a more active engagement — encouraging viewers to examine the collection on their own using the interface filtering system.[2]

A unique approach was taken for representing the artifacts, organizing the content through visuals, themes, and materials. All of the objects are presented within an interactive matrix, bringing the formal aspects of each object into collision. When an item is interacted with, the user can see the timeframe, location of origin, and additional views of the object.[3]

Objects can be filtered by themes such as "foliage" and "hunters and kings." When a theme is chosen, the matrix rebuilds itself.[4] Objects can also be searched by material, highlighting them within the matrix.[5]

ISABELLA STEWART GARDNER'S TRAVEL ALBUMS
(2009: ONLINE VISUAL ARCHIVE)
Museum Curator: Alan Chong, Curator of the Collection
Museum Project Coordinator: Kristin Parker, Archivist
Dynamic Media Institute Project Coordinator: Brian Lucid
Design: Brian Lucid / Heather Shaw, MFA '03
Development: Brian Lucid

> *I have been arranging photographs in my albums all morning; I hope some day you will care to see them.*

— **Isabella Gardner to Julia Gardner, 1884**

Isabella Stewart Gardner traveled extensively through Europe, Asia, and the American West, leaving behind an extensive visual record that includes 28 travel albums from 1867–1895. The albums contain commercial photography and some anecdotal detailing such as Gardner's notes, watercolors, tickets, and pressed flowers.

Too fragile to handle, the museum wished to make these volumes accessible to the public via an online archive. DMI's depiction of *Travel Albums* satisfies two audiences — scholars and the general public — by capturing the experience of the ephemera without sacrificing utility for research purposes. The visual design of the interface was inspired by the detailing in Gardner's books, while structurally organizing the albums on a timeline.[1] When a user chooses a book, they have access to more information about the individual pages, and can view each page at four scales: thumbnail, medium, enlarge, and extreme detail.[2]

NAVIGATING THE MUSEUM EXPERIENCE:
The Isabella Stewart Gardner Museum Site Audit
Dynamic Media Institute Team:
Jan Kubasiewicz, Brian Lucid, Heather Shaw, MFA '03

> *We want to expand on the museum experience... and provide access to the collection in a new way.*

— **Gardner Museum Curators and Staff**

In 2009 DMI performed a *Site Audit* of the Gardner Museum's main website. The museum needed a dynamic online presence that reflected their robust programming initiatives, and facilitated relationships and re-contextualization of museum works that is not possible within the tangible space. The multi-phased analysis included assessment and diagramming of the content and information structure for the original Gardner site, and the proposal of a new site architecture and navigation scheme.

The process involved an in-depth examination of the existing ISGM website content and information structure. This included the development of a visual diagram mapping the major sections and pages on the current web site.[1] Additionally, DMI identified two primary goals for the site architecture. First, the website needed clear taxonomies to support find-ability and usability for first-time and returning users. Second, the creation of a dynamic information structure that would reflect the rich, multisensory experience of a physical visit to the Gardner Museum — inviting users to browse and explore relationships between content they may not have seen before.

In response, DMI proposed substantial architectural changes via three illustrated models. Each view presented the same content and structure, but in different visual contexts:

The Conceptual Model is an isometric diagram illustrating general groupings of content, and content flow. It brings categories together as physical volumes, and exhibits how such volumes can be connected to create exciting and unexpected relationships for the user.

The Structural Model is a hierarchical tree diagram marking general categories, sections, and main navigational items for the new site. It defines the site's overall hierarchy, major sections and subsections.

The Experience Model diagram (wireframes) visualizes the experience of a user navigating through a single path. This particular user scenario begins at the front page (1), through specific areas of proposed content (2, 3), ending on a page that showcases specific work from the collection, and its context to other things within the museum. (4)

The three models addressed the two primary goals necessary for the new site architecture. First, a clearer system of categorization would enable users easy and direct access to desired content. Second, to create a more "sensory experience," DMI proposed a dynamic architecture that is designed to conceptually frame current programming in context to the permanent collection. This unique approach allows users to "navigate sideways" through subject matter. Designed to intrigue and engage them deep within the content of the site, users are immersed directly into the Museum's collection and related programming. In addition to the three models, DMI presented a formal documentation to the Museum citing the comprehensive examination and results.

BUILDING ON A LEGACY: THE ISABELLA STEWART GARDNER MUSEUM NEW BUILDING PROJECT

Museum Project Coordinator: Kendra Slaughter
Dynamic Media Institute Project Coordinator: Brian Lucid
Design: Brian Lucid / Heather Shaw
Development: Brian Lucid

> *We intend to build on the extraordinary legacy we have inherited.*

— **Anne Hawley,** Norma Jean Calderwood Director, Gardner Museum

Building on a Legacy documents the Gardner Museum's expansion with the construction of a new building. Designed by architect Renzo Piano, the New Building Project has two goals: first, to preserve and protect the original palace, and second, to provide an additional physical space accommodating all the museum's initiatives — contemporary art, music, education, and horticulture.

The site needed to embody the spirit and design of the New Building. It features an interactive overview showing highlights from the project. Museum curators, architectural critics, and Piano contributed essays discussing important historic and contemporary issues related to the Museum's expansion. The site also features Piano's sketches and vision, and pays homage to the project team.

The museum needed a website that captured the dynamics of an evolving process. Built upon a content management platform, DMI created a system of rules that structure the content; programmed by design to easily and efficiently handle site updates. This enables the Gardner staff to populate the website with new content in tandem with the building's progress. An "Updates" section documents the construction process; allowing viewers everywhere to witness the project's transformation. Additional essays by curators and critics can be added, and "Recent Press" features current articles about the project.

1. The "Updates" section is designed to be easily populated by Gardner staff.
2. "Narrative Chronology" features all updates sequentially.
3. "Vision" features essays from curators, critics, and architect Renzo Piano.

The site needed to reflect Piano's aesthetic, while incorporating elements from the original palace. The color palette is inspired by the construction materials from the New Building. The mastheads and quotations visually combine textures from modern building materials, contrasted with textile patterns from the palace.

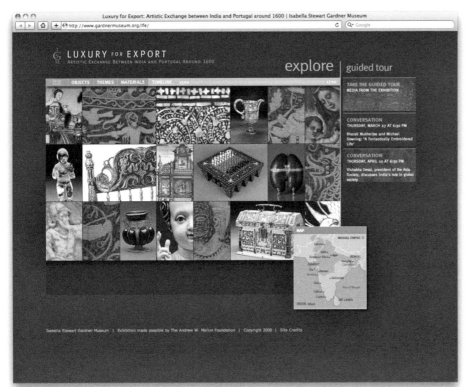

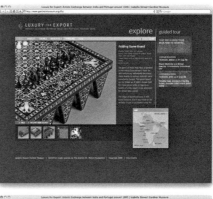

(top) A unique approach was taken for representing the artifacts, organizing the content through visual themes and materials.

(bottom) The interface was inspired by the detailing in Gardner's books, while structurally organizing the albums on a timeline.

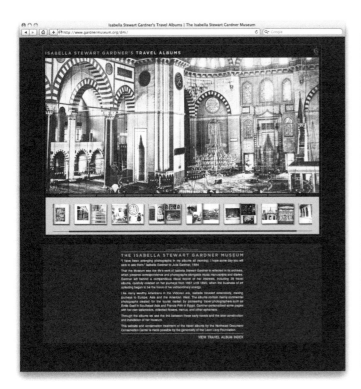

Massaging Media 2:

Graphic Design Education in the Age of Dynamic Media

JOE QUACKENBUSH

AIGA Design Educator Conference
World Trade Center
Boston, April 4–6, 2008

E-mail. Web sites. Text messaging. Instant messaging. Blogs. Podcasts. New media is newer all the time. How do we prepare design students to communicate in this age of new media? How do we adapt graphic design studies to the new media landscape? How do we create fresh curricula that address the unique communication problems new media poses? What can graphic designers do to influence the future of new media?

Over 240 design educators from the US and Europe attended the *Massaging Media 2: Graphic Design Education in the Age of Dynamic Media conference* held April 4-6, 2008, at Boston's Seaport Hotel and World Trade Center.

Massaging Media 2 was developed and co-chaired by Dynamic Media Institute Associate Professors Brian Lucid and Joseph Quackenbush along with Heather Shaw (MFA 2003), Assistant Professor of Design, Curry College. The conference, sponsored by the AIGA and Adobe Systems Inc., extended the series of "*Massaging Media*" conferences started by DMI to a much larger national and international audience. *Massaging Media 2* was the first in the history of AIGA/Adobe Design Educator events that focused exclusively on dynamic media and its role in graphic design education.

Keynote speakers included Jan Kubasiewicz, Professor of Communication Design and Coordinator of DMI, Meredith Davis, Professor of Graphic Design and the Ph.D. program at North Carolina State University, Hugh Dubberly, principal of Dubberly Design Office, and Rick Webb, co-founder and COO of The Barbarian Group. More than 50 other speakers participated in panel discussions, lectures, roundtables, and workshops.

The conference also featured a standing room only Processing workshop by composer, author, and media artist Peter Kirn, who founded the influential blogs *Create Digital Music* and *Create Digital Motion*.

A remarkable team of volunteer students from DMI, MassArt, and the University of Massachusetts, Dartmouth kept the conference running smoothly from start to finish.

Fidelity Investments Gen-Y Project

JOE QUACKENBUSH

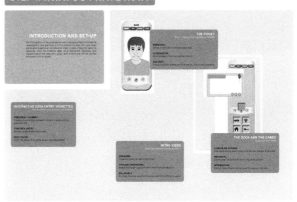

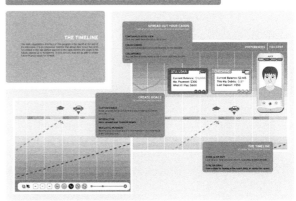

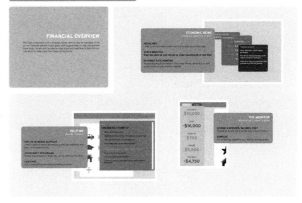

Students in Associate Professor Joseph Quackenbush's Spring 2008 *Information Architecture II* course collaborated with Fidelity Investments to develop an innovative set of online tools for the *Gen-Y* investor.

Our client, David Weisman, Director Systems Analysis, Fidelity Center for Applied Technology posed a clear design brief: create a set of interactive deliverables using rich features and interfaces to attract, educate, and win Gen-Y customers for Fidelity Investments. Unlike many assignments in which students are expected to follow specific design requirements, there were no pre-conceived solutions to this brief. All design deliverables would result from whatever the students proposed as a core business strategy.

Meeting weekly over a period of ten weeks, thirteen students (including Dynamic Media Institute alumni Dan Johnston, MFA 2009) working in groups, proposed, researched, designed, and developed a web-based application that helps address three essential Gen-Y financial problems:

1) What do I have?
2) What is possible in the future?
3) How do I get started?

Final deliverables for the project included analysis of competitive web sites, product strategy, personas, user scenarios, interface design, a video, interactive vignettes, and clickthrough prototypes of the application. Students presented their work on Wednesday, May 7, 2008, to a group of more than twenty Fidelity executives and MassArt administrators. Response to the students' work was overwhelmingly positive.

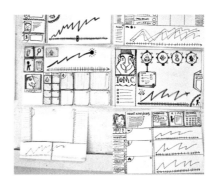

An innovative set of online tools for the Gen-Y investor.

ASCii

COLIN OWENS

A Night of Whimsy, Performance, Music & Art
Student Curated Shows
Massachusetts College of Art and Design
Patricia Doran Gallery
February 23, 2008

OVERVIEW

ASCii was an open one-night show based on a single idea: make art with text.

ASCii "art" uses the computer to create pictures assembled from the original 95 keyboard characters using a fixed-width font. This harkens back to an age when computers could only display text, not bitmap graphics. This technique can also be extended to any text-based art, which was the brief given to the artists.

The night was one of cacophonous audiovisual mayhem intended to overstimulate the participant. We believe it succeeded in doing just that.

WORKS

Oscillocam_TV provided an ASCii audiovisual musical backdrop with accompanying video using specifically designed VJ software.

Jessica Fenlon and Joshua Tonies, staples of the Pittsburg arts scene, came to Boston specifically to show their contributions to ASCii. Fenlon created two simultaneously running videos "*Binary*" and "*Strip*" that explored alphabetical characters of text disconnected from language. Tonies presented two prints from his "*Fireworks*" series that used type as a means to display image.

Scott Murray's "ASCii Photo Booth" prompted people to sit down in front of a web camera with live ascii video display and have a digital portrait taken and printed out for their pleasure.

Mike Golembewski presented a version of his "*Concordance*" that wove through the text of "*War and Peace*" in real time and separated out male and female words into columns on the left and right sides.

{if/then}

COLIN OWENS

Student Curated Shows
Massachusetts College of Art and Design
Patricia Doran Gallery
April 16, 2008

OVERVIEW

On April 16th, 2008, Dynamic Media Institute hosted {if/then}, its first annual student-run show. The purpose of the event was to pull together recent works from Dynamic Media Institute students, recent alumni, faculty, and staff and to create a dialogue between members of the arts and technology communities.

The exhibition space included areas for specific individual work and a Dynamic Media Institute "theatre" highlighting time-based output and documentation of student work.

Student-run shows like this not only showcase works to the outside world, they provide a valuable resource for students in the development of their work.

WORKS

Dynamic Media Institute Professor Gunta Kaza contributed *Map Chain*, a constant work-in-progress fabric of folded interwoven strips of maps. Instruction was provided to viewers, who were encouraged to contribute to the piece, to fold provided pieces of of the map into the growing piece. As the night unfolded, the map grew.

Student David Tames showed *What is the media fabric?* a work-in-progress (a.k.a. dynamic) documentary that played random clips from the interviews intercut with expressionistic images suggesting the concept of media fabric.

Mike Golembewski took pictures with his custom built *Scanner Camera*, an invention that marries a flatbed computer scanner with a traditional 4x5 camera with a specially prepared lens. The camera took pictures of participants and gallery-goers using a slit-scan technique that built the image one vertical row at a time from the left to right. The results were beautiful warbled pictures that captured movement over the course of a few minutes.

Jason Bailey's 3D camera allowed participants to pick up the camera and watch as each picture frame became part of projected 3D object according to its prevalence in the red, green, or blue spaces.

I unveiled *Shapemix*, the culmination of several experiments dealing with sound, visual equivalency, and interface. The program ran on a desktop Macintosh hidden behind a pedestal, with a custom-made box containing a touchscreen that had an accelerometer attached to it. Viewers were encouraged to discover how to use the novel and interface on their own as much as possible and, in some cases (much to my surprise and delight), showed each other how it worked.

Dan Johnston's *Sound Machine* created a musical experience. In his own words:

"The goal of the *Sound Machine* is to give people with limited or no musical background the experience of being a performer. It is designed to challenge users to communicate in ways they may be unfamiliar or uncomfortable with. The absence of a screen allows participants to focus on their fellow performers. I built the *Sound Machine* because I love music, but I am not a musician. I wondered if musical novices would be able to duplicate the modes of communication used by professional musicians."

Student-run shows provide a valuable resource for students in the development of their work.

American Cheese: an Introspection

LOU SUSI

Student Curated Shows

Massachusetts College of Art and Design

Patricia Doran Gallery

January 28, 2010

Humor (is) the process that allows one to brush reality aside when it gets too distressing.

— **André Breton** from his *Anthology of Black Humor*

In the late fall of 2010, I personally reached out to select artists and designers in the Dynamic Media Institute and SIM MFA programs at MassArt asking for work that would respond to the phrase 'American Cheese.' I already arranged a date with The Patricia Doran Gallery to put together a quick-hit collective, theme-based show. My hopeful vision simply aimed to inspire an eclectic body of work that, once assembled in an event-based opening, might serve as the first iteration in a series of prototypical, cross-domain exhibitions. An ulterior and slightly devious motive embedded in the very notion of *American Cheese* — to allow each participating artist to explore kitschy humor — to perhaps bring out what might be considered 'the worst' in us all — to examine certain facets of the notion of 'funny' — and to ultimately create a playful, fun and engaging experience for our audience.

You know, a lot of people come to me and they say, 'Steve, how can you be so fucking funny?' and I tell them, "First you got to feel funny, so before I go on stage, I put bologna in my shoes – so I feel funny.

— **Steve Martin** from the comedy album, *Let's Get Small*

American Cheese successfully brought together 5 works ranging from the dynamic, conceptual, and performative media domains. Much of the work materialized — from concept to finished piece — in a mere matter of days. Energies ran high, both behind the scenes on the day of the opening event, and at the unveiling of the work. We had a fantastic, receptive crowd that responded well to each piece, celebrating the spirit of 'cheese' in its many forms. *American Cheese: an Introspection* included the following work:

Cheeky: Scott Murray

On a high pedestal, in the center of the room, a large monitor displays an interesting linear double curve that seems to move and quiver as you approach. A small crowd stands and stares, all the while talking about the work before them — Scott Murray's interactive installation *Cheeky*. An occasional burst of laughter follows the culmination of the viewer-participants exchange with the on-screen animation.

Based on Murray's major interactive thesis work in mirroring technology, *Cheeky* takes the interaction model from *Practice* and strips away the serene, more meditative visual and audio rewards to turn the participant into the target of humiliation. As the viewer stands and watches the monitor — if they remain still enough — 2 curvilinear elements (the 'cheeks' of the interface) grow larger in size, creating the illusion of getting closer to the user. You are drawn into the intersection of these 'cheeks.' Small squeaky noises come out of the Mac. Little bubbles squeeze out. The stillness of the viewer and the increasing size of the 'cheeks' work together to build an unbelievable tension until — after a minute or so the lines split and reveal a explosive, farting noise accompanied by a visual, chaotic release of geometric shapes. *Cheeky* expresses perhaps the crudest humor of all, with the viewer-participant becoming the punchline to this self-inflected fart joke. If the user stares for a longer period of time — beyond this initial gaseous humiliation — the flame from a small lighter rises at the bottom of the visual display to 'light it up,' bringing us all into a hypnotic, swirling and extended experience.

Cheeky inspired an interesting blend of intrigue and laughter. Most experienced the installation alone, but with surrounding spectators witnessing the interaction, often beckoning pure laughter and

Cheese Procession by Lou Susi

New Crown by lou Susi

joy from the crowd of bystanders within the social context of The Doran Gallery.

Perhaps the silliest retrospective analysis adds to the humor emitted by *Cheeky*. Here, in the very center of the exhibit we display all the best in technology — a big, beautiful Mac accompanied by the largest high-end monitor and crystal clear speakers. The very embodiment of our finest technological progress, all installed to play a silly practical joke on our unsuspecting participants. And somehow, anthropomorphizing our machinery with such a caricaturish, absurdly obscene behavioral response seemed to cut directly to the funny bone and inspire a universal reaction of happiness and delight from our *Cheeky* users.

Untitled: The Cyber Sir Eel Kolective

Donated to the exhibit by The Cyber Sir Eel Kolective, *Untitled* stood on its pedestal, under spotlight, as an enigmatic artifact inspired by the poem-objects produced by the original Surrealists. A block of cheese stabbed by a knife with a broken handle. A noticeable wound in the cheese is embellished with a common, clear-gel pinkish cake frosting — surely symbolic of bleeding. Bleeding cheese. What could this possibly mean?

An interesting conceptual seed for The Cyber Sir Eel Kolective to plant in the mindFarm of the viewer at *American Cheese*. Should we remove the knife? Or should we cut in further? If we re-situated this artwork closer to the snack and libations area, would the viewer simply consume the block of cheese without any speculation pertaining

to purpose, meaning, or utility? In many of the works at *American Cheese* we see a running theme of the object existing within a social system — of objects that somehow play on existing human emotional content residing in the viewer-participant as it pertains to the larger context of the roomful of other gallerygoers. *Untitled* stood as a subtle 'off-centerpiece' at the show. We identify with the cheese in some strange cosmological way. What's inside? Who is trying to dissect us?

> *In many of the works at* American Cheese *we see a running theme of the object existing within a social system — of objects that somehow play on existing human emotional content residing in the viewer-participant as it pertains to the larger context of the roomful of other gallerygoers.*

standUP simul8: Lou Susi

Standing as a makeshift, octagonal, hanging structure of red theatrical curtains — the participant enters this stand-up comedy chamber and is placed centerstage, in front of an invisible audience. In these rather cramped quarters, the participant sees a stool, a small bottle of spring water, microphone stand, microphone, and a bright, hot spotlight — all of the tools presumably necessary for a successful stand-up act. And, in fact, the participant even receives pre-recorded laughter.

Surrounding *standUP simul8*, 3 boomboxes were strategically positioned on individual pedestals, each playing a slight variation on the recycled pre-recordings from the live score for laughter performance, *laughStream 2.0*. Real and found laugh samples — a variety of similarly non-verbal expressions from men, women, children, and animals — as well as random soundScape accoutrements — came together to set the mood, promising a successful comedy act experience for any participant-comedian entering the curtained stage simulation.

At this point in development, *standUP simul8* was not yet a full-fledged 'dynamic' piece. By building this prototype I quickly discovered how a deeper, more interactive connection from the system back to the user could greatly enhance the humor and play experience for the user. For instance, David Tamés immediately wondered if the microphone was actually receiving a vocal input signal, not only triggering the laughter, but also perhaps capturing 'the act' from each participant. This iteration of *standUP simul8* definitely helped establish direction for the next in a series of comedy room prototypes.

Cheese Procession: Lou Susi

Cheese Procession starts to get a bit messier than our rather tidy laughcell experiment. I wanted to create a ritual experience for our gallerygoers. Using over 400 slices of store-bought, processed american cheese, I created (with the help of my DMI colleagues) a 40 foot walkway across The Doran Gallery floor. This little 'walk of shame' for the viewer | user | participant added an interesting element of both the edible and the grotesque. Even the auspicious aroma added to the overall atmosphere of the exhibit, perhaps even extending the realms of *Cheeky* into an implied olfactory domain due to its

Untitled by Cyber Sir Eel Kolective

together to create a vague and messy found-object installation piece. My intention was to incorporate actual live lobsters in the piece, but unfortunately the little creatures died on the trip from supermarket to galleryspace

I am quite certain that on first examination this amalgamation of disparate, natural elements seemed nonsensical and purposeless, but with *New Crown* I think I was still trying to work out a certain metaphor or an issue I have with technology.

All last semester my pieces in *Design as Experience* seemed to explore the boundaries between nature and machine. I wanted to intersect the 2 domains in an almost cartoonish manner, exploring Kurzweil's notion of The Singularity, a time in the near future when man and machine will merge. Looking at photographs of New Crown — of the quirky details of leaves and twigs and lights and various hardshelled surfaces — implores me to explore this area even deeper — to try to actualize some sense of true biotechnic computing. Or at least construct some series of beautiful lies — some amazing story complex that verges on the sense of magic that technology can sometimes bring to adults, a sense of magic we all seem to naturally believe in as children and that we tend to let evaporate as we begin to contain ourselves away into our adulthoods.

Special thanks to all those that in some way inspired or directly assisted with American Cheese go out to: Scott Murray, David Tamés, Christopher Carroll, Kent Millard, Christopher Borden, Colin Owens, Joshua Dolby, Jan Kubasiewicz, Gunta Kaza, Joe Quackenbush, Toby Bottorf, Katsumi Take, and Dennis Ludvino.
Extra thanks to my wife Carol and our family for always supporting me no matter how impractical and strange these journeys into cyber-surrealism get through The DMI.

Photographic documentation materials provided by Lou Susi, David Tamés, Josua Dolby and mar von janko.

Documentation, reflections and other information regarding American Cheese: an Introspection reside at: http://hotsects.com/cheese.

proximity to the 'procession.' Besides my own personal walk on the trail of hundreds and hundreds of american cheese slices, only two other participants dared to make the journey. Inspired by a quote from Steve Martin, the essential purpose of *cheese procession* was quite literally to make the participant 'feel funny.' I don't think I realized just how funny one might feel taking off their shoes and socks in front of strangers and friends in a public place, only to then walk down a sidewalk of cheesy goodness. Once participants completed their journey, the artist humbly offered a ceremonial foot washing in a series of basins filled with warm, sudsy water. This additional element added yet another opportunity for potential embarrassment, one I had not originally anticipated.

Cheese Procession was another test for the participant. A bit more about social dynamics perhaps and how people might interact with a large mass of cheese as both potential participants and general gallerygoers. As an aside, it was also fascinating to see how comfortable many of our non-participanting visitors felt as they talked over the giant path of cheese — almost like 2 mourners talking over the grave of a recently departed friend, or maybe more like hikers conversing from opposite sides of a small, shallow stream.

New Crown: Lou Susi

Made from a myriad of found, textural objects — *New Crown* was my first experiment in using real biological matter in a piece of artwork. Leaves, pinecones, christmas lights, a wreath of twigs, seashells, a large black container and 3 (recently deceased) lobsters worked

inter-akt

An Evening of Multimedia Design

DENNIS LUDVINO

Student-Curated Shows

Massachusetts College of Art and Design

Patricia Doran Gallery

April 15, 2010

In the spring of 2010 I organized *Inter-Akt,* an exhibition of student work from the Dynamic Media Institute. Following in the tradition of annual DMI thesis shows, Inter-Akt featured numerous projects from first year, second year, and graduating students. The intent of the exhibition was to invite the public to peek, if only momentarily, into the strange world that makes up the DMI program. It had the makings of any good art show — there was dance, a micro-video installation, and paper sculptures that lit up when viewers walked by — but it was mostly successful for providing an opportunity for graduating students to celebrate their work one last time.

Despite all the work I had yet to complete in my final semester, I decided to add one final item to my to-do list: curate a student exhibition. This caused an immediate sense of panic. I had never even participated in an exhibition, so how was I qualified to curate one? In classic panic mode, I over-thought every detail and questions began rifling through mind. Who's going to participate? Will anyone show up? What should the show be called? What kind of food will we have? Eventually I let everything go and asked myself the only important question: why bother to curate a show in the first place?

Immediately after that I began thinking of this less as an exhibition that had to be steeped in an overly intellectual design ideology and more as an opportunity for those of us graduating to celebrate our years of hard work. It wouldn't be a mandatory requirement, but the continuation of a tradition of DMI thesis exhibitions. As an added benefit, we would get the chance to document people outside of our current networks engaging with our projects. The show was a chance for us to step back from our work and see it again through the lens of pure observation — to learn what it means to interact.

The evening was a hodgepodge of interactive installations revealing the diversity and range present in the DMI program. Featured work included a film installation, interactive projections with live dance, a collaborative drawing tool, augmented reality, and numerous others. *Heartbeat,* installed by Audrey Fu, captivated the entire room's attention with music, dance, and projections that evolved based on the level of sound. I had the chance to observe a wide range of people use my collaborative drawing project. It was particularly gratifying to see a 10-year-old boy draw an ocean scene complete with pirates and sharks — something that all the classes, planning, and sketching could never account for.

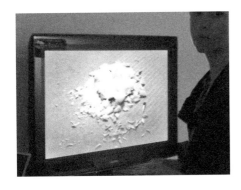

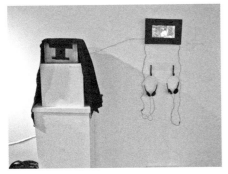

Participating students:
Jason Bailey, Audrey Fu, Dennis Ludvino,
Scott Murray, Kat Take, and David Tamés
Technical support: Lou Susi
Exhibited works from first-year DMI students:
Alexander Wang, Alison Kotin, Andrew Ellis,
Christopher Field, Fan Xiang, Joseph Liberty,
Tania Ostorga and Yaoming Hao.

The "Panorama" Project at **transFORM** Festival in Warsaw

JAN KUBASIEWICZ

Warsaw, September 2009

In the Fall of 2008, I was informally approached by curators from Warsaw, Klara Kopcinski and Jozef Zuk Piwkowski, about a possible participation in the transFORM festival, a series of environmental and exhibition projects associated with the Vistula river. The festival organizers offered a few venues to exhibit art projects and one of them immediately drew my attention — a small geodesic dome that would be erected in a very close proximity to the river to serve as a seasonal exhibition space. After having seen architectural drawings I was immediately convinced that "this was it." It promised a dialog with Buckminster-Fuller space that offered a possibility of a continuous, circular narrative ... and a closeness to the river.

I shared my ideas about the project with Mike Golemewski, Dynamic Media Institute faculty at the time, and soon after we also invited Colin Owens, a student at the time, to form the DMI creative team. By the deadline of the end of 2008, we submitted the official proposal for the "Panorama" project to the Warsaw transFORM festival 2009 and we received the grant.

The "Panorama" project is a kind of map — a recorded journey on the Vistula River in Warsaw, from the Siekierkowski Bridge to the Zeran Bridge and back. Originally, I was hoping that cruising the river between the south and north bridge would reveal the history of Warsaw with its famous "Old Town" in the middle of the footage. However, as Colin Owens described later: "The Vistula in Warsaw is no typical river. Unlike the Thames or the Seine, this river does not pull the city to its banks. There are no major attractions and you see very few people milling about. From a boat you do not see very much of the city. It's almost as if it envelopes you, protecting you from civilization."

In May of 2009, I took an approximately 3-hour cruise on the Vistula river that I documented by a video camera. Sailing down the river I filmed the left bank — Warszawa; sailing up the river the right bank — Praga. While recording views of the riverbanks, the tripod-mounted camera registered other elements too — changing distance to the shore, changing velocity, and rhythmic wave motion and changing light conditions — there were some sun breaks during that mostly cloudy day.

In post-production, the video recording has been translated into a static, continuous image through computer code written specifically for the project by Mike Golembewski. The program scans each video frame and through certain algorithm it compiles an image that is a static representation of the sailing motion. As a result of that transformation the "Panorama" image is a kind of very long "postcard" approximately 15 centimeters high and 25 meters long, printed on Plexiglas panels and mounted in the dome as a full circle. For the exhibition, the Plexiglass panels, each two centimeter deep, were also equipped with an LED lighting strip at the top.

The "Panorama" image, which is somehow reminiscent of a visual sound wave, inspired yet another transformation — image to sound translation. The program, written by Colin Owens, "scans" the "Panorama" and identifies certain visual parameters of the image (such as specific color, shape, etc.). Through a system of equivalencies, specific visual cues trigger various elements of sound

composition. As a result, the image of "Panorama" becomes a map and a musical score of its own soundtrack composed by Colin Owens.

Colin, not having visited Warsaw before, did thorough research on the vocabulary of sound composition associated with Warsaw and the Vistula river. He wrote about it after the project was completed: "The sounds were chosen to symbolize each part of the landscape and section between bridges. Instead of revealing the history of the river, the composition reveals the character of the landscape and the reflective passage of water. In this continuous journey, the music composition mirrors the river. Time reads the panorama continuously like a playhead, from left to right. The river is the composer and the sheet music. Each bridge signals a new song. Each part of the landscape: river, trees, sky and man-made represents a part of the composition."

Dynamic Media Institute team:
Jan Kubasiewicz, Mike Golembewski, Colin Owens

"Code-based Graphics" Exhibition in Cieszyn

JAN KUBASIEWICZ

Cieszyn, June 2010

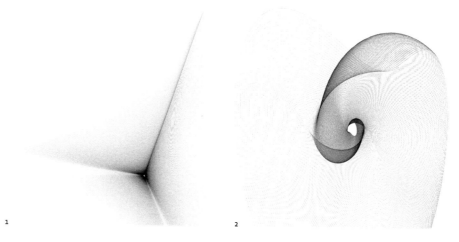

1

2

Cieszyn, on the Poland side, and Tešín on the Czech Republic side are actually two names of the same city, divided by the Olza River and belonging to two different countries, not far from another border with Slovakia ... but in fact there are no borders any more since all three countries belong to the European Union.

The Silesian Castle of Art and Enterprise in Cieszyn is the local government organization situated on the historic Castle Hill. Part of the old castle was renovated and adapted to house the center for design with its conference facilities capable of hosting multiple cultural and educational events, a gallery space, a hotel, a coffee shop, a tea house, and a historic park area.

One of those initiatives conducted by the Silesian Castle of Art and Enterprise since 2005 is the "Educational Meetings" series. It includes public lectures, exhibitions, and workshops that are offered to selective groups of young professionals and design educators coming to Cieszyn for that occasion from Poland, Czech Republic, Slovakia, the UK, Finland, and Germany.

During the last five years, the "Educational Meetings" series included lectures and workshops by prominent European designers: Wolfgang Weingart, Bruno Monguzzi, David Skopec, Remo Caminada, Filip Blazek, Martin Pecina, Gerry Leonidas, Veronika Burian, and Jose Scaglione.

In 2010 for the first time in its history, the "Educational Meetings" curators, Ms. Ewa Satalecka, Professor of Academy of Fine Arts in Katowice, Poland, and Ms. Ewa Golebiowska, Director of the Silesian Castle of Art and Enterprise, invited two designers from the United States to conduct workshops on dynamic media and kinetic typography: Jan Kubasiewicz of the DMI at Massachusetts College of Art and Design in Boston and Dan Boyarski of School of Design at Carnegie Mellon University in Pittsburgh, Pennsylvania. Each of them conducted an intensive five-day workshops with public lecture and exhibition opening scheduled between the workshops, when both professors were present in Cieszyn.

There were two components to the exhibition associated with the workshop by Professors Kubasiewicz and Boyarski, both open to general public. The first was a single-night event—the large-scale projection of student work from Massachusetts College of Art and Design and Carnegie Mellon University. A more than 2-hour movie loop was projected on the walls of the Castle, visible on both sides of the border.

The second component was a three-week exhibition in the Castle of the same dynamic media work displayed on multiple LCD screens, plus the exhibition entitled "The Code-based Graphics" from the DMI in Boston. For that exhibition each image was generated from a digital file as a 35 by 35 cm square, high-resolution, ink-jet print mounted on board. The exhibition included 27 works by the following artists: Jason Bailey, Elaine Froehlich, Jan Kubasiewicz, Dennis Ludvino, Carlos Lunetta, Scott Murray, and Colin Owens. The exhibited work, both dynamic media and code-generated prints, were very well received by the public.

3

4

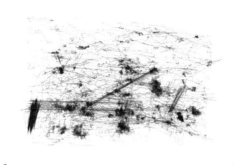

5

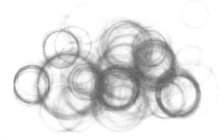

6

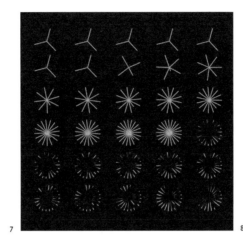

7

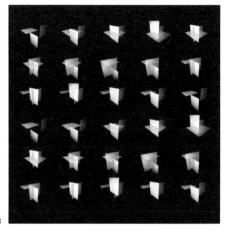

8

1, 2. Carlos Lunetta
3, 4. Jason Bailey
5, 6. Scott Murray
7, 8. Elaine Froehlich
9, 10. Jan Kubasiewicz

9

10

11

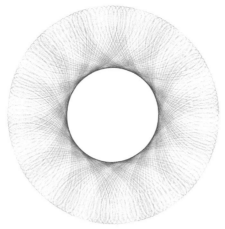

12

13

14

15

11. Jason Bailey & Dennis Ludvino
12, 13. Carlos Lunetta
14, 15.Colin Owens
16, 17. Dennis Ludvino

16

17

student essays

Uninformed Opinions
& Other Observations
on "New Media"
Innovations/Inventors

CHRISTOPHER FIELD

Class of 2011

Throughout the lurid and sundry course of human technological history, mankind has continuously and relentlessly sought ways of improving the human condition. Whether it be figuring out how to fashion a round stone to construct a wheelbarrow to make the carrying of things easier or unlocking the power of the atom to achieve cataclysmic energy sources because we can, the human race does not rest. It hurtles forward at a breakneck pace with little regard for anything but progress, launching rockets at the moon, searching for the next new thing, for transcendence, for efficiency, for transcendence through efficiency, trying to make it easier (and sometimes harder) to be alive on this planet and exist — conscientious objectors, Luddites, and Betamax™ enthusiasts be damned. Does our technology make our lives better or simply more efficient? Does the digitalization of media and the abstraction of the physical realm make it easier to exist as a person in the 21st century?

Many authors, scientists, cultural critics, and computer geek-type people have written extensively about this ongoing quest of salvation through technology. In his 1945 essay "As We May Think," Vannevar Bush, fresh from coordinating The Manhattan Project and apparently ready to turn his attention to something not lighter, but perhaps less heavy, writes of man that "He has built a civilization so complex that he needs to mechanize his records more fully if he is to push his experiment to its logical conclusion and not merely become bogged down part way there by overtaxing his limited memory."

Bush proposes a user-friendly system that will document and present knowledge in a way that will make the information more accessible to the user. He gives this device the shape of a desk and the vaguely futurist moniker "the memex." By cataloguing data "by association, rather than indexing," people would be able to access information as they think, with data being available concurrently with their thoughts. For example, in the midst of, say, an intense thinking session when the user/thinker comes upon a thought or subject worth researching, rather than having to pause to look up the topic in the traditional alphabetical or categorical sense the user would have a sort of thinking buddy alongside him or her — the memex — feeding the user data and associations. Thus, the intense thinking session could continue in an uninterrupted and, theoretically, enhanced way. The device would also allow the user to record these sessions, with the idea being that these associative trails would

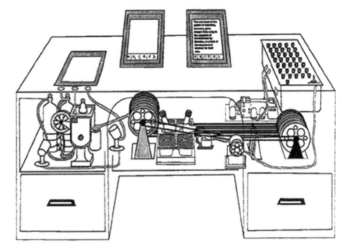

Vannevar Bush, author of "As We May Think," proposes a device called "the memex" to make information more accessible.

become knowledge in and of themselves to be subsequently indexed and associated by other tech-savvy intense thinkers. The process of thinking becomes knowledge.

Obviously, the memex as described by Bush does not yet exist. However, the desktop computer could conceivably function in the same way; certainly the processing power and quantities of data storage that Bush called for can be achieved; today a hard drive with a tera-byte storage capacity can be purchased for $98.95. However, the computer remains more of a data holder/retrieval device than a sort of thinking companion. Perhaps the way we associate things has yet to be understood in a way for a computer to programmatically emulate, or more importantly, associate on its own. Elkhonen Goldberg, in his book *The Executive Brain: Frontal Lobes and the Civilized Mind,* asks whether "human beings recapitulate, consciously or unconsciously, their own internal organization in man-made devices." Computer program-ming is taxonomic and hierarchal because it follows the way we, as people, order and clas-sify things; to diverge from this way of cataloguing would be to, in a sense, diverge from our biology. However, the ability to abstract and associate forms the space between the branches, so to speak, one that we have yet to fill in the computer/database model. So, basically, the memex would likely be totally awesome, but we haven't figured out a way to make its spe-cific kind of awesomeness tangible.

In his 1962 report, "Augmenting Human Intellect," Douglas Engelbart describes the conceptual framework and usability behind what would later be developed into the word processor. In a McInerney-esque second-person narrative, he opines on the user's reaction to such a device, basically the ability to easily edit and maneuver large sections of text: "You are elated by this freedom to juggle the record of your thoughts, and by the way this freedom allows you to work them into shape. You reflected that this flexible cut-and-try process really did appear to match the way you seemed to develop your thoughts."

The word processor is undoubtedly a more efficient tool for the physical act of writing. Even a novice, two-finger-at-a-time typist can produce text at a far faster rate than by writing by hand. And the ability to copy, cut, and paste text renders the editing/revision of a docu-ment as an almost instantaneous action. However, by abstracting the inputted text into a database to be sorted and arranged by the word processor or word processing program, the writer loses a direct physical connection to the work. Consider the novelist Don DeLillo, who continues to use a manual typewriter some thirty years on from the commercial introduction of the word processor. In a 1993 interview, he describes his reason for eschewing the "cut-and-try" wonderland of Engelbert's former imagination: "I don't use a word processor because I like the feeling of touching the paper, of making changes with a pencil or pen, of saving old pages that one can return to in a year or so. I save every note and this, too, is part of the tactile dimension of writing."

Granted, novelists are notoriously habit-intense people who can be change-resistant and who work in a medium that some consider to be dying. However, DeLillo raises an interesting point. Though writing includes the organization of text, it is not the only dimension of the process. At some point the ideas that form the content of the text need to be generated, and the ability to maneuver the text does not specifically engender the creativity of ideas. Most writing is not judged by how quickly it is done or by quantity; it is judged by the content that it contains. The tool of the word processor helps one write more efficiently in a raw-data input sense, but not necessarily better in a content-focused perspective. It ignores the idea of writing as a tactile experience in favor of data input proficiency.

In *The Language of New Media,* Lev Manovich states, "creating works in new media can be understood as either constructing the right interface to a multimedia database or as defining navigation methods through specialized representations." Using this definition, a GPS navigation device can be seen as a new media object. A GPS is essentially an interface, whether it is a touchscreen display or a voice-activated response system, to a multimedia database, which in this case is a series of maps, coordinates, data points, and information. The device is marketed and sold as a tool for people to use to help them find their way, usually while driving. Using a satellite as a beacon to achieve a relative location on a global data grid, the user can plot routes or trips, look up specific destinations, and instantaneously receive directions to those destinations. The arguable intent of the device is to give the viewer a better understanding and knowledge of geography, or at the very least, give the user the fastest route from point A to point B.

When used incorrectly or too dependently, however, the device can function as a sort of confused helper dog, leading the suddenly and somewhat needlessly blind user by an algorithmically programmed leash. Stories of people using their GPS to traverse back-of-the-hand-type routes for possible glimpses of unknown efficiency only to end up on an unnecessary toll road, or the wrong way on a one-way, or worse abound in the public lexicon. Normally navigation-savvy city dwellers can be turned into confused bumpkins when the interface or the database or both fail. However, this hazard occurs when the object is used improperly. As a new media object, the system is constantly being updated and troubleshot; new data is entered and stored in the database as it becomes more accurate and hopefully more useful.

Does the GPS device improve the human condition? When working as a Production Assistant on an independent film project shortly after moving to Los Angeles, I was sent on a run to pick up a piece of lighting equipment. One of the grips programmed the address of the rental house into the device and gave it to me for the trip. At the time, I had very little road/ geographic knowledge of the city and had I not had the device, I might still be lost in the San Fernando Valley or beyond. So, after following the directions of the GPS device, I was able to pick up the equipment and return to the set without incident. However, I didn't learn where I was going or where I had gone; I was, or acted, in a sense, blind; holding on to the leash, hoping the dog would pull me where I needed to be. This new media object but didn't increase my knowledge base or help me think, as, say, the memex theoretically would, but it enhanced my life for a temporary period, and that's something for which I was grateful.

Perhaps that is all we can ask of new media, or of anything: to make each moment more tolerable than the last. Rather than expecting earth-shattering change and transcendence, we should look at ways in which we can improve ourselves and our lives on a micro-scale, moment by moment, billions of ones and zeros at a time.

BIBLIOGRAPHY

Vannevar Bush, "As We May Think" (*The New Media Reader,* Cambridge, 2003), p. 45-47 (originally published in *Atlantic Monthly,* July 1945.)

Douglas Engelbert, "Augmenting Human Intellect" (*The New Media Reader,* The MIT Press, Cambridge, 2003), p. 104 (originally published in Summary Report AFOSR-3223 under Contract AF49(638)-1024, SRI Project 3578 for Air Force Office of Scientific Research, Menlo Park, California: Stanford Research Institute, October 1962.)

Lev Manovich, *The Language of New Media* (The MIT Press, Cambridge, 2001), p. 215

Maria Nadotti, "An Interview with Don DeLillo," (*Salmagundi* 100, Fall, 1993), p. 93

Lawrence Weschler, *Everything That Rises,* (McSweeney's Press, San Francisco, 2003), p. 216.

Telling Stories: Digital Personae and Self-Discovery 1998 – 2000

ALISON KOTIN

Class of 2011

BEGINNING

In 1998, on the precipice of the 2000's dot-com collapse, I was an English major at Brown studying language and gender in contemporary fiction. I struggled to come to terms with my own sexual identity and place within or outside communities defined by sexual orientation, postmodernist theoretical affiliation, and college campus social patterns. At the height of my ambivalence over personal identity and academic affiliation, I became fascinated with the possibilities web design and "hypertext narrative" offered for a reinvention of the self. Close reading of Judith Butler's *Bodies That Matter and Gender Trouble* along with Roland Barthes' *Writing on Language and Pleasure* provided me with a theoretical framework to question the solidity of language and narrative structure, and by inference to consider the conundrum of whether the words we use could in fact shape our perceptions of the world (Butler, 1990).

Coming out as gay in college led me through an extensive personal and academic quest for identity and a stable sense of my place in the world. Shying away from labels and the political weight attached to self-identification with one identity or another, I was drawn to the linguistic ambiguity of postmodernist theorists' and novelists' writing. Cyberpunk stories from Caitlin Sullivan and Kate Bornstein's *Nearly Roadkill* and Grant Morrison's *Invisibles* series to Neal Stephenson's *Snow Crash* and Samuel Delany's 1984 *Stars In My Pocket Like Grains of Sand* together created a picture of an alternate reality populated by nonchalant rebels whose every expression of self or identity was an act of performance. Identifying myself with characters like *Nearly Roadkill's* Winc or *The Invisibles'* Lord Fanny, I aligned my creative practice with people who consciously molded and created futuristic digital identities as artistic and performative works. Although fictional, these characters' experience of fleeing a physical world they found overly restrictive in favor of an unlimited, ever-changing cyber identity offered me a model for melding my own academic and artistic exploration with my evolving sense of self.

EXPERIENCE

As described by John Dewey, "an experience" can be identified as an individual's progression from initial engagement with a series of events through "fulfillment" or closure. When events have run their course, an experience (as opposed to a series of episodes without long-term consequence) is identified as a story arc with beginning, middle episodes, and an endpoint that provides the basis for a retrospective summing-up. "Doing" and "undergoing" are paired in Dewey's model, meaning that a true experience cannot emerge from either passive receptivity or thoughtless action without reflection. Emotion, the "moving and cementing force" of an experience, knits episodes together into a coherent sequence, making sense of conflict, growth, and progression of ideas and relationships (Dewey, 1934). The "aesthetic experience" Dewey describes goes beyond the traditional "doing" and "undergoing" of other experiences to encompass a key element of "making." In creating a new work, an artist participates in his or her own experience as thoughts and concepts are translated through an artistic or performative medium. Ongoing awareness of a potential audience and a desire to facilitate their experience through a work of art sets the act of aesthetic creation apart (Dewey, 1934). A creator who produces an "external embodiment" of his or her own experience enters into a relationship with the audience or receptors of the finished piece, engaging with emotion, conflict, and growth to transmit a story or idea. The experience of the self-aware artist goes beyond the act of creation to encompass a dynamic, shifting relationship with an idealized or imagined other, who will in turn experience the finished artistic work and form his or her own story arc of creation and engagement.

MIDDLE

I began to learn HTML near the end of college, saturated with literary theory and dizzy with excitement over the simultaneously personal and political significance of reinventing my identity to my own specifications. In a writing seminar I learned the Storyspace software, a program created in the 1980s to simplify the process of authoring interactive "hypertext narratives." Rather than the linear structure of a written page (or even the vertical "stacks" of Hypercard), Storyspace is designed to facilitate the creation of densely woven, web-like structures with nodes of content connected by links (Eastgate Systems, 2007). The underlying assumption of the Storyspace interface is that any work authored will reject traditional linearity in favor of data interconnected by relationships too complex to hold simultaneously in mind. This assumption, both liberating and intimidating (examples of similar narratives included canonical works from Jorge Luis Borghes' *Garden of Forking Paths* to Umberto Eco's *The Name of the Rose*) led me to question the essential components of a story, recombining photographs, poetry, maps, and sound files into hybrid works.

Working with Storyspace, a simple interface to HTML coding, I had the experience of finding that the media with which I interacted became a transparent window into a new, non-corporeal space. The branching narrative structures that Storyspace made visible encouraged me to see web-based writing as a space that an imagined body could enter and explore. As I became more adept with HTML and digital storytelling, the web became a space that I imagined could be navigated and constructed as well as interpreted and conceptualized. I created elaborate personal websites, casting myself in the role of a mysterious, ambiguously gendered emcee in ever-evolving galleries of curiosities ranging from the literary to the zoological. The online format allowed me to combine my writing with other kinds of artistic creation, taking me first unconsciously, then with greater intention, down a path of artistic study that eventually led to my current design career.

In experimenting with the creation of new identities and personae, I became conscious for the first time of an audience for whom I could create an experience. I imagined that the invisible audience of fellow web travelers interacting with my digital persona could be vast (although in reality it was likely modest). The unseen presence of visitors and users of my work led me to consider the impact of my words and images on strangers. The performative aspects of my roles took on greater significance, as did the possibility that visitors to my online spaces would not distinguish between my imagined virtual identities and the "real me." In creating an experience for users of my work, I was in some way altering reality, making myself in the eyes of others into many alternate selves. I was engaging in what Dewey terms an "aesthetic experience of making," channeling my own experiential narrative into artistic works that in turn created an experience for their viewers (Dewey, 1934).

My 1999 engagement with dynamic media was relatively unfiltered. I initially learned HTML and Storyspace and designed spaces for my online selves by laboriously typing tags in Simpletext, then uploading images and HTML pages via modem. The online world I inhabited had no guidelines for how to proceed, and conversely, very little support to make the design and updating process user-friendly. This meant that while technically my work was based on hit-or-miss experimentation, I was able to create narrative, image galleries, and virtual spaces without any significant influence from my online hosts. I was empowered by Storyspace and fictional cyberpunk heroes to conceive of the online realm as a world where I could build, dismantle, reconfigure, and discard puzzle-pieces of my creations that ranged from a virtual museum wing, to a labyrinth, to a visual autobiography, to a poetry anthology.

EXPERIENCE AND DYNAMIC MEDIA

A central characteristic of a "dynamic media" experience is the users' ability to engage with media objects that in turn adapt to, change, and interact with their audience over the course of a sustained interaction. The possibility of choice, reconfiguration, customization, and personalization inherent in the dynamic media interface, and the necessary variability of dynamic media objects when in use by multiple individuals, require the user to take an active role in the creation of his or her own experience (Manovich, 2001).

Can the long-term, variable, and customizable interaction between a user and a dynamic media object result in an experience that follows Dewey's required narrative arc of engagement and resolution? When "an experience" is defined as a series of episodes joined by emotion into a narrative arc, the dynamic media objects that seem most likely to provide that experience are those which facilitate a user's own process of creation. By providing an interface to extensive information resources, customizable to individual users' specific interests and preferences, dynamic media can fuse Dewey's concepts of "doing" and "undergoing." The dynamic media user makes meaning from assembled but perhaps disparate informational resources, and simultaneously constructs a digital persona whose desires influence the experience of media interaction. To the extent that the creation of this persona is an intentional and performative act, potential exists for an "aesthetic" experience as defined by Dewey (Dewey, 1934; Manovich, 2001).

Dynamic media tools from HTML editors to social networking sites facilitate both the creation and continual modification of self-image and public personae online. At the same time, customized marketing campaigns are targeted to individuals, rewarding those who portray a coherent consumerist persona with offers and incentives tailored specifically to their preferences (Manovich, 2001). Online communities such as Facebook or Livejournal provide an easily accessible forum for self-expression whose visual qualities (appearance, composition, information hierarchy, etc.) are rigidly controlled by site administrators. These online communities also provide a conduit for personalized advertising to individual users. A webhost for a personal site provides access to a blank canvas for online self-expression without restrictions on content or aesthetic form, but requires a far higher level of technical skill and creative engagement from creators. In this way dynamic media, and specifically online interfaces for the creation of digital personae, encourage users to take on "the responsibility to represent the world and the human condition in it" while limiting to a greater or lesser extent an individual user's ability to aesthetically express an unfiltered point of view (Manovich, 2001).

My entry into online performance and artistic creation was a liberating and empowering experience. In 1999 I felt that my online experimentation with self-identity and persona was part of a larger movement of questioning the unacknowledged power structures of society. On a deeper emotional level, I felt that I had been given the chance to invent myself in the image of who I wished to be, with full acknowledgement that that persona could remain in a state of constant flux.

Through many iterations of personal websites and nonlinear, web-based storytelling I began to see myself as an artist whose goals extended beyond self-discovery to the creation of

WORKS CITED

Butler, Judith. Gender Trouble: *Feminism and the Subversion of Identity.* London: Routledge, 1990.

Dewey, John. *Art As Experience.* London: Penguin Books Ltd., 1934.

Manovich, Lev. *The Language of New Media.* Cambridge, MA: The MIT Press, 2001.

McAdams, DP. *The Stories We Live By: Personal Myths and the Making of the Self.* New York: The Guilford Press, 1997

Morrison, Grant, Chris Weston, and Ivan Reis. *The Invisibles: Kissing Mister Quimper.* New York: DC Comics, 2000.

"Storyspace." *Storyspace.* Eastgate Systems, 2007. Web. 14 Nov 2009.

Sullivan, Caitlin, and Kate Bornstein. *Nearly Roadkill: an Infobahn Erotic Adventure.* London: High Risk Books/ Serpent's Tail, 1996.

new experiences for an anticipated audience. As my awareness of audience (and my technical skills) increased, I also gained self-confidence in the identity of "creator," an appellation flexible enough to contain the many contradictory parts of myself. This mental evolution let me separate myself from my work enough to allow for the "aesthetic experience" of artistic creation Dewey describes: "to build up an experience that is coherent in perception while moving with constant change in its development" (Dewey, 1934). Rather than identifying my cyber-self with fictional characters, I could draw parallels between my real self and the authors whose works I read.

The experience of creating my digital personae, facilitated through HTML and Storyspace, took place over the course of several years. In retrospect, this was a time of rapid personal growth as well as technological evolution, a path of skill development and self-reflection that connects my current design practice and identity to my self of 12 years ago.

EXPERIENCE AND MYTHOLOGY

Considered in hindsight, my first web design projects and creations of alternate digital personae constitute a central experience in the larger narrative of my path to adulthood. From the present day, I am able to look back on the events of 10 – 12 years ago and reconstruct from them a reasonably straightforward narrative that adheres to the storytelling conventions Dewey outlines in describing "an experience." Although these episodes have become an important part of the longer narrative of my own autobiography, it is unlikely that I have been able to reproduce them here with perfect accuracy or clarity. As with the "experience" Dewey describes, my engagement with digital performance and online spaces has gained a symbolic quality to become an "enduring memorial" that provides a point of reference for my memories of that time of my life (Dewey, 1934).

According to historians and anthropologists, storytelling and personal mythmaking stem from human impulses that are as old as the species. Stories are an accessible format to organize important information, they give meaning to otherwise random events by providing the emotional connections that bind episodes together, and they provide us with a pattern by which to make sense of the events of our lives (McAdams, 1997). The "enduring memorials" Dewey describes stand out from less significant happenings, and act in retrospect as signposts to help us find our way back through the stories of our own past history. In the words of philosopher Paul Ricoeur, "time becomes human time to the extent it is organized after the manner of narrative" (McAdams, 1997). From this perspective, a cohesive narrative that makes sense of experiences and shows their place in the protagonist's larger life story may take precedence over accurate recall of details. In other words, we may need to build memories of "experiences" as defined by Dewey to help us come to terms with the events of our lives, which in turn form the "personal mythology" that sums up our conception of ourselves (McAdams, 1997).

Interaction with dynamic media objects has the potential to create the kind of experience Dewey seeks in engagement with other, more traditional artistic creations. In fact, successful dynamic media objects or interfaces encourage engagement over the long term, changing or reacting to input as a user's desires and interests evolve (Manovich, 2001). This interactive ability alone does not guarantee that the experience will become an "enduring memorial" in the memory of a user: Dewey's balance of "doing" and "undergoing" must still be present. In my personal experience, the dynamic media interactions that have taken a significant place in my autobiographical mythos are those that supported my own self-discovery and personal expression. My experience comes from dynamic media objects that helped me to understand and explore something about myself not previously acknowledged or expressed.

The Observer and the Observed

ANDREW ELLIS

Class of 2011

To the perfect spectator, the impassioned observer, it is an immense joy to make his domicile amongst numbers, amidst fluctuation and movement, amidst the fugitive and infinite...to be away from home, and yet to feel at home; to behold the world, to be in the midst of the world and yet remain hidden from the world.

— **Charles Baudelaire**

One of Facebook's intrigues is to awaken a curiosity within the user to communicate with others. However, interaction with the interface falls short of 'an experience' as explained by John Dewey. The navigation through profiles provides the user with superficial histories of a person that never materialize into either a complete story or a conclusive journey. The thrill is in the freedom of movement and gazing passively into another world or another person's life. It ultimately fails as an experience because there is no depth. The end is very much like the beginning and its attraction is the cyclical pattern of observation.

Dewey discusses "an experience" as a unity of a continuous flow of events with pauses but no holes (38). This is an important element of "an experience" as it illustrates the essential movement and rhythm of the one having the experience. The movement is in the expectation and anticipation of finality; that it will conclude. In an experience with new media objects, our interests control our selection of the narrative, for example, clicking on a hyperlink or killing an enemy in a video game. The thought processes of the event or experience happening is inconclusive until there is an adaptation between the person in the experience and the entity or object. "Interaction of the two constitutes the total experience that is had, and the close which completes it is the institution of a felt harmony"(Dewey 45). This structure creates a consonance and balance resulting in an experience.

Facebook does not have a sense of a before or after. There is no other narrative except for the inconclusive one the observer has in his own response to the people he sees. These responses are infinitely incomplete but endlessly intriguing. The lure of amassing more and more connections and inviting them into one's space is addictive. It easily becomes an equal exchange of glances in one's metaphorical and virtual living room (that has been tidied up for guests). One can roam though Facebook's countless profiles and peer briefly into another person's life without real interaction.

The shift from small traditional communities to modern society signifies a change in an individual's behavior. There is a compensation for the loss of identity in a small community by placing oneself impersonally in the multitudes (Manovich 269). On Facebook, users choose to show themselves to an audience. The addiction of the social profile is that one becomes uninhibited and moves through a virtual space by inserting themselves into the group; free of the constraints of day to day life.

Charles Baudelaire's term *flâneur* describes one who walks to experience the urban landscape. The *flâneur* operated as a non-identity; an artist of roaming the streets and enjoying the masses. He had the privilege of always being home without ever being home. His mobility through the public sphere was accessible to him as an anonymous observer. "The movements of the Baudelairean *flâneur* produced a "mobilized gaze," a moving nowhere, neither here nor elsewhere" (Friedberg 30). The modern day *flâneur*, or virtual navigator, has this same kind of motivation, to wander aimlessly through the pages of the Internet while remaining hidden. He is now at home with his ability to mirror his feelings or follow his aesthetic observations, not by only observing but with an endless supply of data and links to click on.

> "Like Baudelaire's *flâneur*; the virtual *flâneur* is happiest on the move, clicking from one object to another; traversing room after room, level after level, data volume after data volume." (Manovich 274)

The virtual gaze of the *flâneur* or observer is adrift through the infinite pages of information.

He does not know exactly where he will begin or end up and the mouse and hyperlink become his compass. A user of Facebook has this quality. His access to data is unlimited and he can drift through the personal information of everyone he passes by. However, he can go no deeper than the qualities another user chooses to show.

Facebook provides a user with personalized advertisements for an individual. It is an organized patchwork designed to blend profiles in an equal space. Everything is on the same plane of existence with no center. A user cannot advance in the sense that a new level is achieved as in a video game and one cannot stand out anymore than the next. It does however have two simultaneous curiosities from differing aspects of the Internet. Facebook has become a tool that breaks down all hierarchies but it is also a communal space where everyone spies on one another. As Lev Manovich states:

"A western artist sees the Internet as a perfect tool to break down hierarchies and bring art to the people. In contrast, as a post-communist subject, I cannot but see the Internet as a communal apartment of the Stalin era: no privacy, everybody spies on everybody else, always present are lines for common areas such as the toilet or the kitchen." (Foreword X)

The *flâneur*, in a sense, is looking through apartments and has not, and never will, find the one to stop and stay at. His walk is not planned but it is purely horizontal. There is no need to deepen the experience of going beneath the surface. A Facebook user has the right to invade and knock down doors into others' lives. Strangely, these doors are left open. They no longer need to be knocked down. The objective is to always let everyone else know exactly where and what one is doing with minute-by-minute updates of that activity. Someone observing these updates can participate by writing comments onto another users profile. They assume a position, not of authority but as a participant while creating their own narrative about someone else's life. However inaccurate it might be, is irrelevant because Facebook is the user's own space to envisage the story.

Perhaps the only realization with Facebook is that one has stopped living their life in order to see how others are living theirs. Dewey suggests that life is a collection of histories and plots; that "an experience" has no holes or mechanical stops. Facebook has only holes and does not provide the opportunity to enter into the real stories of one other. We see only a series of two-dimensional characters with likes, dislikes, and habits. The continuous observation is frustrating. It becomes an unresolved exploration and comparison of character traits without ever choosing a definitive path to follow.

BIBLIOGRAPHY

Manovich, Lev. *The Language of New Media* Cambridge, Massachusetts: The MIT Press, 2001.

Dewey, John. *Art As Experience.* New York, New York: Penguin Group, 1934.

Friedberg, Anne. *Window Shopping: Cinema and the Postmodern.* Berkeley, California: University of California Press, 1993

Baudeliare, Charles. *Selected Writings on Art and Artists.* New York, New York: Penguin Books, 1972.

Why Dynamic Media?

JASON BAILEY

Class of 2010

I am fighting an urge to start this paper with some witty quote from a media theorist describing the importance of dynamic media.

Sometimes, after weeks of heavy reading and research, I find myself adopting a set of beliefs that are entirely detached from my own personal experiences and my own body of work. We can't escape our own history and we cannot adopt the history of another. I think this is particularly important to recognize in developing a thesis.

So in answering the question "Why Dynamic Media" I felt like I needed to start by going back in time to reassess how I got here before projecting into the future.

I grew up in a house divided by two religions, Mormonism and Objectivism. I wanted to make sure that it was fair to define both of these childhood influences as a religion, so I looked for a reliable and scholarly definition to judge them by. Wikipedia tells us that "religion is a system of human thought which usually includes a set of narratives, symbols, beliefs, and practices that give meaning to the practitioner's experiences of life through reference to a higher power, deity or deities, or ultimate truth."

Sure enough, my house had two such systems of human thought, each complete with narratives, symbols, beliefs, practices, deities, and higher powers. My parents were both raised Mormon, met at church, and were married as teenagers. Shortly after getting married, my dad left the Mormon church and started his own religion. Like Martin Luther and other great prophets before him, my father would base his religion on his own misgivings about the system from which he came.

From what I can tell, my dad's religion was based heavily on physics and engineering interspersed with liberal doses of reading paperback editions of Ayn Rand's Objectivist philosophy (every faith needs its bible). His doctrine could be summarized as "all things are knowable through logic; emotions and faith are dangerous; everyone earns their position in life through effort, so if you are not successful, it's because you are not working hard enough."

Best I can remember of the Mormon church, it was based on a guy named Joseph Smith who found a golden book buried in his backyard in upstate New York. Angels came down and told him to put the book inside a hat and read the book using special glasses. Although the main body of the church stopped the practice of polygamy many years ago, it is still the first thing that comes to most people's mind when they think "Mormons." I only have only one mom. (I swear I will get to the dynamic media part soon; this is just the background.)

Shortly after the great Bailey schism, my brothers and I were born. There are three of us; I am the middle child. My older brother has always been mechanically inclined and had early propensities for math, so he spent a lot of time in the Church of Dad learning how to solder wire, build circuit boards, and write computer programs back when almost nobody had a computer. I remember thinking that when I got to be my brother's age, I too would work on such high-tech projects, but alas it was not to be (more on this later). To this day if I need something fixed around the house or help fixing my computer I call my dad or brothers (yep, the younger one has the gifts as well).

The benefit of having two household religions is that if I was not good at one, I could certainly try my hand at the other. Every Sunday for 14 years I spent five to six hours at church. The first hour or so would be spent in a large chapel where high-ranking Mormons would discuss the business of the day, we would all then sing for a bit, and then everyone would be invited to come up and talk about God. This last part was kind of like a sacred open-mike session.

Turns out I had even less of an attention span for testimony and gospel than I did for math and engineering. I found that making drawings on the pamphlets they gave us on the way into the chapel was much more entertaining. I would bring my drawings to the class portion of Sunday service which would last another four hours. While grown men and women would take turns reading stories about man-eating whales and pillars of salt, and then quizzing us on the long list of things that Mormons should never do, I would continue to work on my drawings. And so it went for 14 years, five to six hours of drawing, every Sunday.

I spent time drawing pictures outside of church, as well. I found it to be a great way to pass the time. Math, engineering, and religion were unforgiving practices, each demanding singular correct answers at which I was rarely able to arrive at. If I did a math problem wrong, I was dumb; if I did not live righteously, I would go to hell. Drawing was something I could do that brought great joy to me and it felt like it was outside the realm of the harsh judgments that accompanied these other activities.

So in unfairly limiting my parents' to only a description of their religious beliefs, I have left out many of the positives attributes I owe to them; foremost, their passion for life, poetry, philosophy, and art. They recognized and fostered my interests in art from the beginning. I remember when I was younger and money was tight, my dad would say there was always going to be money for me to take classes. It was a priority for both of them to encourage this in me. So I did take many classes from cartooning to painting to sculpture and even a class in Logo, the early computer drawing language designed by Seymour Papert.

I remember I took this Logo class at night at my middle school sometime in the late '80s. Despite having a house full of electronics and computers and living with engineers, I had spent little to no time using computers for anything other than playing video games. Logo class was fun. I remember the big black floppy disks and the tiny computer monitors. We spent weeks learning how to make the turtle (the name given to the triangle in the center of the screen) move around the screen to create complex visual patterns. These results reminded me of drawings I made on my Spiralgraph toy. Although this was probably the beginning of my career as a "Dynamic Media" designer, I can hardly say it was love at first sight. It was fun, but I did not seriously return to the computer as an art-making tool for many, many years. Sure, I tried Mac Paint at a friend's house (we always had PCs), and later in high school I used an early version of Photoshop on a friend's computer to spherize my face, but that's about all.

I continued my passion for drawing and painting into college where I studied fine arts. I really enjoyed the opportunity to develop my skills in painting, drawing, printmaking, and sculpture. Although my parents were still very supportive of my interests, the specter of a career loomed somewhere on the horizon. What is Jason going to do when he graduates? My dad made it a weekly exercise to look at the help-wanted ads in the Sunday paper and he would tell me about all the jobs that were out there for graphic designers and web designers. It was the middle of the Internet boom and it must have seemed like a way he could coach his artist son towards a feasible career. After some heavy suggesting, I signed up to take a class in HTML programming. Much like my experience with Logo over a decade earlier, I thought it was fun, but was not enamored by any measure. I made a website that I could use to post scanned-in pictures of my artwork and the artwork of my friends, and that was that.

So if it hasn't become obvious, I had little to no interest in computers. Computers were used to do math really fast. I hated math at any speed. I failed most of my math classes, and it almost kept me from getting into college. I thought that most computer-generated art looked like shit by fine arts' standards. The work I had seen was mostly ugly pixilated images of wizards and fairies. I was disinterested in technology in general. I did not have an e-mail address or a cell phone until 2001, years after all my friends and even my grandparents had started using them. So how did I end up just eight years later working towards my master's degree at DMI?

I needed a job. I had graduated with a fine arts degree and worked in various retail stores serving coffee and carrying boxes, and had no clue what I could do with my degree. I knew I needed to make enough money to pay for a place to live and to pay for food, but I had never sold a painting and never met an artist in the flesh who could live off of their artwork.

A friend of the family was starting up a small medical device engineering company and asked me to come in and have lunch. He was impressed with my communication skills and he knew that I got along really well with engineers because I had been living with them my whole life. He offered me a job as a technical reporter that would require me to make and edit digital video updates of engineering progress within the company. In retrospect, this seems more absurd now than it did then. I was neither technical nor a reporter, and I had never worked with digital video, or any video for that matter. So I took the job.

I wanted to do right by the company for taking a chance on me so I studied digital media 'round the clock. First I learned Adobe Premiere video editing software by reading manuals and website forums. Digital video was a lot more complicated back then and I made a lot of mistakes but eventually got the hang of it. After that I went back to my notes from my undergraduate HTML class and learned web programming. I convinced the company to buy me a copy of Photoshop and learned the basics during a couple of weekends. Although I was learning under tremendous pressure, I enjoyed discovering all the things that computers could do.

Post-9/11 I was laid off and found myself needing a job again, only this time I had a mortgage. I didn't actually know what it meant to be a designer, but I had enjoyed my job while it lasted. I decided that designers were artists who knew how to use software and understood typography. So while unemployed I got pirated copies of as much design software as I could, including Flash, Illustrator, and Quark, which were all new to me. I continued to work like crazy, teaching myself actionscript programming, motion graphics, basic print principles, and the bezier tool. I had no real model of what I should know so I was driven by anxiety to learn as much as I could lest anyone find out I was a fraud.

I eventually landed another job as a new media designer at a scientific and engineering firm that did accident-reconstruction work. I was still not entirely clear on what a new media designer was supposed to know, so out of fear that they would discover that I was faking it, I just agreed to do whatever they asked. This usually meant more late nights of self-training after work. They eventually asked me if I could make 3D animations of accidents based on the evidence and theories they had accumulated. I thought this must be something new media designers know how to do, so I tried to teach myself Maya 3D. No amount of dedication was going to help me learn that software package; it was easily more complicated than the sum of all the other software tools and programming languages I have taught myself to date. I spent two semesters commuting to RISD after work to take night classes in Maya while working on 3D projects during the day at work.

At some point in the five-year span I was at that job, I realized that never sleeping had paid off, and I was getting pretty good at what I was doing. I still didn't think I was a graphic designer (this mysterious profession I had been trying to understand since the days when my dad was circling graphics jobs for me in Sunday paper). More likely, I was some kind of new media guy with a focus on technical illustration/information visualization and some digital video editing chops. I had acquired a ton of new technical skills in a short amount of time but never had a chance to apply them to anything other than work assignments. What would the old-media me have done with these new media tools? There was a huge and rapid disconnect between the work I was doing professionally and the work I had done in undergrad, and I wanted an opportunity to bridge that gap. I saw the Dynamic Media Institute program as an opportunity to explore that disconnect, and use my new media skills to create the kind of work I am most passionate about, *my* work.

Why Dynamic Media?

DENNIS LUDVINO

Class of 2010

Most of my early 20s took place in dimly lit bars talking about writing. There were three of us in the writing group. We'd show up late in the evening and pass around our new pages. Each of us took turns buying rounds until we ran out of money. I'd play sad Tom Waits songs on the jukebox and smoke a dozen cigarettes — I always wanted to be a writer.

Pat worked at a thrift shop downtown where he discovered many of his inspirational characters. The man who shot-up in the dressing room, the daily visit by the old woman frantically babbling about dolls with no faces, and the dreaded obese metermaid he referred to as Maid Kong. One of his favorite characters was the guy with a teardrop tattoo under his eye — Pat was convinced this symbol commemorated the icing of a rival gang member.

Kate was a poet. She beautifully strung together complicated relationships between people, god, and a sad city. She tenderly cared for each syllable. She could spend hours pondering a single word and each line read like a new language.

After a number of drinks one evening, someone mentioned the idea of self-publishing our work in a collected volume. A collected volume? Why hadn't we thought of this staggering idea before? Writers publish. We were writers, so why shouldn't we publish? By the end of the night the single volume ballooned into a semi-annual literary magazine.

To gauge interest we put out a call for submissions. We ran around the city posting flyers, sent emails, and told our idea to anyone who would listen. Soon a flood of submissions started pouring in and eight months later we published our first issue. Over the next three years, we put out five additional print issues and numerous online editions containing the work of hundreds of local and regional writers.

I became the designer by default because I had a computer. In the first issue alone I broke every rule of good typography. I stretched typefaces and kerned lowercase letters — a good thing actually. I didn't know what leading was or that line measurements existed. Although it was a monster — I created it and I loved it. After that moment I wanted to be a designer.

One fall afternoon during my first year of college I decided to go out for a run. I remember it so well because running wasn't part of my normal routine. In fact, I probably hadn't run outside since they forced us to do the mile in gym class. I hated the mile, but on this day running seemed to be the right thing to do.

I slogged through the first mile saying to myself, "Damn idiot. What the hell was I thinking going for a run? I'm not a runner." But after another ten minutes or so my legs went numb and the miles started breezing by. The rhythm of my feet hitting the pavement entranced me and I was so deeply focused on the present moment that all other thoughts faded.

I didn't know how far I had run, but it must have been somewhere around eight miles. After catching my breath I started stretching and decided that I could run farther — fifteen or twenty miles, maybe even a marathon.

A year later I was amidst a crowd of people waiting for the gun to sound. The sun hadn't come up yet and the air had a cold bite. There were clouds of foggy breath pouring from our mouths. The leaves were turning a deep orange and my feet crunched loudly on those that had already fallen. I tried to focus on my breathing. I ran in place to stay warm. Bang.

A year after college I ended up in a design department at a publishing company. I shared an office with my manager, Matt. We spent most of our days complaining about the head of our department who we referred to as The Sheriff. She would stealthily poke her head into our office, look around, and leave without a word. In order to remind us of who was responsible for our income, she personally delivered our checks on payday. Some days The Sheriff would stalk down to our area and do laps around the department monitoring what we were working on.

We designed newsletters, books, and bland conference materials. Each week our group drudged through hundreds of projects. Twelve-page newsletters were our bread and butter. I had it down so that I could do an entire layout in about an hour and spend the rest of my afternoon devising elaborate schemes to mess with Matt.

One day I took a screen shot of his desktop and set it as his background. He thought his computer had frozen and unleashed streams of curse words. After he rebooted and his problem persisted, he began throwing anything he could get his hands on.

As files and books soared through the air, I realized that designing for a publishing company stuck in the age of the newsletter wasn't for me. With all of the interesting electronic-based publishing services already available, two-color print newsletters seemed like a terminal media format — a sick dog desperately waiting to be taken out behind the barn.

After I pretended to fix Matt's computer issue (I really just removed the photo from his background), he was convinced I was a genius. He asked me what I did and I just strung together a bunch of technical words. Something like, "Oh I just reset your RAM cache and double booted your hard drives." He shook his head in amazement.

That year I received the highest pay raise the company hands out, but it didn't matter. My mind had already been made up — I was quitting. It was time to go back to school.

Why Dynamic Media?

SCOTT MURRAY

Class of 2010

I remember facing a monumental ethical dilemma at age five. I wanted to attend a summer class on LOGO, the early computer graphics programming language, but it was for ages six and up only. At my parents' suggestion, I lied about my age to the friendly staff at the Junior Museum in Palo Alto. This deceit caused me a great deal of distress, but perhaps the anxiety motivated me to learn as much as possible before being found out and removed from the classroom.

So began one of my first computer programs, although I didn't realize it was programming at the time. All I knew was that I could tell the computer what to do, and it would do it. Also, it would do it correctly, every time. If a mistake was made, it was my own, and I could correct it. My simple circles, triangles, and squares weren't beautiful, but they existed because I had learned to speak the computer's language. There was something attractive and intriguing about that. Maybe part of it was feeling like an insider, knowing a secret language that only I, the computer, and my classmates spoke. Part of it, too, was satisfaction from solving the puzzle — figuring out how to write a program that would execute my vision. But it was also about simply providing instructions, and watching the machine carry them out. The more complex the instructions, the more complex the final image. Using recursion (a word I didn't know at the time), I could even repeat parts of the instructions, building up patterns with spirograph-like complexity.

That same year, my family bought its first computer. Our Macintosh 512KE was very friendly to regular users, but not to aspiring programmers. My neighbor's Commodore 64 was the opposite — just switch it on, and begin entering BASIC commands at the prompt. I remember returning home, excited to try BASIC on my own computer, only to be sorely disappointed by the Mac's non-responsive and indifferent blinking question mark.

Two years later, I discovered HyperCard, an application that made it easy to create buttons, text fields, and pictures, and write code so that behaviors could be attached to those elements. I played around with HyperCard for hours. I made "Cipher," a program that could encrypt or decrypt text using a basic substitution cipher. (This was perhaps my first project to incorporate audio. When encryption was complete, which could take minutes, a prerecorded sample would play: "Sa-sa-sa-sa-cipheeeerrr...") In sixth grade, I made an interactive, choose-your-own-adventure style adaptation of Lois Duncan's book *Killing Mr. Griffin*, in lieu of a traditional, linear, written book report. Ms. Dolan didn't totally "get it," but she understood enough to know that this was a new form of creative expression. (Many creative liberties were taken, as the hidden cave and massively explosive finale don't actually occur in the book.) Even though it didn't resonate with her, she encouraged me to pursue similar projects, and she still gave me an A.

Much later, after earning my college degree in Environmental Theory, I worked in web design and development for six years. The web was not my passion, although some of the same techno-visual-geekery was involved, but it paid the bills, and since my first job after school was web-related, that's all anyone would hire me to do. I had made my first website in 1995, back in the days of NCSA Mosaic and the world wide web. I continued to make sites for myself and others during college, always advocating for clear organization and navigation, although I didn't consider myself an information architect or usability expert at the time. So when graduation day came, although "saving the world" was my passion, no one offered to pay me to do that. So I made websites instead.

Six years and three jobs later, I had learned a great deal about web standards and usability research, but I left work every day with a headache, bored in a position that was about 10 percent creativity and 90 percent bureaucratic struggle. So I applied to graduate programs in design. My focus was on graphic design programs (I had a fantasy of being a type designer, which has since passed), but I knew that technological expertise was my primary asset. I couldn't speak the language of letterpress, but hoped that Illustrator and InDesign would get me in the door.

Thankfully, I was encouraged to look into MassArt by a friend of a friend at RISD. The language on the Dynamic Media Institute website made perfect sense to me, contrasting with other art schools' self-important copy. So I applied, and at the interview I had the most interesting, comfortable conversation with George, Jan, and Joe. Right away, I could see that we were speaking the same language. But I still thought that DMI was a graphic design program, and I didn't understand the distinction between that and dynamic media design until halfway through my first semester. Time-based, interactive, non-static, databased, generative, systems, all these terms floated through my brain until I suddenly got it: This isn't about posters, books, business cards, or even websites! This is about designing the point of interface between people and their machines. The machine needs a system of rules to follow, and the people need a pleasant, satisfying psychological experience. I gradually began to see how all my past experiences had prepared me for this new direction.

During that first semester, though, I grew restless creating only conceptual designs — I had come to school to get creative and make new things, and I wanted them to actually work! Keynote was not bad for faking it, but my ears perked up when Jan mentioned Processing, an open-source, free application then emerging from MIT. I downloaded it, bought a book (the best $40 I've ever spent), and got cracking.

What a surprise: This was the modern-day LOGO! The triangular turtle had been superseded by far more advanced visual capabilities, but it was essentially the same idea: a programming language for creating visual art, digitally. Processing, unlike LOGO, could also be programmed to accept user input and react in kind. So the process of using LOGO may have been dynamic, but its output was not. But Processing could "output" both static images and dynamic experiences. The system designer interacts with Processing by writing code, while the participant (e.g. end-user, client, visitor) interacts with the finished, compiled work. I enjoy both roles, but the latter is much more limited. As the designer, I get to not only engage in the creative puzzle of translating a concept into computer-speak, I also get to define the terms of the puzzle itself. I decide which elements and influences will be included in the system, and then I enjoy watching others interact with that system and figure it out.

Processing's version 1.0 was finalized only last year. LOGO was first created 43 years earlier, in 1967, although I didn't discover it at the Junior Museum until 1986. Today, my career path in generative art and design seems appropriate and obvious. Having felt uncertain about my life path for many years, I am incredibly grateful for this newfound clarity.

thesis abstracts

thesis abstracts
2010

Jae Chul Bae

Using Dynamic Media to Create and Augment the Experience of Narrative

"Narrative serves to inform, educate, and entertain. It provides meaning, background, and context, and it incites interest in what is next." [1]

Narrative is everywhere. We talk, read, watch and imagine stories each and every day. One day, as I entered the lobby of MassArt, I saw several yellow colored post-it notes hanging from the windows. As I looked closer, I realized that each of these notes had a personal story written on them. It was touching to see such a massive collection of personal stories in a single place, and even more engaging to read them. Whether the story is an important secret, or someone's mundane life story, each one tells us how we all live.

Today's media offers new and numerous ways for communicating such narratives. I am interested in the use of dynamic media and interfaces for the purpose of transforming an audience's experience of a story, an experience that augments its author's original intent.

This thesis explores that interest through the means of three case studies where "narrative" is used as a device to create interactive and engaging experiences for its participants. My case studies take the following forms:

1. As an interactive learning tool to explore the narratives in two films.
2. As a documentary through experiments using a physical interface.
3. As a poetic experience through personal expression

The results of these three case studies show how a participant can gain an entirely new, and perhaps unique individual perspective far beyond what I originally conceived for them through experience and interaction.

[1] Mark Stephen Meadow
Pause & Effect: the Art of Interactive Narrative (pg.36)

Jason Bailey

Drawing in Code: Pixels, Pencils, Process

Throughout my life I have changed the tools I use for drawing, starting at a young age with markers, crayons, and pencil, eventually learning to paint with oils and watercolors. Painting is a process which I still consider drawing, only with a brush. In my undergraduate studies I learned printmaking. And then it happened...about eight years ago I started using the computer as a drawing tool. Now I use it almost exclusively. It wasn't until the last year of my graduate program that I asked myself, "Why?"

I decided computers are good at illustrating space and time, facilitating interaction by managing input and output, storing and presenting data, running and storing complex algorithms, and distributing information to a large audience at little or no cost.

When I thought about this list relative to the history of drawing, I made a dramatic realization that these issues have long been of primary interest to artists using analog drawing tools. The computer was not just a fancy calculator for crunching numbers, but also a natural extension of the history of drawing.

Audrey Yen-Ning Fu

Perceiving Interaction: Between Light and Illusory Perception of Space

This thesis focuses on light as a tool to re-create the perception of space.

I created a series of experimental case studies to observe the interaction between light, physical filters, and space. The experimentation was based on a three-layer projection system with light sources, physical filters, and spatial surfaces including balloons, paper waves, and foam core triangular structures, among others. For each layer of the system, I used a manifold projection of image, motion, and sound content, as well as various materials, textures, and shapes, to test multiple variables and possibilities.

For my main thesis projects, human motion is the key variable of the experiment. Humans interact with projected light manipulating our illusory perception of space and creating a sort of performance.

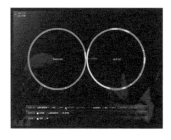  

Dennis Ludvino

PostScript: Writing in the Late Age of Print

My thesis is an exploration in nontraditional digital writing and mark-making environments. Looking at physical surfaces such as bathroom walls and their virtual counterparts like instant messaging and text messaging, my work straddles two worlds: the virtual and the physical. By conducting a series of experiments studying written forms, multimedia environments, and collaborative writing surfaces, I will expand our definition of the writing space and uncover new methods of communicating.

In *Orality and Literacy*, a seminal text exploring the differences of oral and literate cultures, Walter Ong writes, "[Writing] initiated what print and computers only continue, the reduction of dynamic sound to quiescent space, the separation of the word from the living present, where alone spoken words can exist." When first written in 1982, on the cusp of the personal computer and many years before the Internet became a cultural staple, this statement was inarguable. Almost 30 years later, however, we have witnessed an emergence of digital technologies that has reshaped our writing environments. The inactive print surface, a characteristic of writing for thousands of years, has suddenly come to life on the computer screen.

The story of writing is marked by many transformations: From cave wall to clay tablets or pen to linotype. None, however, have had such a dramatic impact as the refashioning of communication through digital writing environments. The digital surface provides an immediate connection to networks of other users. Chat rooms, texting, and instant messaging have blurred the lines between written and oral communication. Web sites like Twitter and Facebook keep us connected with millions of other users at all times. Experimental installations like

Mark Hansen and Ben Rubin's *Listening Post* illustrate the potential for an emergence of algorithmic or collective writing. While these examples highlight the vast potential for virtual writing, the rigid structure and constraints of the digital world can significantly decrease the writer's role and control over the writing surface.

The difference is striking when comparing a digital space such as Twitter to an analog space like the writing found on bathroom walls. While the sheer volume and constant presence of users on Twitter is impressive, when we look at the expressive qualities of bathroom wall writing the division is clear. The digital environment is a controlled and structured space. For the most part programmers decide how and where the writing appears. Writers on a bathroom wall, however, are free to make marks: they can draw, write, cross out and edit other writing, use scale, and change colors. There are no rules and no restrictions.

There is no question that the printed word is in a period of decline. Reading and writing on digital devices becomes more commonplace each day and the craft of penmanship is moving into the realm of the letterpress and other obsolete printing technologies. My thesis is a series of experiments studying the various qualities of the virtual word and its future within our culture. I am also interested in examining the space on which we write and its influence on the writing experience. Many scholars and authors will argue that handwriting is dead, however, my thesis illustrates that there is life after print — and it is fascinating.

Scott Murray

Dynamic Systems of Engagement

We now have the tools and technology to create just about any interactive system imaginable. But how can we ensure that our designs are engaging? *Dynamic Systems of Engagement* illuminates how dynamic, interactive, computationally based systems offer new opportunities for engagement with participants and third-party observers. Through numerous case studies, I explore three core themes: data visualization, dynamic systems, and engagement.

I consider data visualization broadly as a process of interpreting and expressing data of all kinds, not just numbers and text. I explore principles of systems design to illustrate how dynamic systems differ from works of static, pre-composed media, like painting, film, and television. Finally, I connect these themes to methods of interaction and engagement.

My past projects illustrate a range of design possibilities grounded in these ideas. From *Gesture Project,* which responds to physical gestures with patterns of rotating, color-changing discs, to the *ASCII Photo Booth*, a high-tech, low-fi interpretation of a traditional photo booth, these interactive studies illuminate non-traditional uses of data visualization, systems design, and interface concepts.

Although the concepts are valuable, more important is how real people respond to the designs. That is, what is the experience like? I conduct extensive user research with each project, the findings of which are used to refine the designs and inform future projects.

I adopt a framework of challenge and reward for sustaining engagement, which I then employ for two primary thesis projects, *Practice* and *Cheeky*. Although each project has its own distinct content and approach, both elicit engagement by employing visual mirroring, establishing tension and ambiguity, and finally resolving that ambiguity, providing closure to the experience.

Both projects address the questions: how can we challenge someone while keeping them engaged, and how can we incentivize participants to overcome the discomfort of the challenge?

Practice is a new interactive video piece that employs metaphors of stillness (physical and psychological) and reflection (visual and personal). While most interactive video installations reward motion, *Practice* rewards stillness, and in so doing tests participants' tolerance for physical discomfort and emotional ambiguity.

Practice employs computer vision methods of face detection and face tracking to identify participants' presence and level of engagement, so that mere visual stillness, without engaged users, elicits no reward. Visual and aural cues incentivize users to overcome the discomfort of the challenge, by establishing anticipation of the rewards to come. And through it all, the system collects data on participation, which is analyzed and visualized.

Cheeky, a second interactive video piece, is introduced and shown to apply the same principles of experience design to engaging and humorous ends.

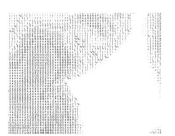

thesis abstracts 2009

Mahesh Gudapakkam

A Learner-Centered Approach to Teaching Programming

Learning to program is difficult, and of particular challenge to an audience of artists, designers, and educators. These learners may have a limited background in mathematics and programming logic and also vastly different motivations from a student majoring in computer science. Yet the pedagogy we use to teach them programming is the same as for everyone else.

While traditional programming languages and environments are powerful in their capabilities to address a variety of programming needs, they are often ill-suited to teaching programming to beginners because of their complexity and rigidity of syntax.

So what is the best approach to teaching programming to such an audience? What combination of pedagogy and tools best responds to their particular needs?

This thesis proposes a learner-centered approach to teaching programming — an approach that combines the use of visual representations for explaining abstract programming elements, and a thoughtfully designed interactive learning environment for working with these elements and verifying a student's understanding.

By tying the abstract program logic to its more tangible visual output within the setting of an interactive visual learning environment, the learner-centered approach tries to make the process of learning how to program more engaging, intuitive, concrete, and ideally, more successful.

Dan Johnston

Creative Communities: Designing to Invite Participation in the Creative Process

How do you define creativity? Creativity is not defined by the best looking poster or slickest packaging. Creativity is the capacity to identify a problem and then move quickly to deliver a solution. I believe many people have this creative capacity within them, but not everyone is in a place to express it. My role as designer is to create conditions that invite people to explore this creative aspect of themselves.

Over the course of my studies I have designed and built several systems that attempt to bring people together to create and share something. Each case study explores new ways that groups or communities can bridge gaps between digital and physical experiences. I am particularly interested in systems that allow a community of users to make their own creative decisions and draw their own conclusions.

Why? In order to move forward as a society, we must forever become more specialized. Take a job title from another generation, Computer Programmer. This industry has seen such explosive growth that the original title no longer conveys enough meaning to include it in a job posting. Programmer has evolved into modern job titles like: Lead UX Consultant, SEO Specialist, and iPhone Application Developer.

As we become more specialized, we need to find new ways of connecting. The human being is a social animal after all. I am interested in using dynamic media to create a shared experience for our specialized world. The kind of experiences a physical therapist and an iPhone application developer can share are the same things our grandparents did: a song, a conversation, a meal.

Mingxi Li

Sensing At The Periphery: Human Experience In the Age of Dynamic Media

My thesis research focuses on exploring the possibilities of dynamic media design to facilitate a more human and natural way to access information and to communicate.

In my thesis, I researched the historical, theoretical, and psychological aspects of communication and technology and developed six case studies to determine how dynamic media design can incorporate the human senses in modern communication.

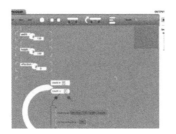

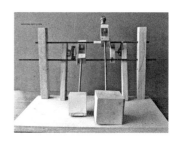

Brian Moore

Interactive Narrative Journalism

Narrative journalism goes beyond mere reporting to tell stories and uncover purpose. It creatively presents in-depth news through the use of literary writing techniques and personal style while maintaining a goal of objectivity. In the digital space, interactive narrative journalism is the combination of artful storytelling and dynamic reporting through the use of multiple media types — text, photos, videos, audio clips, animation, interactive elements, and motion graphics. Interactive narratives have the potential to enrich a story, extend the user experience, and create custom relationships through the use of non-linearity, variability, personalization, participation, and other elements unique new media.

As journalism and storytelling evolve in the digital space, these numerous media options and enhanced capabilities present opportunities as well as challenges to telling stories and creating experiences. My thesis investigates how the combination of personal narrative and the narrative created by the collection of data, experienced in a dynamic online environment, can enhance the overall experience for an audience and tell a more complete story.

Colin Owens

Synaesthesia as a Model for Dynamic Media

Throughout human evolution our senses have evolved, and the tools we have invented have augmented our sensory exchanges with our surroundings. The extent to which we engage with the tools we invent, and how we use our senses to engage with them, has had a tremendous impact on our understanding of how these tools function.

This research examines the interrelationship between our senses as a means of more intuitive control of the computer-based tools we create and use. It challenges historical assumptions about audiovisual synaesthetic relationships, and proposes the adoption of perceptual relationships based on natural metaphor for building more useful experiences with these tools.

I have focused on the computer audio mixer interface in my research as an example of the type of human-computer interface that can be created by using natural motion and spatial cues, as well as other cues found in both the auditory and visual realm.

Agata Stadnik

Body in Motion: A Powerful Tool for Creative Learning and Social Interaction

In my thesis, I explore the power of body language and nonverbal communication with respect to social learning and interaction. I create physical and online spaces with the tools that encourage people to interact freely and spontaneously. An essential part of my thesis is to provide ways and means for people to be active, move their bodies to be more natural, and possibly, to have fun.

According to educational researchers, we now live in a "Creative Society" in which people must develop and enhance their abilities to interact meaningfully with one another. People also need to acquire skills for using the tools offered by new media. Online exchange and collaboration allow people with multicultural backgrounds to exchange ideas and negotiate meanings. The social games I designed, such as *Tell Me Your Secret* and *Jumping Squares,* foster physical playfulness and social interaction, whereas *Cinemagic* and *Motionary* encourage creative learning and online collaboration. The learning experiences I design involve activities, concepts, playfulness, improvisation, and cultural exchange.

In my work, I facilitate opportunities for people to negotiate spaces and meanings while finding new forms of expression. I design experiences where people can switch roles and either they remain in the audience as a passive observer or join the game as both active participant and teacher. Giving people the opportunity to challenge each other by negotiating the rules, meanings, and the interpretation of certain words results in dynamic communication.

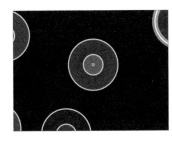

thesis abstracts 2008

Juan F. Burgos-Chaves

**Mapping Science:
Overlapping Science and Design**

Mapping Science documents the different steps in the elaboration of prototypes of interactive visualization tools for scientific data manipulation. The thesis focuses on the interaction between scientists and their data, and in the application of design principles to achieve better results when scientists organize, structure, input, store, and visualize scientific data.

Mapping Science relies on a Ph.D. thesis on bat behavior to assess its needs and to study scientific thinking processes that are later compared to those used by visual thinkers. The goal is to demonstrate the importance of visual thinking processes in the creation of hypotheses and the exploration of data.

Erich Doubek

The Enhanced Object

The functional analog objects of our lives — the clock, coffee maker, telephone, and countless other devices — have seen the benefits of infusing technology into their daily functions. This has allowed us to create an interactive life where we coexist with intelligent objects.

My thesis investigates how we interact with common objects, which are enhanced, augmented, or distorted by an interactive visual and audio experience. This added interactive element changes the user's relationship with the object, expanding the user's established definition and associations.

With the object as the interface, the user's interaction can enable the object itself to tell its own story, its very form and language of interaction enhancing the richness of the experience.

Mary Kathryn Murray

**Interactive Environments:
Bridging the Digital and Physical**

My thesis project, *Falling Up*, is motivated by my fascination with the difference between reality and how we perceive reality, how we make sense of that perception, and finally how we represent that meaning.

The statement above is reflected in my thesis project in two ways:

One: Regarding how we make sense of reality and how we represent it, digital media interests me because it's able to re-create in the material world the actions of our minds in a way that previous media could not. Digital media, because of its interactive and time-based nature, makes it possible for people to move both forward and backward in representations of time — something we do all the time in our thoughts. A major goal of my thesis project is to take this element of the internal thinking process — our ability to mentally move through time — and to make it as external and physical as possible.

Two: A secondary goal of my thesis project is concerned with exploring the difference between reality and our perception of reality. Our eyes and ears are only capable of perceiving information within a certain range. With my thesis project I was interested in creating a playful interaction that made it clear how technology can expand and change our perception.

With both goals, my desired outcome and my methodology remained the same. I wanted to create an interactive environment that people found easy and engaging to use.

In developing this environment I researched two fields with a history of creating interactive spaces: art installations and science exhibits.

From examining those fields and pursuing my own work, five strategies emerged that became important to me in developing my own exhibit: Body as Interface; Mirroring; Multi-user Interactions; Immersive Environments; Playful Interactions.

thesis
abstracts
2007

Carolin Horn

Natural Metaphors for Information Visualization

My thesis research investigates how one can use metaphors of natural form and behavior for information to support a better understanding of data systems.

In everyday life we receive information mediated by behavior patterns and forms of appearance. For instance, if someone is crying, we can infer that the person is sad or may be happy. We can interpret this kind of information and set it in context because of our previous experiences. This is part of our human perception and supports a better understanding of situations and information.

Users are confronted by constantly growing and changing amounts of data. There is a need for new visualizations that support understanding of information and its dynamic nature.

I use natural metaphors to represent information. This includes the structure, navigation, interactivity, visualization, and presentation of content. Visual and behavioral metaphors breathe life into information, creating rich, memorable experiences for users.

Juan Carlos Morales

A Sense of Place

My thesis is about creating a sense of place through photography and sound.

In a larger context, it also focuses on how visual language and sound combine in a new media context to make this sense of place experiential and memorable. In the process, it looks at how photographers, filmmakers, composers, and new media designers can and do encode this sense of place into their work.

In the process, this thesis examines form, visual language, and the expansion of communication vocabularies into sound and motion to explore these concepts.

Katie Westgate

Perceiving the Present: Stimulating Awareness of Present Time and Space through Physical Interactivity with Sound and Light

My thesis explores how perception of present time and space is stimulated. Distractions from the here and now abound. By truly being present, one benefits from moments of centered focus. This stillness of mind creates an important and meaningful connection to the self. Inspiring this connection through engagement with interactive systems is the goal of my thesis projects.

My interactive media installations follow models of meditation and yoga—methods to achieve lightness of mind through concentration on ambient information or by holding unfamiliar body postures.

In my projects, bodily engagement with sound and light increase the awareness of a space. They offer a new experience, turning the mind upside down and allowing the unfamiliar and unexpected to engage the user in the present moment.

 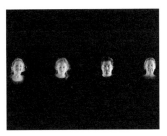 

Ting Zhi

Dynamic Illusion: Designing Unpredictable Interactive Experiences

thesis abstracts 2006

Lauren Bessen

Visualizing Visuality: Interactive Tools for Visualization

Elizabeth Lawrence

Ancient Divination Parallels New Media: Cartomancy in an Interactive Context

My thesis investigates the vocabulary and role of dynamic illusion in the interactive environment. I am particularly interested in utilizing visual illusion to create an immersive, exploratory, unpredictable, poetic, and meaningful experience that activates both physical and mental participation by an audience.

Visual illusion is an indispensable communication approach that has been broadly exploited in traditional art and design for centuries. It surprises viewers, leads them to stop, stare, explore, rethink, and re-evaluate beliefs by engaging their mind.

However, traditional media, largely a broadcast paradigm, limits the potential for illusion. New media, due to its dynamic and interactive natures, brings infinite possibilities to employ illusion as a compelling communication strategy. By incorporating visual illusion in the digital environment, a designer can arouse audience's curiosity, inspire their imagination, evoke their emotion, guide their thinking, enhance their experience, and reinforce their memory by encouraging multisensory engagement.

My thesis examines the potential of illusion in new media through extensive research and two major projects: *Live Painting: Bamboo Garden* and *On Your Way — Blowing Away the Myth of Illusion*. In *Live Painting: Bamboo Garden*, I explore interactive behavior as a metaphor for the way we look at things and challenge traditional art forms by creating immersive three-dimensional illusive experience. In my *On Your Way — Blowing Away the Myth of Illusion* case study, I create a poetic interactive environment that allows an audience to break illusion and discover truth by literally blowing away metaphorical obstacles.

To become literate and articulate in the domain of images, to be competent in understanding the nature and structure of visual messages, is to be keenly aware of one's vision. It also means mastering a common set of terms attached to what one sees and creates. Attaining this comprehensive understanding of visual form is the task of a design student.

Drawing on analog pedagogical precedents, this thesis sets out to examine the ways in which dynamic media can be used as a unique aid to vision, a means to impart greater insight into the designer's vocabulary. Through two interactive tools, *RandStudio* and *LetterForm*, my thesis investigates how using motion and the principles of interactivity to visualize information can complement traditional approaches to teaching visual literacy.

RandStudio is a system designed to help students analyze the work of master designer Paul Rand. By letting users manipulate practically all of the visual elements in a classic Rand poster, the project guides them to discover the formal mechanics behind Rand's refined simplicity. *LetterForm* is an interactive tool that illustrates typographic terminology and allows students to explore the elemental formal properties of the letterform. Both case studies help students to become more aware of the communicative potential of formal decisions — of the dynamic correlation between form and communication — by providing the opportunity to drive dynamic transformation of form on screen.

For centuries, the tarot has been an interactive narrative system employing such new media principles as nonlinearity, randomness, modularity, and algorithm. As a visual system employing symbolic "open imagery," cartomancy facilitates cognitive processes such as analogical thinking, pattern recognition, and communication with the unconscious — processes which serve to foster creativity, intuition, and psychic integration in the participant. The exploration of creating personal meaning through interactivity was explored through the development of a contemporary tarot featuring original photography.

Kate Nazemi

Through Hand, Through Mind: Multi-Sensory Approaches to Form, Interaction and Language Through Objects and Dynamic Media

In order for design to communicate, it must relate content through the senses. By interacting with design — being able to handle, hear, see, and change it — we arrive at our own understanding of it. In this way design leads to a form of knowledge that is affective, immediate, and visceral.

The focus of this thesis is on developing communication through the hand, the senses, and through the mind, simultaneously through sight, sound, touch, and motion. This is made possible through the unique qualities found in objects and dynamic media.

An object's ability to communicate openly through synthesized communication channels is explored through structured interactive environments where physical responses are explored. The case studies put forth in this thesis explore this through the investigation of the concepts of form, interaction, and language.

Karolina Novitska

forWordPlay: Experiential Learning of a Foreign Language via Interactive Play

My thesis research investigates how play can influence learning a foreign language and how the interactive medium can serve as a bridge between the actions of learning and playing.

As children we learn our first language through a very natural, playful, and exploratory process in which all our surroundings serve as stimuli for this process. However, as adults, we typically learn a foreign language in a much more systematic and reflective manner, applying our existing life experiences to contextualize the new language.

While the latter method can be valuable at advanced levels of language development, when we are ready to build and reflect upon our basic understanding of a foreign language, the difficult task of learning the primary building blocks of a new language can be more rewarding from a child's approach — learning through experimentation and play.

Playful, exploratory learning requires us to become active participants in the process rather than to passively receive information. Participatory learning can manifest itself in new media. Due to its modular, responsive and non-linear nature, new media allows content and curricula to be combined, remixed, and customized in the most effective manner for each individual student. New media also allows infinite possibilities to surprise, engage minds, challenge perceptions, transcend time and geographic location, and to create a personal connection by appealing to our specific interests. I believe new media has a remarkable advantage over the analog world to provide an effective setting for these playful, exploratory learning experiences.

As a case study for my research, I have developed a range of prototypical modules for an interactive language learning system. My objective is to foster continuous exploration and stimulate participatory learning, while attempting to replicate the subconscious and relatively effortless learning we experience as children acquiring *our first language*.

Meifen Tsai

Intimacy in Digital Communication

Leaving my home, my country, a comfortable womb, I start a new communication journey. I'm the person who loves to express myself well. I love to build up relationships with people by talking to them. Having intimate relationships with good friends makes me feel comfortable and happy. As a foreign student in United States, communicating in my second language and keeping in touch with friends in Taiwan brought challenges to me in building up and maintaining relationships. For keeping in touch with friends in Taiwan, I used instant messenger intensively. However, the more I rely on it, the more I feel insecure. This communication technology brings little warmth. In my thesis, I investigate the need for intimacy in digital communication and the role of media in human intimacy.

about dynamic media institute

what we do

The Dynamic Media Institute at Massachusetts College of Art and Design offers a creative and intellectually stimulating environment wherein graduate students focus on the role and possible new uses of dynamic media in communication design. Each student's unique vision and passion for design develops into an original body of ideas and fresh practice.

OVERVIEW

The Dynamic Media Institute is a 60-credit MFA graduate program in communication design. DMI offers students three tracks to accommodate various individual schedules and allow working professionals to participate in the program either full-time in four semesters or part-time in five or six semesters. The only difference between tracks is the distribution of elective credits. DMI also offers a one-year fellowship "non-matriculating track" to which candidates are accepted based on specific project proposals.

CURRICULUM

First Year (or completion of 30 credits)

The first year of study is devoted to developing the intellectual foundation and creative processes for dynamic media design. Students gain expertise in interface and experience design through individual or team projects and through research in design history and theory, structured within required design studio and seminar courses. It may take a student a minimum 2 (full-time) or maximum 4 semesters (part-time) to reach the 30-credit benchmark, which, together with the approved preliminary thesis proposal is a prerequisite to proceed with MFA thesis development.

Second (or third) Year / MFA thesis

All students in their second (or third year) of study in the DMI MFA program are required to develop a substantive thesis that identifies, researches, and solves a communication problem using dynamic media. The majority of work toward the MFA thesis is structured within thesis project courses by individual agreement between the student and faculty advisor, who guides the program of study, and provides ongoing feedback and evaluation. In addition to major project work, students develop a comprehensive written thesis document within thesis seminar courses. The final thesis document becomes a part of the graduate design archives.

POST-BACCALAUREATE PROGRAM

DMI proudly offers a one-year Post-baccalaureate Program in Communication Design with a focus on dynamic media. The program gives professionals from outside the design field an intensive educational experience that will prepare them for new opportunities, including possible application to graduate schools or continuation in the DMI. Focusing on fundamental design skills, theory, and history, the Post-baccalaureate curriculum provides students with a core understanding of the principles of dynamic media, preparing them for the next step in their education.

CURRICULUM

The post-baccalaureate is a one-year, 24-credit, immersive educational program. After successful completion, students will graduate with the "Dynamic Media Institute Post-baccalaureate Program Certificate." Those who choose to apply and are accepted to continue graduate study at DMI will be allowed to transfer up to 6 credits.

The post-baccalaureate program is designed specifically to prepare students for the DMI MFA program and is not recommended for those who are primarily interested in traditional print design. Students work with a faculty advisor to develop an appropriate curriculum that may include undergraduate classes like Information Architecture I and II, and graduate classes such as Elements of Media.

who we are

DMI's faculty includes tenured professors from the Massachusetts College of Art and Design, as well as visiting lecturers and critics who represent a diverse group of designers, theorists, technology specialists, and media historians. They are demanding and determined that you grow intellectually as well as professionally.

FACULTY

Jan Kubasiewicz	*Professor of Communication Design, Massachusetts College of Art and Design, Coordinator of the Program*
Gunta Kaza	*Professor of Communication Design, Massachusetts College of Art and Design*
Brian Lucid	*Associate Professor of Communication Design, Massachusetts College of Art and Design*
Joe Quackenbush	*Associate Professor of Communication Design, Massachusetts College of Art and Design*
Toby Bottorf	*Visiting Faculty, Principal, Digital Design, Continuum*
Mike Golembewski	*Visiting Faculty, Ph.D. Candidate, Horizon Doctoral Training Centre, The University of Nottingham*
Evan Karatzas	*Visiting Faculty, Founder, Proximity Lab*
Dennis Ludvino	*Visiting Faculty*
Colin Owens	*Visiting Faculty, Founder and Managing Partner, Shapemix Music*
Scott Murray	*Visiting Faculty, Principal, Aligned Left*
Heather Shaw	*Visiting Faculty, Assistant Professor, Curry College*
Ronald Bruce Smith	*Visiting Faculty, Professor of Music, Northeastern University*

VISITING LECTURERS, CRITICS AND ADVISORS

Joseph Auner	*Chair, Professor of Music, Tufts University*
George Creamer	*Dean of Graduate Education, Massachusetts College of Art and Design*
Hugh Dubberly	*Principal, Dubberly Design Office*
Amber Frid-Jimenez	*Associate Professor, Kunsthøgskolen, Bergen, National Academy of the Arts, Norway*
Christopher Graefe	*Founder, Bluewhale Studios*
Al Gowan	*Professor Emeritus, Massachusetts College of Art and Design*
Margaret Hickey	*Professor of Architectural Design, Massachusetts College of Art and Design*
Hubert Hohn	*Director of Computer Arts Center, Massachusetts College of Art and Design*
Hiroshi Ishii	*Muriel R. Cooper Professor of Media Arts and Sciences, Massachusetts Institute of Technology*
Peter Kirn	*Composer/Musician, Editor of the blog Create Digital Music*
Christina Lanzl	*Project Manager, Urban Arts Institute, Massachusetts College of Art and Design*
Krzysztof Lenk	*Professor Emeritus, Rhode Island School of Design*
Margaret Livingston	*Professor of Neurobiology, Harvard University*
John Maeda	*Director, Physical Language Workshop, Massachusetts Institute of Technology*
Dana Moser	*Professor of Media and Performing Arts, Massachusetts College of Art and Design*
Chris Pullman	*WGBH, Vice President of Design*
Elizabeth Resnick	*Professor of Communication Design, Massachusetts College of Art and Design*
Mitchel Resnick	*LEGO Papert Professor of Learning Research, Massachusetts Institute of Technology*
David Small	*Small Design Firm, Founder*
Sherry Turckle	*Abby Rockefeller Mauzé Professor of the Social Studies of Science and Technology, MIT*
Mara Wagner	*Director of Admissions, Boston Graduate School of Psychoanalysis*
Carrie Wiley	*Senior User Experience Designer at Microsoft, Founder, Sixth Sense Studio*
Frank R. Wilson	*Peter F. Ostwald Health Program for Performing Artists, University of California School of Medicine*
Krzysztof Wodiczko	*Professor of Visual Arts, Interrogative Design Group, Massachusetts Institute of Technology*
Fred Wolflink	*Associate Director of Computer Arts Center, Massachusetts College of Art and Design*

where we are

DMI is housed in the Tower Building of the MassArt campus and includes multi-function studio, lecture, and presentation spaces. Students enjoy access to an array of technology including servers, touchscreens, high-definition projectors, professional video cameras, synthesizers, wide format ink jet printers and plotters, high-resolution digital SLRs, and a greenscreen studio.

MASSACHUSETTS COLLEGE OF ART AND DESIGN

MassArt's seven-building campus complex on Huntington Avenue accommodates specialized studio programs in all areas of the fine arts and design. MassArt students use state-of-the-art facilities to explore the traditional materials, as well as computers, video, film, photography, performance and installation. The campus features two professional galleries, several galleries programmed by student organizations or departments, including the Patricia Doran Graduate Gallery, and the Morton R. Godine Library with online access.

CITY OF BOSTON

Situated in Boston, one of the world's centers for learning and research, DMI has a unique position to draw on various local resources. MassArt has numerous formal and informal connections with the Boston's leading educational institutions, such as the HYPERLINK "http://www.colleges-fenway.org/," Colleges of the Fenway Consortium, MIT, Harvard and Tufts, offering our students limited course selection for cross registration or access to consultants and adjunct thesis advisors.

HOW TO APPLY

DMI enrolls approximately 8 to 10 students in the program annually. The number is limited because our philosophy values small group interaction. Applicants to the program are expected to have an undergraduate degree and at least two years of professional experience related to design practice. Applicants are strongly encouraged to visit the college, tour the facilities, and interview informally with the DMI faculty prior to formal application.

APPLICATION PROCESS

Admission to the DMI is extremely competitive. To apply to the program, candidates must submit: An application form and the graduate application fee (you may apply online, or download application forms); Official transcript(s) showing the awarding of your degree(s); A professional portfolio in digital format on Mac or PC compatible CD or DVD or online; A Statement of Purpose to indicate the reasons for selecting the program, the direction of future work, the support and facilities sought in a graduate program, and those questions that may be addressed in studio and academic pursuits; Current resume outlining professional experience; Letters of recommendation from three individuals who can comment on your qualifications for advanced study.

ENGLISH PROFICIENCY

Graduate study demands competency in English writing, reading, and conversation at an advanced level. Applicants whose first language is not English must present TOEFL scores of 223 (computer test); 563 (paper test); or 85 total with minimum scores of 21 reading, 19 listening, 23 speaking, and 22 writing (internet-based test). For applicants taking the IELTS test, a score of 6.5 is required.

APPLICATION DEADLINE

The deadline for application is January 15. Late applications will be accepted through March 1. Selected candidates are invited to the college for interviews with faculty and advanced graduate students. Applicants can expect to be notified in early April.

ASSISTANTSHIPS

The college awards three different types of assistantships to graduate students: technical, administrative, and teaching. All assistantships are assigned as either quarter, half, or full assistantships; the award amount is based on the number of hours worked per week. All assistantships are determined by student need and ability, departmental needs, and budgetary allotments. Although most graduate students receive at least one assistantship for which they are qualified, there is no guarantee that a student will be awarded an assistantship.

course descriptions

REQUIRED COURSES

DSGN 601 Design Studio I (6cr.)

Advanced program of study and research in communication design focuses on fundamental principles of visual communication in the context of interactive media.

DSGN 611 Design Seminar I (3cr.)

Students examine socioeconomic and technological context of design disciplines. Students write a comprehensive paper that analyzes history of design concepts and movements and their impact on current design practice.

DSGN 602 Design Studio II (6cr.)

Advanced program of study and research in communication design focuses on complex information structures for various contexts and audiences. Subjects of study emphasize interactive media in the context of information design.

DSGN 612 Design Seminar II (3cr.)

The course wherein students examine, explore, and debate current issues of communication design and design education. The seminar content may include lectures, studio projects, readings, and discussions with emphasis upon the intellectual context of design. The requirements of the course include a comprehensive paper and a preliminary thesis proposal presented to review board for approval.

DSGN 697 Review Board (0cr.)

Public presentation of graduate credit work by each student to a panel of reviewers comprising MassArt faculty, guest critics, and moderated by the coordinator of the program.

DSGN 603 Thesis Project I / DSGN 604 Thesis Project II (6cr. each)

The thesis project de 503 / de 504 courses provide a supportive context for the development of the project component of the thesis. The class, limited to 5 students, is a forum to articulate and debate the issues associated with individual thesis projects. The work in class is structured by a specific agreement between the student and faculty advisor, who guides the program of study, and provides ongoing feedback and evaluation. The student selects a particular course/faculty upon approval of the preliminary thesis proposals. The faculty advisors may further define their own specific criteria, process, and schedule of thesis development.

DSGN 613 Thesis Seminar I / DSGN 614 Thesis Seminar II (3cr. each)

The Thesis Seminar courses provide a supportive context for the development of the document component of the thesis. The class is a forum for students to articulate, debate, and record the results of their research and design process and provide critical discussion of historical and contemporary context of their work. The final thesis document becomes a part of the graduate design archives.

NOTE: Thesis Project and Thesis Seminar are concurrent courses — they can only be taken simultaneously. Prerequisites: completion of 30 credits and approval of "Preliminary Thesis Proposal."

DSGN 698 Thesis Defense (0cr.)

Public presentation of thesis project and document evaluated by a panel of reviewers comprising MassArt faculty, guest critics, and moderated by the coordinator of the program.

GRADUATE ELECTIVES

DSGN 631 Elements of Media (3cr.)

This course is focused on developing a better understanding of the complexities of the re-synthesis of visual, oral, aural, and temporal information as they exist in time-based and interactive media. Through lecture and in-class demonstration students will learn the technological processes necessary to begin temporal explorations in sound and image.

DSGN 633 Design as Experience (3cr.)

A multidimensional and multisensory research-based course, focused on creative processes, that integrates form and content generated within and outside of the class experience. Students will re-examine and explore various temporal, spatial, visual, and verbal aspects of communication process. Work will consists of both static and dynamic media presentations and individual and group projects.

DSGN 635 Design for Motion and Sound (3cr.)

Exploration of motion literacy — the act of understanding of how the "language" of moving image and sound can be used to communicate effectively. The course will focus on cinematic vocabulary in the context of time-media by creating linear and nonlinear narrative structures.

DSGN 637 / DSGN 638 Interactive Media Project I and II (3cr. each)

The goal of this class is to explore various dimensions and possibilities of dynamic digital media in the context of user experience and human-computer interaction. Students will research and develop a project, which involves advanced programming for interactive media and various aspects of sound, sensors, and robotics.

DSGN 639 Thesis Exploration (3cr.)

This course goal is to allow students entering into, or currently engaged in, thesis research to develop a more focused vision of their thesis topic, a better understanding of the contextual landscape of their study, and an awareness of the relevant technologies that apply to their area of investigation.

DSGN 699 Independent Study in Design (3cr.)

Independent Study in Design offers students the opportunity to pursue a specific studio or seminar project by working with a faculty member on an independent basis. Students must provide a description of the project and schedule of at least six meetings with the faculty during the semester. The project must be approved by the faculty advisor and program coordinator. Students may take only one 3-credit directed study per semester.

DSGN 660 Design Symposium (6cr.)

Design Symposium is an extended (6-credits), graduate-level studio elective focused on exploring unconventional approaches and possible new uses of dynamic media in communication design. Working with multiple resident and visiting faculty students will research and develop experimental models of multisensory experience, communication, and interaction within three-dimensional environment.

DSGN 636 Sound Design for Dynamic Media

This is a course that examines the use of sound in communication design and dynamic media. Through lecture, demonstration, and in-depth exploration students will learn the fundamentals of sound design and musical structure in temporal and spatial dimensions.

DSGN 641 Interactive Prototyping for Dynamic Media

This course will introduce Processing as an accessible programming environment for quickly prototyping interactive ideas. Students will develop original interface concepts and execute them in code with a different project each week. Each student will complete the course with six working applications, including one self-directed project of their choosing.

FREE ELECTIVES

NOTE: Students choose free electives from the offerings of various MassArt departments as well as Fenway Consortium offerings, for instance:

CDGD 311 Information Architecture I

Introductory course to basic concepts, methods, and procedures of information organization focused on managing information complexity. The course addresses the issues of information structures developed for various contexts and audiences. Subjects of study include printed and interactive media, and both static and dynamic approaches to information design.

CDGD 321 Information Architecture II

Advanced course in information architecture focusing on the organization, navigation, design, and management of complex interactive systems. The course content represents professional methods in solving design problems of interface for dynamic media.

CDGD 364 Dynamic Typography

In dynamic (pertaining to, or caused by motion) typography, students explore visual narratives in reference to time-based media. The course emphasizes conceptual, visual, and technical aspects of typography in motion.

HART 386 Communication Design History

Communication Design History, spans the Industrial Revolution to the present, with selected references to pre-industrial developments. The course investigates diverse languages and technologies of visual communication to help students understand their own role as producers and/or consumers of communication design.

MPSM 375 Electronic Projects for Artists

The purpose of this studio course is to provide skills and information that will be useful for artists who use electronic devices in their artwork.

MPSM 311 Electronic Projects for Artists II

This course introduces students to computer interfaces for connecting interactive sculpture, performance, and installation with software. Course content includes micro-controllers, electrical sensors, custom-made circuits, and programming.

full-time
4-semester track

15cr. per semester

FALL
DSGN601 Design Studio I (6cr.)*
DSGN611 Design Seminar I (3cr.)*
DSGN631 Elements of Media (3cr.)
DSGN633 Design as Experience I (3cr.)
DSGN697 Review Board (0cr.)*

SPRING
DSGN602 Design Studio II (6cr.)*
DSGN612 Design Seminar II (3cr.)*
DSGN660 Design Symposium (6cr.)
DSGN697 Review Board (0cr.)*

FALL
DSGN603 Thesis Project I (6cr.)*
DSGN613 Thesis Seminar I (3cr.)*
DSGN660 Design Symposium (6cr.)
DSGN697 Review Board (0cr.)*

SPRING
DSGN604 Thesis Project II (6cr.)*
DSGN614 Thesis Seminar II (3cr.)*
DSGN6xx graduate elective (3cr.)
DSGN600 Directed Study (3cr.)
DSGN690 Thesis Defense (0cr.)*

* Required courses

part-time
5-semester track

12cr. per semester

FALL
DSGN601 Design Studio I (6cr.)*
DSGN611 Design Seminar I (3cr.)*
DSGN6xx graduate elective (3cr.)
DSGN697 Review Board (0cr.)*

SPRING
DSGN602 Design Studio II (6cr.)*
DSGN612 Design Seminar II (3cr.)*
DSGN6xx graduate elective (3cr.)
DSGN697 Review Board (0cr.)*

FALL
DSGN660 Design Symposium (6cr.)
DSGN6xx graduate elective (3cr.)
DSGN6xx graduate elective (3cr.)
DSGN697 Review Board (0cr.)*

SPRING
DSGN603 Thesis Project I (6cr.)*
DSGN613 Thesis Seminar I (3cr.)*
DSGN600 Directed Study (3cr.)
DSGN697 Review Board (0cr.)*

FALL
DSGN604 Thesis Project II (6cr.)*
DSGN614 Thesis Seminar II (3cr.)*
DSGN600 Directed Study (3cr.)
DSGN698 Thesis Defense (0cr.)*

part-time
6-semester track

9 – 12cr. per semester

FALL
DSGN601 Design Studio I (6cr.)*
DSGN611 Design Seminar I (3cr.)*
DSGN697 Review Board (0cr.)*

SPRING
DSGN602 Design Studio II (6cr.)*
DSGN612 Design Seminar II (3cr.)*
DSGN697 Review Board (0cr.)*

FALL
DSGN660 Design Symposium (6cr.)
DSGN600 Directed Study (3cr.)
DSGN697 Review Board (0cr.)*

SPRING
DSGN660 Design Symposium (6cr.)
DSGN600 Directed Study (3cr.)
DSGN6xx graduate elective (3cr.)
DSGN697 Review Board (0cr.)*

FALL
DSGN603 Thesis Project I (6cr.)*
DSGN613 Thesis Seminar I (3cr.)*
DSGN600 Directed Study (3cr.)
DSGN697 Review Board (0cr.)*

SPRING
DSGN604 Thesis Project II (6cr.)*
DSGN614 Thesis Seminar II (3cr.)*
DSGN698 Thesis Defense (0cr.)*

DMI participants since 2000

Dirk Albrecht	DMI Fellow 2002	
Carlos Avila	Class of 2004	
Jae Chul Bae	Class of 2010	
Claudia Baeza	Class of 2005	
Jason Bailey	Class of 2010	
Lauren Bessen	Class of 2006	
Julio Blanco	Class of 2003	
Kate Brigham	Class of 2002	
Juan F. Burgos-Chaves	Class of 2008	
Chris Burns	Class of 2001	
Alex Candelas,	Class of 2002	
Coleen Crawford	Class of 2003	
Erich Doubek	Class of 2008	
Lynn Faitelson	Class of 2005	
Audrey Yen-Ning Fu	Class of 2010	
Geraldine Garrido	Class of 2003	
Julia Griffey	Class of 2005	
Mahesh Gudapakkam	Class of 2009	
Carolin Horn	Class of 2007	
Dong-Keun Jang	Class of 2001	
Sue-Ellen Johnson	Class of 2004	
Dan Johnston	Class of 2009	
Evan Karatzas	Class of 2005	
Dusan Koljensic	Class of 2005	
Elizabeth Lawrence	Class of 2006	
Jun Li	Class of 2000	
Mingxi Li	Class of 2009	
Dennis Ludvino	Class of 2010	
Carlos Lunetta	Class of 2005	
Kelly McMurray	Class of 2002	
Isabel Meirelles	Class of 2003	
Gauri Misra	Class of 2001	
Leila Mitchell	Class of 2003	
Sam Montague	Class of 2003	
Brian Moore	Class of 2009	
Juan Morales	Class of 2007	
Keiko Mori	Class of 2005	
Mary Kathryn Murray	Class of 2008	
Scott Murray	Class of 2010	
Kate Nazemi	Class of 2006	
Karolina Novitska	Class of 2006	
Colin Owens	Class of 2009	
Elif Ozudogru	Class of 2004	
Christine Pillsbury	Class of 2005	
Harun Razith	Class of 2005	
Judith Richland	Class of 2003	
Heather Shaw	Class of 2003	
Stephen Spiridakis	Class of 2005	
Agata Stadnik	Class of 2009	
Chris St.Cyr	Class of 2000	
Fenya Su	Class of 2003	
Meifen Tsai	Class of 2006	
Katie Westgate	Class of 2007	
Mike Wiggins	Class of 2003	
Ting Zhi	Class of 2007	

Class of 2000	Jun Li
	Chris St.Cyr
Class of 2001	Chris Burns
	Dong-Keun Jang
	Gauri Misra
Class of 2002	Dirk Albrecht
	Kate Brigham
	Alex Candelas,
	Kelly McMurray
Class of 2003	Julio Blanco
	Coleen Crawford
	Geraldine Garrido
	Isabel Meirelles
	Leila Mitchell
	Sam Montague
	Judith Richland
	Heather Shaw
	Fenya Su
	Mike Wiggins
Class of 2004	Carlos Avila
	Sue-Ellen Johnson
	Elif Ozudogru
Class of 2005	Claudia Baeza
	Lynn Faitelson
	Julia Griffey
	Evan Karatzas
	Dusan Koljensic
	Carlos Lunetta
	Keiko Mori
	Christine Pillsbury
	Harun Razith
	Stephen Spiridakis
Class of 2006	Lauren Bessen
	Elizabeth Lawrence
	Kate Nazemi
	Karolina Novitska
	Meifen Tsai
Class of 2007	Carolin Horn
	Juan Morales
	Katie Westgate
	Ting Zhi
Class of 2008	Juan F. Burgos-Chaves
	Erich Doubek
	Mary Kathryn Murray
Class of 2009	Mahesh Gudapakkam
	Dan Johnston
	Mingxi Li
	Brian Moore
	Colin Owens
	Agata Stadnik
Class of 2010	Jae Chul Bae
	Jason Bailey
	Dennis Ludvino
	Scott Murray
	Audrey Yen-Ning Fu

The Experience of Dynamic Media:
Works from the Dynamic Media Institute
at Massachusetts College of Art and Design
2006 – 2010

ISBN 978-0-9772411-1-8

design: Jan Kubasiewicz, Joseph Liberty, Katelyn Rezza, Rumiana Williams

printing and binding: Capital Offset Company

fonts: Melior and Vista families

Established in 1873, Massachusetts College of Art and Design was the first, and remains the only, freestanding public college of art and design in the United States of America. The college is nationally known for offering broad access to a quality professional arts education, accompanied by a strong general education in the liberal arts. A major cultural force in Boston, MassArt offers public programs of innovative exhibitions, lectures, and events.

MASSART
MASSACHUSETTS COLLEGE
OF **ART AND DESIGN**